FINANCIAL SECTOR OF THE AMERICAN ECONOMY

edited by

STUART BRUCHEY
ALLAN NEVINS PROFESSOR EMERITUS
COLUMBIA UNIVERSITY

A GARLAND SERIES

THE POLITICS OF PORK

A Study of Congressional Appropriation Earmarks

SCOTT A. FRISCH

GARLAND PUBLISHING, INC.
A MEMBER OF THE TAYLOR & FRANCIS GROUP
NEW YORK & LONDON / 1998

Library of Congress Cataloging-in-Publication Data

Frisch, Scott A., 1964–
The politics of pork : a study of congressional appropriation earmarks / Scott A. Frisch.
p. cm. — (Financial sector of the American economy)
Revised edition of the author's doctoral dissertation . . . Claremont Graduate School.
Includes bibliographical references and index.
ISBN 0-8153-3258-0 (alk. paper)
1. Waste in government spending—United States. 2. Government spending policy—United States. 3. United States—Appropriations and expenditures. 4. United States. Congress. I. Title. II. Series.
HJ7537.F77 1998
336.3'9'0973—dc21

98-37454

Printed on acid-free, 250-year-life paper
Manufactured in the United States of America

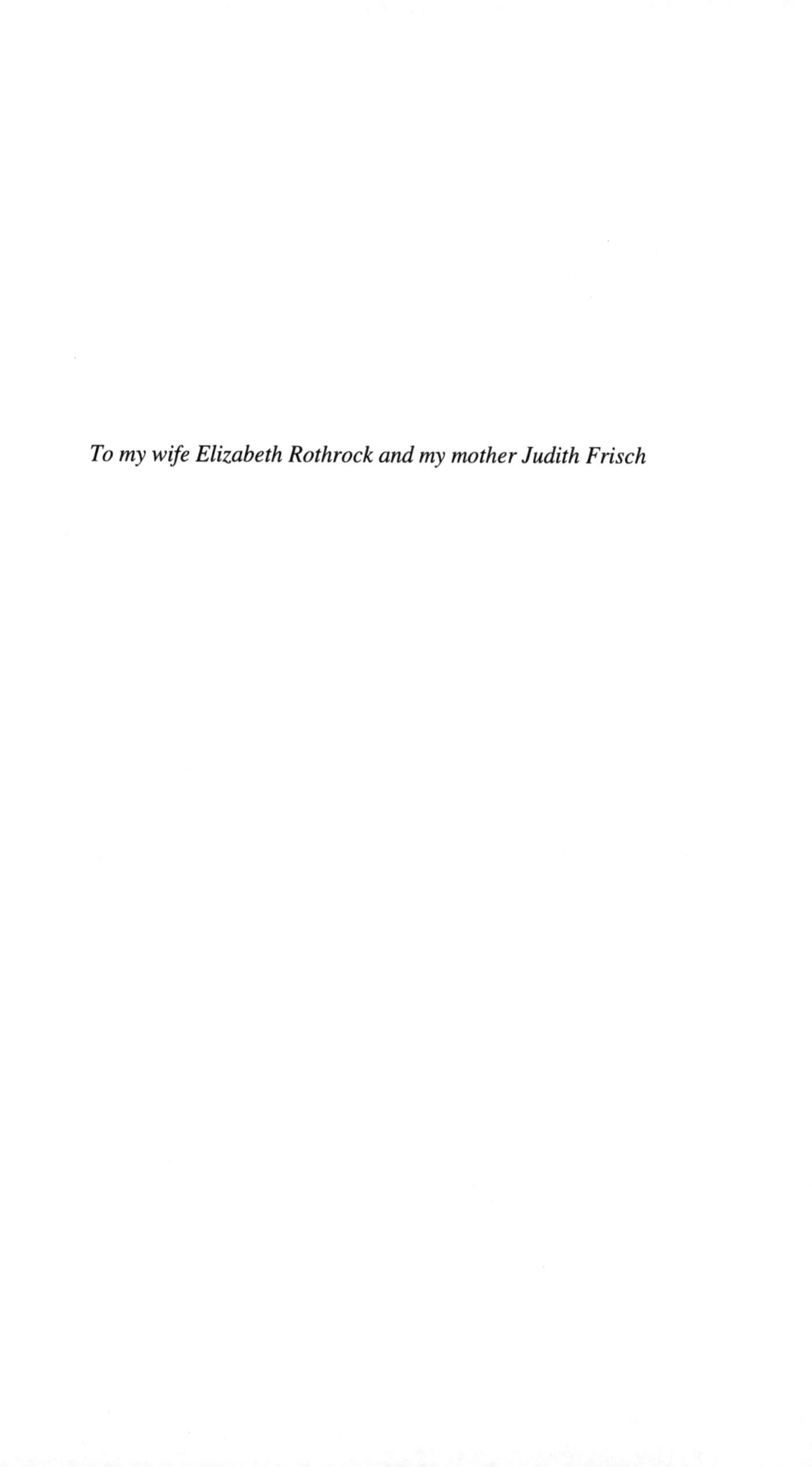

To my wife Elizabeth Rothrock and my mother Judith Frisch

Contents

Preface

This study is a revised edition of a doctoral dissertation that was originally submitted to the faculty of the Claremont Graduate School. When I began this study, I believed that popular attitudes towards congressional behavior were being formed on the basis of anecdotal evidence of several particularly well known examples of distributive spending (the Lawrence Welk museum, for example) rather than a thorough understanding of federal spending. Much of the scholarly debate on congressional spending was taking place within the context of formal models of behavior, rather than through the use of empirical evidence of government spending. I believe that this study fills an important gap in the literature by systematically studying the most common form of pork barrel spending, congressional appropriations earmarks.

This study provides a clearer understanding of pork barrel spending in America by identifying where congressional influence is most apparent in location specific spending—congressional appropriations earmarks—and by analyzing the predominant theories of distributive spending using data on the seven most popular earmark programs. This study also serves as a critique of the rational choice approach to the study of Congress, especially the theoretical assertion that Congress is designed to maximize the likelihood of member reelection through a committee system that institutionalizes the capture of gains from exchange. While the appropriations earmark system fits the theoretical predictions of this distributive model, Congress has opted for delegated distribution of spending in the vast majority of program areas, often through the creation of formulas or the reliance on the discretion of others, including bureaucrats and experts outside of government (peer review).

Recent events are supportive of the major conclusions drawn in this book. For the first time since 1969, there will be no federal budget deficit in fiscal year 1998. Yet the passage of the 1998 Highway Reauthorization bill containing 1,850 specific earmarked road projects at a five year cost of more than $9 billion reminds us that the association between congressional pork barrel spending and federal deficits, which is so commonly depicted in the media and accepted by the public, is inaccurate and overblown. Distributive (pork barrel) spending continues, even as the budget has come into balance.

The short history of the federal Line Item Veto Act also illustrates the lack of association between distributive spending and government deficits. Billed by its supporters as a powerful deficit reduction tool, in actual operation the line item veto made very little difference in overall spending. From the time the procedure became effective (January 1997) until it was declared unconstitutional by the Supreme Court (June 1998), President Clinton was only able to identify 79 items of wasteful spending worth $477 million to eliminate from the federal budget. This amounts to only .09% of total 1998 discretionary budget authority, and a mere drop in the bucket in a $1.7 trillion budget. It is now even clearer that the large deficits of the 1980s and early 1990s were functions of a combination of factors including slower than expected economic growth, rapid growth of entitlements, and fiscal policy changes enacted during the early years of the Reagan administration, rather than wasteful local congressional spending.

The perception that Congress is designed to distribute pork barrel spending and the impression that pork barrel spending is the dominant method of resource allocation and is out of control lessens faith in government. It is my hope that readers of this book will think more critically about media and scholarly accounts of a Congress made up of legislators so intent on reelection that they sacrifice the public good. While there are certainly examples of distributive congressional spending that the public would be better off without (some of these are described below), the question that future researchers may want to address is not "why does Congress waste so much taxpayer money?" but instead "why does Congress allow the vast majority of allocation decisions to be made by others?"

Acknowledgments

I would like to thank the members of my dissertation committee for their helpful comments and their assistance in completing this project. My advisor Jean Reith Schroedel, and committee members Paul Peretz and Gary Segura each contributed a different perspective to the project which I am sure improved the final product greatly.

I am also indebted to the many colleagues in government and academia who gave me encouragement and advice along the way. My fellow Claremont Graduate School student Bruce Snyder read and commented on the entire manuscript. My friends and colleagues at the Department of the Treasury encouraged me to pursue an academic career, and helped give me the confidence that was necessary to leave a secure job in the federal bureaucracy, for the very uncertain world of higher education. Several members of the staff of Senator Frank Lautenberg, especially Bruce King and Sharon Waxman taught me more about Congress in the six months that I served with them as a legislative fellow, than I could have learned in a lifetime in a library. My colleagues at East Carolina University have been very supportive during the final stages of this study. I would also like to thank my students at the various colleges where I have taught who facilitated completion by continually reminding me why I chose this profession.

The years spent researching and writing this book were a time of great joy and great sadness. I have dedicated this project to my wife Elizabeth Rothrock, and to my mother Judith Frisch who have shared the emotional journey, and without whose support this project never would have been completed.

Acknowledgments

The Politics of Pork

CHAPTER ONE
Introduction

Congressmen are not single-minded seekers of local benefits, struggling feverishly to win every dollar for their districts. However important the quest for local benefits may be, it is always tempered by other, competing concerns.

R. Douglas Arnold (1981b)

Pork is not the do-all and end-all of legislative behavior, legislative organization, or legislative policy outcomes. Thus, legislatures will be reluctant to commit to parliamentary arrangements that "institutionalize" gains from trade.

Keith Krehbiel (1991)

Pork barrel spending by Congress is an issue that is receiving a great deal of attention from the media, the public, and politicians. Popular accounts of wasteful congressional spending designed to ensure reelection of members have become staples of the weekly news magazines, television tabloid exposes, and have even cracked the bestseller list.[1] Each of the three daily network news programs currently runs a periodic segment highlighting wasteful government spending: NBC, for example, calls their reports "The Fleecing of America." [2] There was even a cable television program devoted exclusively to the topic—"Pork"—which aired *daily* on the now-defunct America's Talking Network. A February 1994 cover story in *U.S News and World Report* entitled "The Pork Barrel Barons" summed up the perspective that is typical of this type of journalism:

"Congress, as everyone knows *likes* to spend—particularly members of the House of Representatives. Facing reelection every two years, House members need to be able to show constituents that they can bring home the bacon. Highways, new courthouses—these are the tangible results that lawmakers can show those who elected them." The article is subtitled: "Here's the inside story of how one powerful congressional committee wastes millions of tax dollars" (Pound and Pasternak 1994).

Recent survey research indicates a wide-spread belief among the American public that the federal government engages in wasteful pork barrel spending. A national survey conducted in June, 1995 (Kay, Henderson, Steeper, Greenberg, and Blunt 1995: 6) concluded:

> The public firmly believes, more strongly than any other such attitude, that "government wastes too much of our money;" this is far and away the number one reason people give for mistrusting the government. Eight in ten say they strongly agree with this proposition, and a total of 93% agree at least somewhat. Only 3% disagree. It is difficult to conceive of an attitude shared as universally as this one, or a more clearly articulated explanation for the public's frustration with our leaders in Washington.

It is also apparent that members of Congress and the President are aware of the media and public fascination with pork barrel spending. On April 9, 1996, President Clinton signed into law the Line-Item Veto Act, giving the President authority to eliminate congressional spending deemed wasteful.[3] In the Report accompanying the legislation, the Conference Committee described the need for the legislation as follows:

> The American people consistently cite run-away federal spending and a rising national debt as among the top issues of national concern. Over the past fifteen years alone, the national debt of the United States has quintupled. From 1789 through 1981, our total national debt amounted to $1 trillion. Yet today, just fifteen years later, that debt exceeds $5 trillion, and without significant reforms an additional $1 trillion will be added over the next four years. This astonishing growth in federal debt has fueled public support for measures to ensure greater fiscal accountability in Washington. This legislation along with other measures to balance the federal budget considered in the 104th Congress, moves to meet that demand by enhancing the

> President's ability to eliminate wasteful federal spending and to cancel special tax breaks. (Line Item Veto Act—Conference Report 104-491: 15)

Political scientists are also interested in pork barrel or distributive[4] spending. The literature on distributive spending has been dominated by scholars writing from the rational choice perspective.[5] Most of the formal rational choice work on the U.S. Congress describes a legislature organized and structured to facilitate and preserve gains from exchange associated with localized federal spending.[6] According to this perspective, legislators are modeled as utility maximizers seeking reelection as their primary goal (Fiorina 1977; Mayhew 1974).[7] To best pursue the reelection goal of its members, an institutionalized system of decentralized committees has developed whereby members self-select seats on committees that will provide them with the best opportunities for obtaining particularistic benefits for their constituents (Shepsle 1978). Each members' desires are met through a process that provides universal benefits to cooperators both within individual legislation, and throughout the decentralized legislative system (Weingast 1979; Weingast and Marshall 1981; Fiorina 1981 Niou and Ordeshook 1985; Inman and Fitts 1992).[8] According to this line of analysis, the inevitable results of a system that universalizes distributive benefits to all legislators are government growth, wasteful government programs and deficits (Fiorina 1977; Shepsle 1984, Shepsle and Weingast 1984 and 1985, Fitts and Inman 1990).[9]

The distributive model is summed up nicely in the following passages from Shepsle and Weingast (1984):

> Today's key budgetary problems can be understood only as an integral part of the congressional system. The roots of our fiscal problems—budgetary growth, deficit financing, inexplicable programmatic forms, attention to special interests— are anchored in Congress; unless this fact is understood, reforms are unlikely to be effective.

They continue:

> In arguing that policies are the by-product of the legislator's pursuit of election and power, we shall give special prominence to the way legislators have organized the Congress. Some important elements of

> our story are the division of labor of the committee system, the self-selection to committees of what we call "preference outliers" by the committee assignment process, the institutional bargains that constitute reciprocity among committees and universal distributive tendencies, and relative weakness of institutional regulators like parties and leaders (pp.344-345).

The model of distributive politics outlined briefly above leads to conclusions similar to the popular conception of a Congress obsessed by inefficient local spending, often at the expense of what is in the best interest of the nation and the economy. If correct, the distributive model would legitimate the call for major changes to the American political system, especially the Congress, and may even require changing the institutional designs and processes established by the Constitution.

This research attempts to emphasize the difficulties of examining congressional behavior on the basis of the assumption that members are motivated by a single overriding reelection goal and the hazards of drawing universal conclusions regarding congressional organization and behavior based on this assumption. I will undertake to do this through a closer examination of five key premises upon which the model of the distributive Congress (which will be referred to as "distributive theory") outlined above is based:

Premise 1: Legislatures are composed of committees comprised of self-selected preference outliers. Members of committees reap disproportionate benefits from the programs within the jurisdiction of their committees.

Premise 2: Legislatures are organized into committees and subcommittees to provide pork barrel benefits to all members (In the language of formal modeling, they institutionalize norms of universalism and reciprocity to secure gains from exchange).

Premise 3: All legislators seek pork barrel spending to help secure reelection.

Premise 4: Universalism of benefits is directly associated with government growth, inefficiency, and deficit spending that plague the modern Congress.

Premise 5: Legislators are single minded seekers of reelection.

Using the previous empirical literature on Congress structured according to these premises, as well as new research on congressional appropriations earmarks and case studies from the modern Congress, I will examine each of these premises. The first four premises are testable, and have been tested using various methodologies by others. The fifth is an underlying assumption that guides scholarly work, and upon which this study will have implications. Although there is some empirical support for the premises, especially when Congress is directly responsible for district specific spending decisions, evidence will be provided that lends doubt to the predictive strength of each of the first four premises as an overall description of Congress. This in turn seriously weakens the generalizability of the fifth premise as well as the overall conclusion that the institutional arrangements and self-interested desires of Congress leads to wasteful spending and especially budget deficits and accumulated debt.

ORGANIZATION

This research is presented in a structure that flows from the five premises outlined above. Chapter Two will present a discussion of the definitions of pork barrel spending, emphasizing the differences between the theoretical literature, with its focus on projects, and the tendency of empirical studies to concentrate on spending that is not driven by congressional allocation of projects, but instead looks at programs that disburse expenditures on the basis of grants, broad-based formulas, as well as aggregate district spending totals. The chapter will conclude with a discussion of how congressional appropriations earmarks best fit the definitions of distributive politics proposed by Lowi (1964) and especially Weingast (1994). Chapter Three is a detailed description of the seven policy areas that are studied in this research, and serves to justify their inclusion in this study as examples of congressional distributive policy.

Chapter Four begins an evaluation of the five premises outlined above. The contention that congressional committees are composed of preference outliers who receive disproportionate shares of pork of the variety best suited to the demands of their districts, will be evaluated using evidence from the existing literature. Chapter Five will examine the same hypothesis discussed in Chapter Four empirically, using a study of congressional earmarks. From the literature it appears that the claim that members are preference outliers is supported most strongly for government programs where Congress retains the capacity to make project by project decisions. In cases where the decisions are made by formulas or by bureaucrats in grant issuing agencies, there is less evidence that funds are allocated disproportionately to members of related committees. This finding will be tested by comparing the distribution of earmarks, with the distribution of non-earmarked expenditures in the same policy area. As only a small minority of allocative decisions are made directly by Congress through earmarks, any effect on overall government spending resulting from the institutionalization of preference outliers is small indeed.

Chapter Six is an examination of the concept of universalism as it applies to distributive theory. The crucial question to be resolved is: do all (or nearly all) members cooperate to produce omnibus legislation that showers each district with projects? Again, this claim will be evaluated with evidence from both the existing literature and congressional earmarks, and again evidence suggests that universalism may only pertain to project specific (earmarked) distributive spending and only when viewed across the entire appropriations system. As earmarked spending is only a small fraction of total discretionary spending (not to mention an even smaller fraction of total spending), the importance of the concept as the guiding principle of legislative organization is questionable. In addition, three short case studies from the contemporary Congress (the effort to strip highway demonstration earmarks from the fiscal year 1992 appropriation proposed by Senator Robert Smith, spending cuts proposed in the Penny-Kasich Amendment of 1993, and the failed economic stimulus package of 1993) will be introduced to support the claim that universalism and reciprocity are largely confined to those areas of congressional policy making where Congress makes location specific funding decisions, and even in those areas, universalism and reciprocity does not always characterize the modern Congress.

Chapter Seven casts doubts on the widely held belief that there is a strong link between pork barrel spending and reelection, that it is universally acknowledged and pursued by members of Congress, and that the association is unchanging over time. Although largely literature and anecdotally based, this section will also include evidence on the electoral connection between earmarks and electoral margins.

The relationship between universalism, pork barrel spending, and deficits will be examined in Chapter Eight. There does not appear to be convincing evidence that pork barrel spending is related to deficits. In addition to the empirical evidence and evidence drawn mainly from the literature on federal government budgets, this study will look at the impact that the spending caps imposed by the Omnibus Budget Reconciliation Acts of 1990 and 1993 (OBRA90 and OBRA93) have had on earmarked and other discretionary spending to argue that gross spending totals and especially domestic discretionary totals are not a function of pork barrel spending, and pork barrel spending may at times allow Congress to make painful cuts in overall spending. This study will also explore the hypothesis that the desire for pork barrel projects (as measured over time), is dynamic, and has shown a decrease following the 1992 election, and a change in composition following the election of a Republican congressional majority in 1994.

This study will conclude (Chapter Nine) with an evaluation of the overall relevance of distributive theory as a predictor of legislative behavior. While there is little predictive value to the model as an overall (universal in a different sense) way to characterize the organization and policy output of the U.S. Congress, the model does offer insight into congressional behavior in some circumstances. Although all committees may not be composed of homogenous high demanders, there is evidence that some committees are, and that a system of universalism has arisen in the areas most responsible for congressionally specified spending. This result has implications on two claims closely associated with the research of Fenno (1966 and 1973). While Fenno's conception of the House Appropriations Committee as the guardian of the Treasury may no longer be accurate, this research does lend considerable support to both the idea that congressional committees differ systematically, and the depiction of members as possessing multiple goals (good public policy, institutional prestige/power, as well as reelection). Often the goals that aren't related to reelection are more important factors in decision-making and the organization of Congress, therefore reducing the importance of the distributive theory as a universal model.

Importance of Study

It is apparent that much of the climate of distrust of the federal government in general and Congress in particular stems (at least in part) from the perception that wasteful distributive spending is out of control. It is the aim of this research to bring about a better understanding of the cause, effects and extent of congressional distributive spending. Some academic research appears to support the popular conception that wasteful government spending is out of control, and is a contributing (if not the main) factor driving the country's chronic deficits and mounting debt. Distributive theorists often advocate dramatic changes designed to curtail the geographic impulses of members of the U.S. Congress.

The relationship between the congressional system, distributive policy, and budgetary shortfalls is important and worthy of further study. This issue is important for reasons that involve questions of public policy as well as questions of political theory. In terms of policy, there are several popular policy proposals on the national agenda that take as their starting point the assumption that congressional distributive spending is ultimately responsible for recurrent budget deficits. The most notable of these is the recently enacted presidential line-item veto.[10] This policy option is based on the assumption that the President will keep the national interest forefront by striking congressional expenditures that are purely local in benefit, but national in cost. Following this logic, serious deficit reduction can be achieved through the line-item veto. The findings of this research will have implications for the potential of the line-item veto and other policy options aimed at reducing or eliminating federal budget deficits by controlling congressional pork barrel spending.

From a more theoretical point of view, the central question of this study is important for what it says about the Constitutional design of the American political system as well as the current institutional organization of American democracy, especially the structure and distribution of power within Congress. The basic Constitutional design of this country (Article I, Section 9) stipulates: "No money shall be drawn from the Treasury but in consequence of Appropriations made by law." The Framers of the Constitution were well aware of the importance of the spending power to the survival of any government, and chose to give the power to Congress.[11] The Presidential veto was designed to be a check on congressional discretion. If the modern Congress cannot overcome the distributive pulls of the geographic constituency which are attributed to the desire to be reelected to serve the common good, and the Presidential veto (or veto threat) is insufficient to suppress parochial spending desires, the Constitutional design is called into question. Proposals to amend the Constitution, such as a call for a balanced budget amendment and the imposition of term limits may be necessary if congressional distributive spending is uncontrollable and in fact the cause of large deficits.

The institutional arrangements that have evolved to implement the American Constitution must also be questioned, if a majority of the members of Congress will always act in the best interests of their districts at the expense of the nation. Are the internal structures of Congress (committee and subcommittee autonomy, decentralization of leadership, weak parties) capable of supporting the common good and controlling parochial interests?

Finally, there is an ongoing debate in the field of political science regarding the empirical accuracy of theoretical predictions of rational choice models.[12] Green and Shaprio (1994), in a work that is being hotly debated within the scholarly community, offer a critique of rational choice theory in which they emphasize the lack of empirical support that characterizes many theoretical claims. Green and Shapiro maintain:

> To date, a large proportion of the theoretical conjectures of rational choice theorists have not been tested empirically. Those tests that have been undertaken have either failed on their own terms or garnered theoretical support for propositions that, on reflection, can only be characterized as banal: they do little more than restate existing knowledge in rational choice terminology (p.6).

I seek to enter into this debate by examining critically the rational choice literature on distributive politics. This study will evaluate the predictive strength of the distributive theory of Congress which is based on formal modeling, in two ways. The study will systematically review the previous empirical literature on distributive policy. It will combine this literature review with an empirical study of what I have determined to be the clearest example of pork barrel spending in Congress today—congressional earmarks. Formal models have produced some insights into the behavior of Congress in the distributive realm; however, there has been a tendency to draw overall conclusions regarding congressional behavior, policy output and organization. This study will show that many of these conclusions are flawed.

Morris Fiorina (1977 and 1989), in a work that is still required reading in many undergraduate political science classes, paints a picture of Congress based on the distributive model which is consciously cynical. According to Fiorina: (pp.68-69)

> Public policy emerges from the system almost as an afterthought. The shape of policy is a by-product of the way the system operates, rather than a consciously directed effort to deal with social and economic problems. Congressmen know that the specific impact of broad national policies on their districts is difficult to see, that effects are hidden, so to speak. They know that the individual congressmen are not held responsible for the collective outcome produced by 535 members of Congress. Thus, in order to attain reelection, congressmen focus on things that are both more recognizable in their impact and more credible indicators of the individual congressman's power—federal projects and individual favors for constituents. In order to purchase a steady flow of the latter, congressmen trade away less valuable currency—their views on public policy. The typical public law is simply the outcome of individual bargains to build a majority.

I frankly do not agree with this statement. Certainly, some members of Congress are primarily interested in seeking reelection and pursue this strategy through providing pork barrel spending (and casework). However, through examination of the literature on distributive spending, as well as an analysis of the congressional behavior most often associated with pork barrel spending, I will show that the pork barrel tendency is not nearly as strong as is claimed by advocates of the distributive theory, and is best considered as one of the competing motives of members of Congress.

NOTES

1. See for Example Gross 1993; Perot 1993. Other mass market books on the deficit and debt are: Calleo 1992; Peterson 1994; and Miller 1994.

2. For a discussion of television news coverage of wasteful government spending see Cohn 1996. Cohn maintains that: " . . . the relentless pursuit of even the most petty examples of excess frequently simplifies complicated policy issues while crowding out more worthy targets, particularly those in the private sector. You can't turn on a news show without hearing about a $500 toilet seat, but good luck trying to find a story that reports the untaxed benefits top managers get from their companies" (p.13.).

3. The Line-Item Veto Act (PL 104-130) passed the House by a vote of 237-177 and was approved by the Senate with a voice vote. The procedure, which became effective in January, 1997, required the president to sign entire

appropriations and tax bills into law. The president could then cut spending and targeted tax breaks from appropriations bills and reports and other legislation. Cuts took effect automatically unless Congress voted specifically to overturn presidential decisions. The U.S. Supreme Court ruled the procedure unconstitutional on June 25, 1998 (See Clinton v. City of New York).

4. Theodore Lowi (1964) used the term distributive policy to describe policies "characterized by the ease with which they can be disagregated and dispensed unit by small unit . . . patronage can be taken as a synonym for distributive in the fullest meaning of the word." Other synonyms for distributive common in the literature are divisible, particularized and pork barrel (which is usually pejorative).

5. Throughout this research, I will rely on the description of rational choice provided by Fiorina in what is certainly one of the most widely read (and accessible) accounts of congressional behavior that is explicitly from the rational choice approach—*Congress: Keystone of the Washington Establishment* (1989, Second Edition), pp.101-107. According to Fiorina: "This approach views individuals as the fundamental actors in politics and seeks to explain political processes and outcomes as consequences of their purposive behavior. Political actors are assumed to have goals and to pursue those goals sensibly and efficiently . . . individuals have goals appropriate to the institutional positions around which their careers are centered. Congressmen are assumed to have a predominant reelection motive."

6. The major exception to the model describe below is Krehbiel, 1991, who proposed a model of self-interested legislators pursuing information rather than localized benefits. See Baron (1996) for the argument that a theory of legislative organization and policy product should be focused on collective goods (i.e. entitlements) rather than particularized benefits. Baron offers such a theory. See also Kiewiet and McCubbins (1991) and Cox and McCubbins (1993) on the failure of distributive theory to account for the role of political parties.

7. Although Mayhew is closely associated with the idea of understanding Congress exclusively on the basis of the legislators' desires to be reelected, the formal rational choice modeling of behavior based on the supremacy of the reelection goal follows more closely on the work of Fiorina.

8. For current purposes, this simplistic presentation of the distributive model is sufficient. More detailed discussions of concepts such as instability of coalitions, cycling and uncertainty are included when they become relevant to the discussion.

9. For more extensive reviews of this model see: Collie (1988); and Shepsle and Weingast (1994); for a critique see Krehbiel (1991, Chapter Two).

10. Although the Line Item Veto Act was declared unconstitutional in June, 1998, its supporters are certain to propose alternative policies (legislative and/or Constitutional) to achieve the same result.

11. Madison in Federalist 58 wrote: "This power over the purse may, in fact, be regarded as the most complete and effectual weapon with which any Constitution can arm the immediate representatives of the people, for obtaining a redress of every grievance, and for carrying into effect every just and salutary measure" (p.359).

12. On this debate see especially: Green and Shapiro (1994) and Friedman (1996). See also: Fiorina (1989), Kelman (1987), Mansbridge (1990); Grofman (1993) and Munroe (1991), and Bessette (1994).

CHAPTER TWO

Legislative Earmarks and Other Evidence

> *Earmarks flourish because members of the Appropriations Committees would rather decide where funds are to be spent than let executive agencies make the determination. They flourish because the chief political value of serving on the Appropriations Committees is to bring home the bacon, not guard the Treasury. They flourish because a spending bill with a lot of projects spread across the country is easier to pass than is one without them. They flourish in good times, when incremental resources are bountiful, and it seems even more in hard times when the budget is tight.*
>
> Allen Schick (1995)

> *Several representatives remarked on the ease with which earmarked funds could be obtained. "I used to plead endlessly for grants from agencies," said one, "but I've since learned that it's far quicker and less complicated to approach the cardinal directly"*
>
> Richard Munson (1993)[1]

WHAT IS EARMARK DATA

The purpose of this chapter is to introduce a measure of distributive politics that differs from the data used in most previous studies—congressional appropriations earmarks.[2] It is necessary to introduce this concept of pork barrel spending at this point because each of the subsequent chapters includes an empirical analysis using earmark data. It is my contention that earmarks most accurately reflect the concept of legislative project decision making that is incorporated in many models from the rational choice approach, and this chapter will make the case that earmarks present a purer empirical test of the various hypotheses generated by formal models, than do previous empirical attempts that rely on grant expenditures or other gross measures of district specific spending.[3]

Allen Schick defines an earmarked expenditure as: "appropriations dedicated by an appropriations act or the accompanying committee report to a particular project or activity" (Schick 1995: 210).[4] Earmarks typically are included in Appropriations laws or committee reports at the request of a member or group of members of Congress. It is important to note that earmarks frequently are placed in report language rather than as individual line items in the appropriations bills themselves. In fact Brown (1994) quotes former Senate Appropriations Committee Chairman Robert Byrd as stating: "Most earmarking is done in committee reports, not in the appropriations bills themselves" (p.24). The fact that earmarks are often not written into law does not mean that agencies do not follow them closely. There is considerable evidence that agencies follow report language as if it had the weight of law.[5]

An institutionalized process for including appropriations earmarks has developed in the modern Congress. Members of the House and Senate from both political parties typically notify their Appropriations Subcommittee Chairs (through key staff known as clerks) in writing of their desire to include funding for specific local projects in the report language. According to Daniel Franklin (1993):

> An annual Spring ritual in most congressional offices . . . is the writing of a letter to each of the subcommittee cardinals in which the member spells out in detail each special funding request that falls within the jurisdiction of that subcommittee. Subcommittees are literally deluged with requests. As a rule a member can expect that at least a portion of his or her requests will be deleted by the Subcommittee Chair. This being the case, the member without being too ham-fisted, will often make requests for more money or projects than are actually needed (p.163).

There is considerable anecdotal evidence that Subcommittee Chairs receive many more requests for project funding than money available.[6] Individual members also will testify at Subcommittee hearings and or contact the cardinal (as the powerful chairs of appropriations subcommittees are often called) directly for especially important requests. Through interviews with key Appropriations Committee staff, Savage (1991) has concluded that cardinals essentially decide which (if any) earmarks will be included in the report language that is presented to the Subcommittee at markup.[7] The secrecy of the draft report preparation process, the very short time periods common between when the subcommittee members see the draft language and the scheduling of the mark-up, and the 602b budget rules which require additional expenditures to be achieved only through offsetting spending reductions, all conspire to protect the choices made by the cardinal.[8] Therefore, the cardinals have a great deal of control over the content of earmark language under their subcommittee's discretion.

A typical earmarked appropriation might take the following form, which is drawn from the Senate Report on the Departments of Veterans Affairs and Housing and Urban Development, and Independent Agencies Appropriations bill for Fiscal Year 1993 (S. Rept. 102-356: 51):

Special Purpose Grants.—The Committee recommends $126,275,000, and bill language, for the following special purpose grants whose activities are consistent with the criteria established by the community development block grant program:

> +$1,500,000 for the Tacoma, WA, job opportunity and neighborhood revitalization program
>
> +$1,350,000 for the Seattle community action capitol project for social services and working capital to assist four areas in Seattle Washington . . .
>
> +$150,000 for the North East Community Center Association in Spokane, WA.
>
> + . . . (the list of earmarks continues through page 56).

The list of projects continues until the pot of funds is exhausted. The only reference to these earmarks that appears in the appropriations bill that is voted on by each chamber and presented to the president, is a single line item appropriating a total funding level for special purpose grants. Frequently the Conference Committee accommodates both House and Senate requests for earmarks, which often differ due to the different priorities of House members and Senators. In the case of the report cited above, although the House did not include any earmarks in its original report, the Conference Report includes earmarks from the House in addition to those already specified by the Senate. The total amount allocated for earmarked projects is increased to $260 million, and pages 21-31 of the Conference Report include itemizations of both Senate and House earmarks (H. Rept. 102-902; see also p.4).

PROBLEMS WITH OTHER MEASURES OF PORK

Much of the previous academic research on distributive or pork barrel spending relies upon empirical evidence that is made problematic by the inclusion of cases where what is being measured is not pork barrel or distributive spending in the purest sense. At least one of the following problems typically are present:

1. Grant programs (such as the Community Development Block Grant and Federal Aid Highway programs) where spending decisions allocate funds on the basis of geographic formulas based on demographic statistics (such as poverty rate and number of highway miles) are included. Formulas are not doled out piece by piece making manipulation by individual members of Congress extremely difficult. In addition, credit claiming opportunities are limited in that the legislator cannot realistically take credit for benefits brought to the district through formula grants.

2. Large scale entitlement programs (such as Social Security and Medicare) that distribute funds or in-kind benefits to individuals are included. These programs are purely redistributive and include the classic examples of redistributive policy. They are allocated on the basis of eligibility requirements which are rarely subject to political manipulation once enacted.

3. Data is aggregated at the state rather than district level, obscuring actions of individual legislators. While this is necessary in some cases (when federal government funds go to states rather than projects or localities), it is frequently difficult to draw many conclusions based on an N of 50.

4. Spending decisions for project grants are made largely at the discretion of administration bureaucrats (frequently based on objective requirements and peer review) with members of Congress playing only an indirect role in the decision making process. This most common form of federal assistance program involves the establishment of broad program guidelines by Congress, and individual funding decisions are determined within the agency.

5. Programs that provide legislators with minimal opportunities for credit claiming are included. True pork barrel spending must in some way have value for a legislator.[9]

6. Data that does not isolate new spending for a given year or Congress, but instead uses gross measures that have accumulated over time, are included. This may more accurately reflect the pork barrel performance of previous Congresses than the current institutional balance of power.

The recent work of Stein and Bickers (1997, 1996, 1995; 1994a; 1994b) is a considerable improvement over earlier empirical studies of distributive politics, many of which used gross measures of district or state specific spending as their data.[10] Stein and Bickers have developed a data set based on the Catalog of Federal Domestic Assistance (CFDA) and the Federal Assistance Awards Data System (FAADS). In analyzing distributive policies, Stein and Bickers include all domestic assistance programs where there is some degree of discretion; therefore they correctly exclude the most obvious redistributive programs such as Social Security, Medicare, Medicaid, Food Stamps, and AFDC from their data set. They use the congressional district rather than the state as the unit of analysis, which allows for more specific examination of spending patterns. They use change in awards to exclude benefits obtained by previous legislators. However, Stein and Bickers' research still provides an example of how empirical studies deviate from the depiction of the pork barrel spending model common in the distributive theory literature.

Stein and Bickers' measure of pork barrel spending includes certain "domestic assistance awards" to congressional districts. By including all programs that spend funds based on bureaucratic decision, they include many programs that may involve little congressional influence.[11] Programs where geographic allocation decisions are made by bureaucratic agencies often rely on objective criteria and frequently peer review, in determining awards. Peer review is now the most pervasive method for evaluating grant proposals to determine awards (Kalas 1987: 83). Professional experts outside of government review grant proposals and make funding decisions in many policy areas. Peer review is often associated with the evaluation of scientific research, but it is also used for other types of programs such as education, social services, economic development, medicine, the arts and humanities.

The National Science Foundation is one of many agencies that relies on peer review for grant determination. According to a report on grant decision making at the National Science Foundation: "NSF's current policy is that all formal proposals for grant funding are subject to peer review by appropriate experts external to the agency, with minor exceptions . . . " (National Science Foundation 1994: 62). Current review criteria include: 1) Competent performance of research; 2) Intrinsic merit of research; 3) Utility or relevance of the research; 4) Effects of the research on the infrastructure of science and engineering. Stein and Bickers (1995: 185-186) include thirteen separate programs administered by NSF in their data set as examples of pork barrel spending. While NSF may be subject to some political pressure to award grants, it is likely that the process of peer review eliminates most of the congressional influence.[12]

In addition, Stein and Bickers' model does not make any distinction between programs that provide considerable amounts of credit claiming opportunities to legislators, and those programs that are less appealing from a reelection perspective. Arnold (1979: 29-30.) claims that there are three ways that allocation of federal expenditures can affect the reelection prospects of an incumbent: 1) by influencing the direct beneficiaries; 2) through favorable publicity; and 3) through the impact that funds have on the local economy. While some of the programs included in Bickers and Stein's data appeal to the reelection concerns of members of Congress, many of the included programs have little impact on either of the three groups described by Arnold. Compare, for example, the reelection appeal of a labor intensive public works project that improves the quality of life for residents and stimulates economic development, such as Construction Grants for Wastewater Treatment, with a program that has small and largely invisible benefits such as Grants for the Promotion of the Humanities. Large scale public works programs tend to be much more desirable as they provide visible reminders of a legislator's clout in the form of district specific employment and improved infrastructure, yet Stein and Bickers' analysis treats all programs as equals.

Stein and Bicker's model of congressional influence over distributive spending involves the aggressive promotion of grant applications by members of Congress. Members influence the flow of federal funds by stimulating grant applications from their constituents. "The key is how hard a legislator works in identifying and assisting potential grant applicants in his or her district" (1994: 382). Their model explicitly excludes direct pressure on agencies by members of Congress seeking approval for member generated grant proposals. They assert: " . . . agencies take special pains to avoid appearing partisan in their review and award activities" (1995: 123). This model does not fit well with the model of distributive theorists who explicitly assume projects are favored by members of Congress.

Bickers and Stein may reject the criticism made above regarding the use of peer review, claiming that the important factor is the decision on the part of a grant recipient to apply for a grant. It is at this stage, according to Bickers and Stein, that members of Congress differ in their distributive efforts and successes. However, even a cursory examination of the grant programs included in their analysis leaves this observer skeptical. Do more social scientists apply for grants because their members of Congress encourage them to do so? Most observers would agree that many members of Congress do encourage constituents to apply for grants from the federal government. However, direct evidence on magnitude and variance of congressional impact on the stimulation of grants compared to other factors is not provided.[13] Cain, Ferejohn and Fiorina (1987: 73) report that of a survey of 102 congressional offices, " . . . 33 did not actively search out grants for their district." Apparently, one-third of all congressional offices do not even solicit projects from their districts. The level of resources devoted to this task by those offices that do search out grants is not reported.[14] A model that relies so heavily on such a novel definition of pork barrel spending needs clearly to provide empirical evidence supporting its importance. Stein and Bicker provide none.

In a recent exchange of articles that appeared in Political Research Quarterly, Robert Stein and Kenneth Bickers (1994a, 1994b) and Barry Weingast (1994) discussed the state of theoretical and empirical research on distributive theory (with special attention paid to universalism). Bickers and Stein (1994a) present an empirical analysis that does not support distributive theory and universalism as an explanation of congressional behavior, organization and policy output.[15] Bickers and Stein conclude that an analysis of domestic assistance awards reveals little support for universal distribution of benefits across congressional districts. They fail to find evidence of universalism at the program level, as each grant program included in their data set tends to be concentrated in less than half of the 435 congressional districts. When their analysis is extended to the subsystem level (which they define as multiple spending programs within the same federal agency), they continue to find little evidence in support of universal distribution of pork barrel programs across policy areas.

Weingast (1994) responds to this analysis with a critique, (to which Bickers and Stein were given the opportunity to respond). In his critique, Weingast claims that part of the difficulty (of Bickers and Stein as well as others) involved in finding empirical support for the theory of universalism (and by extension, other aspects of distributive theory) is attributable to the failure of researchers to use data that meet a careful definition of distributive policy. Weingast outlines three essential and one additional desirable criterion for a policy to be considered distributive. According to Weingast, the four hallmarks of distributive policy are: (D1) Divisibility: Its projects are local and can be varied in size scope, and dollar amount independently of one another; (D2) Omnibus: Legislation is an omnibus of many divisible projects within a policy area; (D3) Expenditure: The legislation is an expenditure policy; its main task is to allocate a given amount of funds. The fourth criterion, which is said to be "desirable" is (D4) Scope: A large, supramajority of districts is eligible for funds.

According to Weingast, empirical studies such as Bickers and Stein are flawed in that they do not accurately isolate policies that are distributive. Bickers and Stein for example, include in their research a number of policies (Indian Education, undersea research, national agricultural libraries etc.) where benefits are only available to a small number of districts. The omnibus quality of the data is, however, where the real difference between Weingast, and Bickers and Stein becomes apparent. Weingast is concerned with congressional discretion at the legislative stage. What Bickers and Stein are concerned with is the results of activity of members of Congress in stimulating grant applications. These are two very different models of congressional pork barrel behavior, yet it is not apparent from their exchange of articles that either side recognizes that they are comparing apples and oranges.

Weingast is concerned with the legislative behavior of members of Congress that results in omnibus pork barrel programs. Bickers and Stein view pork barrel behavior as occurring "at home" rather than in Washington through stimulation of grant applications.

The research presented here attempts to avoid the problems associated with previous attempts at operationalizing distributive theory (including the work of Bickers and Stein) by using a data set that meets all four of the criteria developed by Weingast. Congressional appropriations earmarks provide a data set that fits the definition of distributive policy outlined above. Each earmark is divisible; addition or elimination of a given earmark has no impact on other projects. Appropriations bills (and report language) are omnibus; a cursory look at any of the seven subcommittee reports will reveal spending and policy changes in many different program areas. All federal discretionary spending is contained in thirteen annual appropriations bills.[16] Appropriations are expenditures; in fact with few exceptions, they are the only policy type that must result in an outlay of federal funds.[17] Finally, each of the seven areas that are the subject of this study have the potential to be located in virtually every congressional district. While some areas offer less potential for geographic spread than others, even a policy area like National Park Service funding (which would on the surface appear to be limited to only those areas where a large and visible National Park is located), has some presence in virtually every congressional district in the country.[18]

Stein and Bickers (1995: 6) claim: "members of Congress need agencies to provide benefits to their constituencies." As this study will show; this is not necessarily true.[19] Earmarks represent direct congressional action. In addition, congressional appropriations earmarks represent a popular source of congressional spending that is traceable directly to the actions of a particular member or members. The action is ultimately a legislative one, as written instructions are included in a congressional document. When government spending decisions are made by an administrative bureaucracy, there is no direct link between the dollars and the legislator. If the president is from a different party than a legislator, there are incentives for executive branch officials as well as congressional challengers to also claim credit for a grant expenditure. Therefore, legislators will prefer the traceable credit claiming opportunities provided by earmarks.

In addition to Stein and Bickers, virtually all of the existing empirical literature on distributive politics (with the exception of studies of water resources legislation) examine policy areas that rely heavily on bureaucratic rather than congressional decision-making. Although members of Congress influence the decisions of executive branch officials, congressional pressure is only one of many factors influencing bureaucratic decisions.[20] Pressures from the President,[21] the courts, interest groups, differing local needs for government benefits,[22] as well as the desire to implement efficient public policy[23] are among the other factors that influence the decisions of bureaucrats.[24]

Congressional earmarks more accurately reflect the will of Congress (or at least some members of Congress), in that geography-specific decisions are part of the traceable legislative history of a program. The introduction of earmark data allows the existing theories of distributive politics to be tested in a new way. Arnold (1990) maintains that voters hold representatives accountable for actions only when there is a traceable effect (p.47). He specifies three conditions that make an action traceable: 1) there is a perceptible effect; 2) there is an identifiable governmental action; and 3) (most important for my purposes) there must be a visible contribution on the part of the legislators. Although Arnold uses the concept of traceability to outline the types of actions that legislators avoid, the concept works just as well in describing the actions that legislators value in the distributive environment.

Earmarks are traceable actions—there can be no disputing a legislator's claim of credit for an earmarked local project, as all three conditions are met. For a legislator to claim credit for a grant issued by a bureaucratic agency is more problematic. Traceability is no longer clear, as the decision is ultimately made elsewhere. A legislator may attempt to claim credit for a grant by making a formal announcement, but there is no proof that the source of the government spending depends on the actions of the member of Congress. The link between congressional and bureaucratic action is more tenuous when the legislator is not from the same party as the president.

As a final note on identifying the source of pork barrel spending in the contemporary Congress, it is useful to consult the scholar credited with introducing the concept that policies in this area result in different congressional behavior than in other areas. In the introductory text book that he co-authors (Lowi and Ginsburg 1996), Lowi discusses pork barrel spending in terms of congressional earmarks: "The most important of these opportunities for direct patronage is in the legislation that has been described half-jokingly as the pork barrel. This type of legislation specifies both the projects or other authorizations and the location within a particular district . . . A common form of pork barreling is the 'earmark' . . . " (p.164).

Identifying Where Earmarks are Common

Earmarks have not been distributed evenly throughout appropriations bills and committee reports. At least 1,400 location specific earmarks were placed in the Energy and Water Development FY 1997 Appropriations report, yet according to a General Accounting Office Report (GAO 1987a), only three instances of congressionally earmarked funds were identified in a study of all National Institutes of Health (NIH) research funds in eleven appropriations acts that were analyzed between 1966 and 1985. The question then becomes, which spending categories have been favorite targets for localized spending, and why are these categories preferred over others?

In order to answer these questions, a two pronged research strategy was undertaken. Initially, the descriptive literature on Congressional appropriations was studied to determine likely locations for earmarked spending. In addition a more systematic study involving a content analysis of congressional newsletters during the 103rd Congress was undertaken to identify credit claiming for distributive benefits by members of Congress. By analyzing a sample of congressional newsletters, patterns in the projects for which members claim credit can be identified. These results can then be compared to the descriptive literature to better understand the nature of the programs that are favorite locations for pork barrel spending.

Results of Newsletter Content Analysis

There is considerable agreement among congressional observers that congressional newsletters serve the reelection needs of incumbent members of Congress.[25] Research indicates that newsletters serve not only the advertising needs of members, but also are vehicles for extensive credit claiming. In the most detailed analysis of congressional newsletters to date, Yiannakis (1982) identifies "credit claiming for particularized benefits" as one of the most frequent and distinctive categories of congressional communication included in newsletters. According to House member Ted Strickland: "With few exceptions, mass mailings [i.e. newsletters] contain self promotional materials . . . the privilege of being able to send these to every constituent's household is without question unfair to nonincumbents" (Congressional Record October 27, 1993).

Copies of congressional newsletters were requested from all 435 voting members of the 103rd Congress. As recently adopted Senate rules make it very difficult (and in some cases impossible) for Senators to mail state-wide newsletters, this analysis will concentrate on the House of Representatives, which maintains more liberal rules on mass mailings.[26]

Responses were received from 207 members of the House, or 47.6% of the total.[27] Of those responding, 52 (25.1%) indicated that they do not currently use newsletters. This is roughly consistent with Johannes and McAdams (1986) who reported that 72% of members in their sample used newsletters during 1977-1978, and slightly lower than the 84% of members who reported using newsletters during 1982. Partisan representation in the sample roughly mirrors the partisan composition of the House, with Republicans slightly overrepresented and Democrats slightly underrepresented. Newsletters mailed by Representatives from forty-five states are included in the study.

Content analysis was performed on the newsletters of the 155 members who do send newsletters. Every reference to a grant, project, or other tangible asset that benefits the specific congressional district without imposing a distinguishable cost on any taxpayer was coded as a distributive benefit. Distributive benefits were further distinguished by the source of decision making that resulted in the benefit. Projects were considered to be earmarks if there was apparent congressional (legislative) action to produce the benefit; projects that were the result of bureaucratic action or formulas were considered to be grants.

Of the members of Congress in the sample who use newsletters to communicate with their constituents, 93 (59.2%) describe at least one distributive project or program that spends federal government funds in their district. It is clear that a majority of the sample see newsletters as an opportunity to claim credit for distributive benefits. In addition, it is apparent that legislators are much more likely to claim credit for projects that require their traceable action, than for projects that allocate funds on the basis of executive discretion or statutory formulas. Of the members of Congress who claimed credit for distributive benefits, 87 (93.5%) referred to benefits that required legislative action, almost always, appropriations earmarks. Distributive benefits that are allocated on the basis of formula, categorical, or block grant were much less likely to be included in congressional newsletters. Only 24.8% of the members mentioned local grant allocations.[28] The preference for earmarks becomes more apparent when the number of times earmarks are mentioned is compared with the number of mentions for grants. Total earmark mentions in the sample outnumber grant mentions 294 to 87.

Of the 294 separate earmark mentions, the great majority (97.9%) fall into one of the seven different appropriations categories which form the basis of this study. Transportation appropriations (especially appropriations for demonstration projects for bridges and highways) account for the largest volume of earmark credit claims. Table 2.1 summarizes the number of references by appropriations area included in the newsletters that were studied. A detailed description of each earmark category is the subject of the next chapter.

Table 2.1: Earmark References in Newsletters

EARMARK CATEGORY	EARMARK MENTIONS
Transportation	131
Energy and Water	57
HUD Special Projects	27
Military Construction	26
Interior/National Parks	20
Federal Buildings Fund	11
Agricultural Research	6

Organization of Empirical Literature Reviews

Throughout this study, evidence will be included from both an empirical study of earmarks, and previous studies of pork barrel spending. In order to more precisely understand the findings of prior empirical research, it is important to look at the nature of the data involved in those studies. Comparing research that explores project decisions such as water projects, with studies that look at project of formula driven research often adds confusion in interpreting the results. Chapters Four, Six and Seven include reviews of the relevant theoretical and empirical literature pertaining to the premise of distributive theory being critiqued. When discussing the empirical findings, I will employ a typology that categorizes the empirical literature based on characteristics of the spending data sorted by the source of decision making discretion.[29] The four broad types of expenditures differ in how locational decisions are made (either through statutory formula or through project discretion) and in who makes the decisions (either by the bureaucracy or by Congress). The four possible expenditure types are depicted in Diagram 1 below. They are: 1) Decision by legislators on a project selection basis; 2) Decision by legislators who write a distributional formula into authorizing legislation; 3) Decision by bureaucrats on a project selection basis and 4) Decision by bureaucrats who write general allocational formulas.

Diagram 1: Types of Discretion

	PROJECT DECISIONS	FORMULAS
CONGRESS	Legislative/Project	Legislative/Formula
EXECUTIVE	Bureaucratic/Project	Bureaucratic/Formula

Note: Consistent with previous research, I have not found any scholarly studies using data from bureaucratic/formula programs.[30]

This research will use the framework to organize the empirical literature on distributive politics. A fifth category will include those articles where there is more than one type of delivery mechanism included in the data set, for example studies looking at the distribution of all government outlays across congressional districts. By using this framework, patterns in the literature become more apparent. Previous reviews of the empirical literature on distributive politics that have considered all research together regardless of source of discretion, and have been less successful in finding patterns in the results. It is the contention of this research that those studies which rely on legislative project determination are the purest reflections of congressional pork barrel behavior, and present the most accurate evaluations of existing theory. These studies have thus far been limited to the case of the Army Corps of Engineers water resource projects. Congressional earmarks are also an example of legislative project determination, and will form the basis of the empirical analysis of this research.

NOTES

1. The term "cardinal" is often used by members of Congress and observers in referring to chairs of Appropriations subcommittees. Use of the

word is meant to convey a sense of power accompanying the institutional position. The collective term is often "college of cardinals."

2. Savage (1991) has studied appropriations earmarks as a reflection of distributive politics; however, his study was limited to the impact that Appropriations Subcommittee chairs can have on limiting distributive results. Evans (1994, 1995) examines authorization earmarks for highway demonstration projects; however, her research looks at the use of distributive benefits to win legislative support of non-distributive legislation. Andres (1995) in a largely anecdotal account, argues that earmarks are more common during periods of divided government as legislators can't rely on a cooperative administration to help ensure the provision of their distributive priorities. See also Savage (1992a) and (1992b).

3. It is specifically not my intent to argue either that earmarks are the most prevalent example of district specific spending or the most important from a policy perspective. In fact, I would contend that their policy importance has been overstated by opponents including members of Congress, public interest groups like the National Taxpayers Union, and Congressional Quarterly. The point simply is that virtually all distributive theory models include members who vote on projects, something that cannot be tested using data where the ultimate locational choice takes place after the legislative choice and is made by another entity, typically bureaucrats.

4. A narrower definition of earmarking has been proposed by former House Science, Space and Technology Committee Chairman George Brown in an informal Committee Report (Brown 1994). Brown defines earmark as: "appropriations that are tied to specific locations or institutions and which have not been requested by an Executive Branch Department, approved by the president, and included in his budget, and/or in authorizing legislation approved by the House and Senate and signed by the President" (p.1.).

5. Schick (1995) claims: "What gives appropriations reports special status is not law but the fact that the next appropriations cycle is less than a year away. An agency that willfully violates report language risks retribution the next time it asks for money" (p.162). Former Reagan Budget Director James C. Miller III tried to implement a policy in 1988 to encourage agencies to disregard earmarks in report language. According to Miller (1994), this action so outraged members of Congress that they threatened retaliation. "I eventually capitulated declaring that this was an issue the next president would have to resolve" (p.110). For additional discussion of the importance of non-statutory techniques for spending and spending control, see Kirst (1969), and Fisher (1989).

6. For example, Senator Barbara Mikulski (D-MD) former chair of the Departments of Veterans Affairs and Housing and Urban Development and Independent Agencies Appropriations Subcommittee claimed: "This committee, this subcommittee, received 1,100 individual requests from Senators for line-item projects. That totaled $96 billion. This entire appropriations (sic) is $88 billion to fund VA, space, and all the other programs I mentioned. We said "no" to 90-some billion dollars worth of projects" (Congressional Record, 9/27/94: S13398). References of this sort are quite common. Former Appropriations Committee and Interior Subcommittee Chair, Senator Byrd (D-WV) claimed to receive 3,000 requests for earmarks for the FY 1993 Interior Appropriation (CQ Almanac 1992: 249). An interesting research question relates to the frequency with which legislators request and receive earmarks. I have been unable (for obvious reasons) to obtain this data.

7. On this point, and the importance of the "chairman's mark" see Shuman 1988, pp. 71-72. Shuman claims that over 95 percent of the items in an appropriations bill are decided at a private meeting between the subcommittee chair and the ranking member.

8. See White (1993) and Savage (1991) on the inner workings of the Appropriations Subcommittee process. See also Forgette and Saturno (1994).

9. Not all government programs with local benefits are equally valued by members of Congress. Murphy (1968) cited in Mayhew (1974: 55.) quotes one member as saying :"They've got to see something; it's the bread and butter issues that count—the dams, the post offices and the other public buildings, the highways. They want to know what you've been doing." Another way to interpret the value of a particular program to a member of Congress concerns the "social construction of the target population" (Schneider and Ingram 1993). According to Schneider and Ingram, expenditures that are targeted for the "advantaged" group in society (including those groups that are both politically powerful and positively construed—the elderly, business, veterans, and scientists) will be oversubscribed compared to spending for less powerful and positively viewed segments of society. For example, a member of Congress would much rather add (and take credit for) a wing to the veterans hospital in his/her district than add a new needle exchange program for heroin addicts.

10. In fact, I will argue that Stein and Bickers make a valuable contribution to the literature by providing a database of district specific expenditures, and by analyzing that literature on the basis of new and existing hypotheses. However, I will also argue that it is not accurate to call the expenditures identified by Stein and Bickers pork barrel spending, at least in light of the way distributive theorists model distributive politics. See discussion below.

11. Wilson (1989: 240) claims that: "the detailed regulation of bureaucratic conduct to some degree has given way to the manipulation of legislated constraints on behavior. Where Congress once said, 'open this fort' or 'close this shipyard,' it now says, 'subject the opening of forts or the closing of shipyards to environmental impact statements.' Where Congress once unabashedly directed the War Department to give a weapons contract to the Jedediah Jones Canon Foundry, it now directs the Defense Department to insure that the contract is awarded to an American firm that tenders the lowest bid, employs the correct mix of women and minorities, makes provisions to aid the handicapped, give subcontracts to suitable numbers of small businesses, is in compliance with the regulations of the Environmental Protection Agency and Occupational Safety and Health Administration, and is not currently under indictment for contract fraud."

12. NSF is not the only example of a funding agency that relies heavily on peer review. As another example, Bickers and Stein also include over sixty different programs administered by the National Institutes of Health (NIH) in their data set. NIH also relies on peer review.

13. Johannes and McAdams (1986) test the broader question of whether members of Congress are "entrepreneurs" or "agents" regarding the stimulation of casework. Although casework and stimulation of distributive benefits differ somewhat, Fiorina (1977) explicitly links the two, and it can be assumed that there is at least some relationship between the provision of services to constituents and the provision of pork. Johannes and McAdams conclude: ". . . the bulk of casework volume appears to be a function more of pure happenstance and constituency traits than of anything congressmen themselves do to stimulate case requests" (p.548).

14. Cain, Ferejohn, and Fiorina (1987) also conclude: "Even local politics affects grant seeking. One Republican office complained that 'Democratic mayors don't want to ask a Republican representative for any help on projects.' Thus, staff efforts are only one aspect of the involvement of the congressional office with projects" (p.74).

15. Universalism will be discussed in Chapter Six.

16. Thirteen is the total for a "normal" year. However, most years are not normal. Supplementals can account for additional bills, and continuing resolutions can increase the omnibus nature of appropriations by reducing the number of individual bills.

17. While direct spending does characterize many of the redistributive programs, it is very rare for distributive policies; the main exception is highway authorization earmarks In addition, many more distributive programs are authorized than can be funded.

18. According to Hartzog (1988), with the passage of a series of laws in the late 1960's " . . . the National Park Service has designated a national landmark in private, state or local government ownership, commemorating either an historical event, a natural environment or a nationally significant educational study resource, in every one of the then existing 435 congressional districts."

19. Bickers and Stein (1994a, 1994b, and 1995) ignore the possibility of a more direct distributive connection. It is only in their most recent effort (1996: 1304) that they the acknowledge the existence of earmarking. However, they claim: " . . . the frequency that such earmarking occurs has not been widely researched (the exception is Evans 1994). Our sense is that the folklore about earmarking tends to exaggerate the extent it occurs."

20. Using the terminology of rational choice theorists, bureaucrats can be viewed as agents of more than one principal.

21. For a recent study of the influence of presidential elections on the distribution of benefits, see Mayer, 1995.

22. Local jurisdictions differ greatly in their economic and social need for federal assistance, their eligibility for federal grants, as well as their capacities (political and otherwise) to solicit grants. On this point see Saltzstein 1977.

23. On the motivation of bureaucrats to pursue good public policy, see Goodsell 1983; and Kelman 1987.

24. There is a clear division in the literature between those who view the Bureaucracy as the agent of Congress and those who believe that bureaucratic motivations and incentives extend beyond congressional pressure (dominance). Fiorina (1981a, p.340) summarizes the "congressional dominance" perspective as follows: "Congress has powerful instruments of control over the bureaucracy, and there is ample evidence that the threat of those instruments is seldom far from bureaucratic minds. The effectiveness of those instruments is made all the more real by the establishment and maintenance of the elaborate committee reciprocity system . . . " Additional evidence in favor of the congressional dominance hypothesis is found in Calvert, Moran, and Weingast (1987). In a direct critique of the congressional dominance theory, Terry Moe (1987) argues that congressional scholars may overstate the role of congressional influence in bureaucratic decision making. The public administration literature often emphasizes the competing demands placed on agency bureaucrats. See Rourke's (1993) description of the "joint custody" arrangement between the executive and the legislature in directing the behavior of the bureaucracy for a typical example. See also Aberbach and Rockman (1988), and Neustadt (1964).

25. See Mayhew 1974, Cover 1980, Yiannakis 1982, Parker, 1986, Smith 1985, Cook 1989, Lineberry, Edwards, and Wattenberg 1994, Penny 1995 and Lipinski 1995. The congressional newsletter provides the incumbent member of Congress the opportunity to engage in both advertising and credit claiming in a forum that often reaches every household in the district (Newsletters are also known as "postal patrons" due to the scope of their reach). The conservative interest group National Taxpayers Union (NTU) which tracks congressional spending on mass mailings, finds evidence that members of congress use newsletters to boost their reelection chances. The NTU found that in 1994, lawmakers spent 84% more in July and August (the last two months prior to an election that the current law allows mass mailings), than in the same two months of 1993 (a non-election year). According to David Keating, president of NTU: "The last minute scramble shows the franking privilege is being abused. Many frightened incumbents spent millions of tax dollars to send out propaganda aimed at boosting their image with angry voters." (NTU, 1994) Roll Call the self-proclaimed newspaper of Capitol Hill has reported on the use of the franking privilege and frequently editorialized against its use, on the grounds that it provides an unfair electoral advantage to incumbents. See for example: Curran (1993); Love (1994) and Love and Von Dongen (1994).

26. Both House and Senate rules define mass mailings as "newsletters and other similar mailings (including town meeting notices) of more than 500 pieces in which the content of the matter mailed is substantially identical (see Senate Rule 40 and 39 U.S.C. 3210 (a)(6)(E). During the major focus of this research (102nd, 103rd and 104th Congresses), use of mass mailings/newsletters by Senators was limited and declining. The Legislative Branch Appropriation Act reduced the funds available for mass mailings, while at the same time increasing reporting requirements (Senate Rule 40). While the following quote appears to be a slight exaggeration, Senator Harry Reid stated: "I do not think there is a Senator who now sends a newsletter. I might be wrong, but I doubt it. Because under our franking rules, we do not have enough money to send one letter to every household in our state" (Curran 1993). Telephone calls to several Senate press secretaries in the fall of 1994 confirmed that only a few Senators continued to send newsletters. The Senate subsequently (October, 1994) banned all newsletters. During the time period in question, Senator's were typically allotted approximately fifteen cents per postal addresses in their States, insufficient funds to pay for even one statewide newsletter. A typical House member on the other hand received about 67.4 cents per address, enough to cover the costs of roughly three districtwide mailings (Curran 1993). Attempts to reduce the House allowance for franked mail have been common in recent sessions of Congress. See for example an

attempt by Representative Mark Neumann (R-WI) to reduce postage spending on June 21, 1995 (Congressional Record, pp.H6186-H6189).

27. Requests for newsletters from all 435 voting members of the House of Representatives were mailed in the summer of 1994. Initial requests were addressed directly to the member of Congress. Follow-up mailings were sent to each office that did not respond in the fall of 1994. Follow-up mailings were addressed to each member's press secretary by name (obtained from the Congressional Staff Directory). This was done because evidence indicates (see for example Jackley 1992) that House Offices may routinely discard mail directed to the member from outside of the state or district represented in Congress. Senator Ted Stevens (R-AK), for example, claimed: "I shred all of the mail from out of State. I do not have enough money to answer mail from out of State. (Congressional Record, 23 July 1993, p.S9349)" In addition, all members who still did not respond, and were available through the House email system in January 1995 were contacted via email. I believe that respondents will closely mirror the total House membership. However, it is possible that respondents are also those who are more likely to want to claim credit for their accomplishments as they are more willing to devote resources to dealing with out of state requests for information. This potential bias should not be important to the results of this analysis, as I am not measuring which members are more likely to engage in pork, but only measure what type of pork is favored. One could assume that those who more actively claim credit have an understanding of what is valuable.

28. The total of grants and earmarks exceeds 100% as some newsletters claimed credit for bringing home both type of benefits.

29. This typology is a simplification of the process by which the federal government allocates funds to states and localities, but it covers all four types of discretion that are involved. For example, federal grants can be either categorical (use specific) or block grants which give greater discretion to the recipient in the use of the funds. For a complete list of programs in which the federal government distributes funds, along with a description of the way in which funds are allocated, see the General Service Administration's Catalog of Federal Domestic Assistance. See Arnold 1981b and Anagnoson 1980b for discussions of method of funding allocation. See also Hamm 1983 for a similar typology.

30. The existence of bureaucratically determined formula grants is documented in an extensive General Accounting Office (GAO 1987b) study of formula grants entitled: Grant Formulas: A Catalog of Federal Aid to States and Localities. The GAO was able to identify the origins of 101 formulas that are used to determine the allocation of federal funds (of a total 142 programs that

distributed funds on the basis of a formula). Of those programs where the source of the formula was identified, 87 were developed with at least some congressional guidance. Therefore, at least fourteen (and as many as 55) programs rely on formulas that are arrived at solely through bureaucratic determination.

CHAPTER THREE

Descriptions of Earmark Programs

When members of Congress want to make money move in mysterious ways, they slip an arcane reference or two into the back pages of an appropriations bill. This legislative legerdemain is called earmarking, a word derived from the old herdsman's practice of cutting a notch in the ears of swine or cattle as a mark of ownership. The language, usually inserted in a footnote or short paragraph, demands that money be spent on a certain program in a certain place, usually somewhere in the author's home district . . . To earmark a program, a member must have the ear of one of the 13 chairmen of the House Appropriations subcommittees. The chairmen, nicknamed "the college of cardinals" by their colleagues, have the power to distribute billions of dollars a year in favored programs.

Tim Weiner (1994)

The most visible type of pork barrel spending are the earmarked projects tucked neatly into large appropriations bills.

Rep. Bill Orton, D-UT (1996)

This chapter provides additional details about each of the seven spending categories that have been identified as favorite sources of pork barrel spending. Through a systematic examination of each category, similarities can be identified, which may improve our understanding of the attributes that make a spending program more or less desirable for members of Congress and more or less susceptible to credit claiming. Descriptions of each earmark category follow the same format; they begin with a sample quote illustrating how members value and claim credit for legislative earmarks. These quotes are drawn from member newsletters and press releases from the 103rd and 104th Congress as well as *Congressional Quarterly*. The quotes are followed by a brief description of the spending category, including some history of the policy and evidence that it provides distributive benefits to a congressional district. For each category, there is a chart depicting the scope of spending during the 102nd through 104th Congresses (Fiscal Year 1992—Fiscal Year 1997) in terms of both number of earmarks, and total earmarked expenditures. The descriptions of each earmark type conclude with some discussion of a political controversy surrounding the earmark category related to how it has been labeled an example of pork barrel spending. Each of these spending areas has been subject to attempts by political opponents of pork barrel spending to reduce or eliminate spending on the category.

MILITARY CONSTRUCTION

> The House today passed a conference bill to fund construction at U.S. military bases—including almost $14.5 million for Shaw Air Force Base. The conference measure resolved differences between the House and Senate versions; once it passes the Senate, it will go to the President to be signed into law. U.S. Rep. John Spratt (D-SC), a senior member of the National Security Committee, said $3.3 million would go toward a new security police building, $2.365 million would be used to upgrade the sanitary sewer system at the base, and $8.8 million will be used to improve three airman dormitories . . . Spratt said his goal has been "to make sure that at least one or two military construction projects are approved for Shaw each year . . . " "We want to keep Shaw in the top echelon of all Air Force Bases," said Spratt. "We don't want to wait until we see another round of base closures coming several years from now. We want to make sure that Shaw stays ahead or abreast of its competitors."
>
> Rep John Spratt (D-SC), press release, August 1, 1996

DESCRIPTION

The political importance of military construction funding is underscored by the existence of a separate appropriations subcommittee with jurisdiction over this one area of defense spending. Prior to 1958, military construction funds were included as a part of the Department of Defense Appropriations bill, which continues to fund the rest of

Defense spending including expenditures related to weapons system procurement, operations and military compensation (Bowens 1993). Most of the funds included in the military construction appropriation are used to contract with local construction companies to build such physical assets as: barracks, facilities for weapons, training facilities, hospitals, child care centers, physical fitness centers, and armories for use by active duty as well as National Guard personnel. Military construction in a district therefore provides a representative/senator with a visible short and long-term avenue for credit claiming. Construction jobs are plentiful in the short run, and military employment and the accompanying economic benefits are present in the longer term.

Previous analysts have concluded that spending for military bases is the most politicized aspect of defense spending (Mayer 1991; Soeherr-Hadwiger 1993).[1] The battles in Congress to preserve military bases are legendary, and have led to the creation of an independent base closure commission to remove some of the politics from base closing decisions (Soeherr-Hadwiger 1993). According to Mayer (1991: 7): "No one disputes that military bases are a classic example of pork barrel politics, and members will fight furiously to protect local installations that have no conceivable national security justification."

SCOPE AND FUNDING

Congressional Quarterly's *Congressional Districts in the 1990s* lists 467 military facilities in the United States, located in 241 congressional districts in all 50 states.[2] Every state, and almost 60 percent of all congressional districts, contain military bases or other installations and many more are located close enough to bases so as to receive economic benefits from them. The payrolls and procurement associated with these military bases, an American Enterprise Institute analysis has concluded, 'may provide greater benefits [to communities and members of Congress] than do highly sought after projects for the construction of dams or the improvement of rivers and harbors" (Fitzgerald and Lipson 1984: 13).

Table 3.1: Domestic Military Construction Appropriations Earmarks

	All Military Construction		Non-Requested Earmarks	
Fiscal Year	Earmarks (#)	Earmarks ($)	Earmarks (#)	Earmarks ($)
1992	713	3,776,850,000	179	826,799,000
1993	504	2,689,460,000	250	1,128,680,000
1994	692	3,698,142,000	202	696,904,000
1995	418	2,839,787,000	197	1,105,500,000
1996	425	2,611,366,000	112	705,980,000
1997	389	2,928,998,000	129	737,381,000

Controversies

The tendency of the Military Construction Appropriations Subcommittee to fund additional projects not requested in the President's Budget is frequently mentioned by critics of spending in this area. Facilities for National Guard and the Reserves (such as armories) which are located in areas without large bases are frequently included as unrequested (in the President's Budget) and unauthorized appropriations, thereby increasing the geographic spread of this spending category (Bowens 1993). This practice has been the subject of floor amendments in both chambers seeking to strip some or all unrequested military construction projects. Senator John McCain (R-AZ) has been a vocal opponent of this practice:

> In the past 5 years, from FY 1990 through FY 1994, Congress has added over $4.4 billion in unrequested military construction projects to the Defense budget. This equates to $880 million every year in special interest projects designated for members' districts or States. And every dollar added for these pork-barrel projects had to come from some other program . . . " (Congressional Record, July 15, 1994: S9099).

The non-partisan interest group BENS (Business Executives for National Security) has also been critical of add-on Military Construction spending (BENS 1995). The organization issued a "Pork Alert" on June 15, 1995 which criticized the excesses in the Fiscal 1996

Military Construction Appropriation. "The business leaders suggested that more rigorous legislative barriers might result in fewer but more thoroughly justified add-on projects."

Highway Demonstration Projects

> As a senior member of the House Transportation and Infrastructure Committee, Congressman Bateman continues to make sure the Commonwealth of Virginia's infrastructure needs are addressed. He has secured $14 million in federal funds devoted to helping Virginia pay for widening the Coleman Bridge over the York River. He also is working hard to obtain funding for an I-95 interchange in Stafford County and an extension of HOV lanes on I-95 to the Rappahannock River. Congressman Bateman worked closely with residents of the Northern Neck and the Middle Peninsula to dramatically improve plans to repair the Norris Bridge over the Rappahannock River. He also was an integral part of the federal, state and local team that brought the Monitor-Merrimac Bridge Tunnel to the Peninsula.
>
> Rep. Herbert Bateman (R-VA), Legislative Accomplishments 1995

Description

The Federal-Aid Highway Program, which is administered by the Federal Highway Administration (FHWA) of the U.S. Department of Transportation, is the major program by which states are financially aided to continue construction, repairs and expansion of the national highway system, including completion of the Interstate system. Funds are distributed to states from the highway trust fund based upon a statutorily arrived at formula. In addition to this program which allocates funds to every state, both the Transportation Appropriations subcommittees and the highway authorizations committees of each chamber (Public Works [now Transportation and Infrastructure] in the House; Environment and Public Works in the Senate) have frequently funded highway demonstration projects as earmarks in recent years.

Demonstration projects provide highly visible benefits to constituents in the form of increased mobility, reduced highway congestion, and concentrated construction employment. Due to the nature of the policy type (roads, bridges, etc.), every congressional district is the potential location of one or more demonstration earmark. Unlike Federal Aid Highway funding, national legislators, and not state officials determine where earmarked funds will be spent, and therefore members of Congress have a greater ability to claim credit. Although these projects are justified by their supporters as separate earmarks because they purport to demonstrate a new technology or concept, there is widespread agreement that they are simply an avenue for increased congressional control over distributive spending.[3]

Unlike most other authorizing committees, the committees that authorize transportation spending have the ability to earmark spending directly, through the highway trust fund, without the need for confirming action on the part of the Appropriations committees. Therefore, this one area of pork barrel spending by an authorizing committee will be included in the detailed analyses to follow. However, authorizing committees are only able to earmark projects every five or so years, when periodic reauthorizations take place. During the six years covered in this project, one major reauthorization was enacted. Specifically, ISTEA (the Intermodal Surface Transportation Efficiency Act of 1991) will be analyzed for distributive results.[4]

Table 3.2: Highway Demonstration Projects (Appropriations)

Fiscal Year	Earmarks (#)	Earmarks ($)
1992	127	589,000,000
1993	55	273,750,000
1994	23	6,000,000
1995	127	352,055,000
1996	0	0
1997	0	0

ISTEA contained 539 individual earmarks designating spending from the Highway Trust Fund of $6.2 billion over the life of the law.[5] Highway demonstration earmarks were not included in either of the two most recent appropriations reports covered in this research. This does not mean that the Transportation subcommittee appropriations reports are entirely free of earmarks. Earmarks are now common in programs that fund Intelligent Vehicle Highway Systems (IVHS), mass transit, as well as for regional airports.

Controversies

According to Jon Healy (1993: 127-128):

> No aspect of transportation spending is more controversial than the "demonstration projects" that lawmakers fund to build roads and bridges back home . . . Demonstration projects have been controversial for several reasons. In the past, most were not authorized by House and Senate Public Works committees. In addition, state transportation officials often disliked these projects because they bypass the traditional highway funding method of lump-sum grants, which let states decide how to spend the money. Critics say the projects rarely "demonstrate" novel road-building techniques and force states to put up matching funds to pay for work not considered by state officials to be of priority.

Highway demonstration earmarks were criticized by Vice President Gore in his "Reinventing Government Report" and have been removed from Appropriations Committee reports by Subcommittee Chairman Senator Frank Lautenberg in the 103rd Congress (D-NJ) and subsequently by House Subcommittee Chairman Frank Wolf (R-VA) in the 104th Congress. Authorization earmarks seem likely to continue.

National Park Service

> Solomon also has been successful and gone to great lengths to repair and maintain the national parks that dot the 22nd district and make up much of its charm and character. The Saratoga Battlefield monument has received $3 million directly so that it can be reopened and the FDR and Vanderbilt mansions have received $1.7 million thus far to begin rehabilitation with more to come . . . "These parks are critical to the local communities which surround them," said Solomon. "But they are also a national treasure that deserve to be kept up and by all means remain open. That's why I will oppose any commission or park closing list like the one put forth by President Clinton and his Interior Secretary, Bruce Babbit."
>
> Rep. Jerry Solomon (R-NY), press release, Oct. 25, 1996

Description

The United States National Park System consists of 367 major areas representing over 80 million acres of land in 49 states and the District of Columbia; over 272 million people visited a Park Service site in 1992 (House Report 102—256). If one includes all of the sites that the National Park Service has designated as a national landmark commemorating either an historical event, a natural environment or a nationally significant educational study resource, the Park Service has a presence in each of the 435 congressional districts (as of 1988) (Hartzog 1988: 138).

It is only in the last twenty years that National Parks truly have been considered a pork barrel program. It is largely through the legislative efforts of the late Representative Phil Burton (D-CA) that the packaging of park authorization legislation into large omnibus bills changed the way that Congress viewed the policy area.[6] National Park appropriations have followed the pattern established by Burton. According to Lowry (1994):

> The application of NPS funds to congressionally approved pet projects has historical roots but has become rampant recently. Big Bend [National Park] superintendent Arnberger assessed recent changes: 'The federal budget is becoming more of a line-item process wherein members of Congress take care of pet projects.' Pork barreling was so obvious in 1990 that several agency career officials complained to their political bosses in a memo that the NPS was becoming a 'repository for what are in essence economic development type projects'.

Table 3.3: National Park Service Construction

Fiscal Year	Earmarks (#)	Earmarks ($)
1992	121	271,871,000
1993	135	275,801,000
1994	70	231,801,000
1995	134	201,724,000
1996	44	63,500,000
1997	65	163,444,000

Scope and Funding

Park construction provides tangible benefits to an area through the employment of contractors to build the facilities, increased recreational opportunities for local residents, as well as potential economic development through increased tourism that may result from new and improved park facilities. The National Park Service is funded by the Department of Interior and Related Agencies Appropriations Subcommittee, and a special account for construction at park facilities is annually earmarked to specific locations.

Controversies

Perhaps the most notorious example of pork barrel spending in the National Parks Service construction account is the case of Steamtown, a site honoring the history of railroads in America located in the Scranton, PA district of Representative Joseph McDade (R-PA). The funding of Steamtown is best summed up by Lowry (P.49):[7]

> Historic sites were added as political "pork," the most illustrative example being Steamtown in Pennsylvania. Steamtown became a NPS unit in 1986 when Representative Joseph McDade (R-Pennsylvania), ranking member of the House Appropriations Committee, bypassed slated procedures for unit creation, amending the budget bill to designate a site commemorating historic steam railroading. Since the abandoned railyard had no original equipment and few historic structures, the site came with a huge price tag. Over the five years following its creation, Congress appropriated over $40 million for design and construction. In 1991, a panel of historians testified to Congress that Steamtown, when finished, would be 'little more than a railroad theme park with an eclectic collection of trains.'

Several attempts to eliminate or reduce the funding for Steamtown have been unsuccessful. As Steamtown illustrates, National Parks are now viewed by some members of Congress as tools for economic revitalization of a community. This has fundamentally changed the nature of the budget of the National Park Service.

Federal Buildings Fund

> Federal and local officials gathered today to celebrate the official start of construction on the new 16 story, $142 million federal courthouse building in Sacramento. The first new federal building in the downtown area since construction of the Moss Federal Office Building in 1961 is expected to create at least 1,200 new jobs. Congressman Robert T. Matsui was on hand for the ceremony. "This

> much needed building will be a welcome addition to the Sacramento skyline," Matsui remarked. "The new building will not only overcome the shortfalls of the current courthouse building, but it will also serve as a critical link to future development downtown . . . Over 1,200 new jobs will be created on top of the positions already necessary for the operation of the current facility and federal courts. Furthermore, downtown retail sales are expected to grow an additional $2.2 million annually. Matsui explained. "It was clear that in order to meet the increasing demands on the district court system, we would need to build a new facility. I can't express how pleased I am to be here today to mark the official start of construction on this facility." Representatives from numerous local unions were also on hand to celebrate the occasion. Every contract which has been let for construction has been to a union employer. Over ten local unions will be involved in the construction.
>
> Rep. Robert Matsui (D-CA), Press Release, 1996

Description

The construction of a federal building in a congressional district is a very visible reminder of the federal government's presence. Federal buildings provide employment both in the construction and staffing of a facility, and are typically highly sought after by legislators. Large federal office complexes and courthouses are often viewed as important to an area's economic development, not only because of the construction work and revenue associated with the building, but also because federal buildings tend to attract other firms that need to do business with the government to the area.

The construction of federal buildings is funded through the Federal Buildings Fund in the Budget of the General Services Administration (GSA) which receives its appropriation from the Treasury, Postal Service and General Government Appropriations Subcommittee. According to Congressional Quarterly: ". . . one account in the bill [Treasury and Postal Service Appropriation] gives members opportunities aplenty to bestow favors. That is the Federal Buildings fund which pays for new construction. Courthouses are a particular favorite of members, eagerly sought and vociferously defended" (Taylor 1993).

Scope and Funding

Although relatively few in number, the large amount of funds associated with each building earmark over a multi-year period, makes this type of earmark especially desirable. However, because of the limited scope of the program, options for statistical analysis using this program as a variable is quite limited.

Table 3.4: Federal Building Fund

Fiscal Year	Earmarks (#)	Earmarks ($)
1992	23	271,000,000
1993	34	330,501,000
1994	32	925,000,000
1995	52	601,702,000
1996	27	545,002,000
1997	39	400,544,000

Controversies

Construction of new federal buildings have been attacked by critics on two grounds: 1) that new construction is unnecessary at a time when there is a large surplus of office space in the private sector; and 2) that federal buildings are unnecessarily expensive, and often serve as economic development projects rather than essential facilities to meet the needs of government agencies. The second criticism is especially prevalent, and it is often accompanied by claims that federal buildings are being "gold-plated;" that is that they are more expensive than necessary due to costly add-ons and frills. Courthouse construction, for example, has been criticized for the use of expensive varieties of marble. The following excerpt from a statement made on the House floor by Representative Dan Burton (R-IN) captures this type of opposition to federal building construction:

> This bill contains eight new Federal building construction projects which were not authorized by the administration, and these projects cost $212 million, and they are not needed by Federal agencies. Five of the eight projects are not authorized, they are unauthorized, and they cost $141 million. The worst abuser of these five is the project in Newark, NJ. It is a nine-story parking garage . . . The real purpose of

> this project, Mr. Chairman, is economic development in downtown Newark. The adjacent Federal office facilities are being used as a convenient excuse to bring home $15 million in pure pork. (Congressional Record, July 1, 1982: H5761).

Agricultural Research

> In a letter written by Congressman Sanford D. Bishop, Jr., House members of the Georgia Congressional Delegation requested $400,000 for the Southeastern Fruit and Nut Laboratory in Byron, GA. The entire House delegation, led by Mr. Bishop, asked House Agriculture Appropriations Subcommittee Chairman Richard Durbin (IL) to support funding for a research and development study of entomological pest management at the Byron facility.
>
> Rep. Sanford Bishop, Newsletter, Spring 1994

Description

The primary function of the Cooperative State Research, Education and Extension Service (CSREES) is to administer the Acts of Congress that authorize Federal appropriations for agricultural research carried out by state agricultural experiment stations, 1890 land-grant institutions, and other eligible institutions. In addition to programs that are funded on the basis of competitive evaluation of project merit, the Agriculture Appropriations subcommittees have included a category of "special research grants" in report language which are allocated to universities and other eligible recipients by the subcommittee in a distributive manner. Members of Congress have also earmarked spending for large scale research facilities in the budget of the Cooperative State Research Education and Extension Service, usually for buildings located on College campuses. A second bureau of the Department of Agriculture, the Agricultural Research Service (ARS) conducts basic, applied and developmental research directly.

Scope and Funding

One of the reasons given by advocates of earmarked spending in these areas is to increase the geographic spread of federal research dollars which tend to be concentrated at the elite major research universities when competitive awards are used.[8] There are no restrictions placed on the location of earmarks in this category.

Table 3.5: Cooperative State Research Education and Extension Service

	Research Grants		Research Facilities	
Fiscal Year	Earmarks (#)	Earmarks ($)	Earmarks (#)	Earmarks ($)
1992	133	73,979,000	50	75,270,000
1993	133	73,411,000	42	52,101,000
1994	133	72,917,000	40	56,874,000
1995	121	52,295,000	36	62,744,000
1996	111	49,846,000	27	57,838,000
1997	112	49,767,000	20	61,591,000

Controversies

Agricultural research projects have been a particularly easy program to attack by opponents of this type of targeted spending, as many of the projects concern crops and specific farm related issues that have strange sounding (to the uninformed) names. President's Reagan, Bush and Clinton, have all singled out CSREES earmarks for elimination. President Reagan highlighted this program in his 1988 State of the Union Address (Administration of Ronald Reagan 1988):

> Over the past few weeks, we've all learned what was tucked away behind a little comma here and there. For example, there's millions for items such as cranberry research, blueberry research, the study of crawfish, and the commercialization of wildflowers . . .

According to *Congressional Quarterly:* "For years, the Agriculture appropriations bill had funded hundreds of research projects on agricultural production, pest control, marketing, and rural economic issues. And for just as many years, deficit hawks, and presidents have derided a number of these programs conducted at government facilities, universities, and private sector laboratories as examples of wasteful federal spending" (Benenson 1993: 29).

Housing and Urban Development Special Purpose Grants

> Seldom could I walk on the floor of this House without members asking me to sit down so they could tell me about a special project in their district," Stokes said. He added that he had received more than

> 300 requests for HUD special purpose grants, and more than 1,000 requests for grants in the bill overall. "Earmarking funds for special projects has been a congressional prerogative for a long time," Stokes said. "These are good projects."
>
> Rep. Louis Stokes, D-OH, former Cardinal

Description

The Community Development Block Grant (CDBG) program was established in 1974 with the primary objective of providing adequate housing and a suitable living environment and expanding economic opportunities principally for lower and moderate income individuals. CDBG's are allocated on the basis of a statutory formula using demographic criteria such as population and age of housing stock. In addition, the Departments of Veterans Affairs and Housing and Urban Development and Independent Agencies Appropriations subcommittee has opted to earmark grants to specific projects, called Special Purpose Grants, on the basis of discretionary criteria. According to Congressional Quarterly: "The projects entail a wide variety of purposes, including funding for sewer and water lines; science, health and educational facilities, restoration of railroad stations, municipal plazas and civic coliseums; clinical labs; industrial developments; social services; housing, and unspecified economic development activities" (Congressional Quarterly, September 12, 1994: 2574).

Table 3.6: HUD Special Purpose Grants

Fiscal Year	Earmarks (#)	Earmarks ($)
1992	78	150,000,000
1993	214	260,000,000
1994	0	0
1995	266	290,000,000
1996	0	0
1997	0	0

Scope and Funding

As projects include any loosely interpreted effort at community development all congressional districts are eligible for special purpose grants. A broad range of projects have been funded under the special purpose heading. For example, fiscal 1995 earmarked projects ranged from more traditional community development activities— $600,000 for the infrastructure improvement for a sewer system in St. Louis—to more original examples of community development funding— $2,000,000 to the Jewish Community Federation of Cleveland for a system of support services for the frail elderly.

Controversies

The special purpose grants program has been controversial from its creation. Jack Kemp, Secretary of Housing and Urban Development in the Bush administration opposed these grants on the grounds that they should be allocated through a competitive process. When Kemp threatened to request a presidential veto of the appropriations bill in fiscal year 1991 because of the presence of earmarks, "His complaining so annoyed appropriators that the Senate subcommittee cut his first class travel privileges and zeroed out his public affairs staff for fiscal 1991." (Congressional Quarterly Almanac, 1992: 645). Though Kemp's privileges were later restored in conference, Kemp did not voice similar complaints in subsequent years.[9] No earmarks in this category have been included since the Republican Party gained control of Congress in 1994. However, earmarking continues in the subcommittee; it has shifted to areas more favorable to Republican voters. In fact freshman Representative Mark Neumann (a Republican from Wisconsin), appeared on C-SPAN in September 1996, complaining about the long list of earmarks included in this subcommittee Conference Report for fiscal year 1997.[10]

Army Corps of Engineers Water Resources Projects

> I have worked for many years to solve Orange County's nagging energy and water problems. I am happy to be able to secure the funding necessary to enhance those efforts . . . I am proud to be able to secure $750,000 for the Southern California Comprehensive Water and Reclamation Study . . . The $51 million I got for the Santa Ana River Mainstem is an important step to protect billions of dollars of property and millions of lives from potentially deadly floods . . . I was able to secure $365,000 to complete the San Juan and Aliso Creeks reconnaissance study of flood control issues and will permit the Army Corps of Engineers to move to a feasibility study to correct the flood hazard in the area," said Packard.
>
> Rep. Ron Packard (R-CA), press release, Sept. 12, 1996

Description

The Army Corps of Engineers was established in 1824 as a domestic unit of the Army. Since its inception, it has been responsible for ensuring the navigability of the nation's commercial waterways. In 1936, the Corps was given the mandate to build and maintain civil works projects to enhance flood control, storm damage reduction and environmental restoration. "The major activities of the Corps are the damming, widening, straightening, and deepening of rivers for barge navigation, building harbors for shipping, and construction of dams and levees and reservoirs for flood control. It also works on disaster relief and tries to prevent beach erosion." (Drew 1970: 53)

Army Corps of Engineers water resource projects have long been considered the classic example of pork barrel spending.[11] As a response to the frequent criticism, state and local governments have been required to share costs on federal water control projects since 1986 which is intended to ensure that the projects with the most merit and accountability get funded. In addition, detailed cost-benefit analyses are used in evaluating proposed projects. However, in addition to projects requested by the Corps in the President's annual budget, members of Congress typically earmark additional projects that have not been deemed priorities by the Army Corps.

Funds for water resource projects are typically divided into two major categories—funds for construction projects and funds for operations and maintenance of projects built by the Corps in the past (locks, dams etc.). The sheer size and scope of the program, the tangible benefits that projects provide in terms of flood control and economic development and the addition of programs not requested by the administration (and therefore not as highly ranked by the Corps) provides members of Congress with plentiful credit claiming opportunities.

Ferejohn (1974: 49-50) in his classic study of Army Corps of Engineers policy, sums up the reasons for the huge investment of resources that has historically characterized this funding area:

> Water projects in particular are something that congressmen generally believe can help them get reelected. Basically, the process can work in two ways. In the first place, getting projects can be symbolically

> important in a reelection campaign, since it shows voters that their congressman can do things for them in Washington . . . Perhaps even more important is the fact that projects provide benefits for a few well-organized groups in the district. Construction workers, contractors, and local businessmen receive economic rewards from nearly any sort of construction project; these groups frequently contain important potential contributors to, or workers in, a particular congressman's campaign.

Scope and Funding

Congress makes more location specific decisions for water projects than any other earmark category. The Appropriations Committee Reports typically divide Corps funding into two main sections—one for new construction, the other for operation and maintenance of ongoing projects (for example, locks or dams). The construction account, especially for construction of new projects, is often considered the most susceptible to political manipulation.

Table 3.7: Army Corps of Engineers Water Projects

Fiscal Year	Construction Earmarks	Total Earmarks	Total ($)
1992	515	1239	3,013,795,000
1993	482	1182	2,902,171,000
1994	553	1253	3,297,405,000
1995	518	1223	2,811,402,000
1996	543	1263	2,630,037,000
1997	542	1407	2,932,829,000

Controversies

President Jimmy Carter devoted considerable effort trying to reduce the size and scope of Army Corps of Engineers water resource spending during the early part of his administration. Most observers contend that this cost him valuable political support on Capitol Hill, and contributed to his ineffectiveness in getting his legislative goals through Congress.[12] According to journalist Hedrick Smith (1988: 339-340):

> . . . before getting to the heart of what he wanted to do, Carter got entangled with Congress in an ill-considered fight over pork-barrel funding of public works and water projects, a perennial legislative favorite. However noble Carter's attack on such questionable largesse, it was a sure loser. That fight soured his relations with Congress right away and kept him from getting to his own pet items.

President Clinton has included a proposal in his recent budget submissions calling for Congress to fund only those water projects which have national benefits, that is those projects that benefit more than one congressional district. Not surprisingly, this proposal was rejected by the Republican controlled House Appropriations Committee in July 1995 (Freedman 1995: 1990)

Finally, the political importance of water projects is perhaps best captured by one of this century's most vocal opponents of pork barrel spending—former Senator William Proxmire (D-WI). Drew (1970) relates the following quote from Proxmire discussing the Cross-Florida Barge Canal project:

> One hundred fifty-five million dollars has been spent as a starter . . . that is what it is, a starter—to make many more jobs, to make a great deal of money, and a great deal of profit. That is the essence of pork. That is why senators and congressmen fight for it and win reelection on it. Of course people who will benefit from these tens of millions of pork profit and jobs are in favor of it. That is perfectly natural and understandable.

Conclusion

From the seven programs discussed in this chapter, it is apparent that members of Congress are especially concerned with the geographic distribution of projects that provide highly visible benefits to their district. Large construction projects that increase economic development in the short-run through the infusion of federal government capital and labor and in the long-run through economic development that is directly associated with improvement of infrastructure and the employment of high wage (government) employees tend to be favored. Credit claiming is enhanced when the member can demonstrate personal involvement in the decision to fund the project, and earmarks, more than any other type of program, provide this opportunity.

NOTES

1. On the political nature of base closing decisions even after the creation of a Commission on Realignment and Base Closing see Bernardi (1996).

2. Several of the earmarked appropriations included in committee reports were for locations not included in the Congressional Quarterly volume, indicating an even greater geographic scope for the expenditure category.

3. Evans (1994: 682) claims: "... the primary and most obvious motivation of House members for requesting them [earmarks] was to enhance their chances for reelection through constituency service. As one respondent said, 'Anyone would concede that what they're demonstrating is how a member of Congress can come to the Public Works Committee, get a project, and go home and put out a press release'."

5. In 1998, Congress passed a highway reauthorization that contained 1,850 specific highway and bridge authorization earmarks totaling more than $9 billion (Pianin 1998).

6. Jacobs (1995) relays the following history: "Burton introduced his magnum opus, HR 12536, on May 5 [1978]. The scope, size and cost of Burton's bill was unprecedented. The previous Interior omnibus bill in 1974 was four pages. This had 157 pages and seven titles. Its price tag was $1.8 billion, and its 150 projects affected more than 200 congressional districts in 44 states. It authorized development funds for 34 parks, historic sites, and national seashores. It expanded 12 wilderness areas, created 11 new national parks, historic sites and seashores, and added segments to eight wild and scenic rivers and four new national trails." [Burton said] "'Why not put the whole agenda in here" he said. 'Why not get something for everyone? Christ, we'll pork out.' He would load up the bill until he had enough votes to guarantee passage. Burton thus became the first legislator with the imagination, patience and skill to turn environmental issues into the political equivalent of a water project or a defense contract. Others had used parks for leverage for years, but certainly not on this scale. Bob Neuman an aide to Arizona Congressman Morris Udall, was the first to call it what it was: park barrel."

7. There are numerous other accounts of the Steamtown example. See also: CQ Almanac 1992: 289; Davidson and Oleszek 1995; Lowry 1994b; Kriz 1995 and Zaroya 1996. For an insiders' account of the failed attempt to reduce Steamtown's FY 1994 appropriation, see Penny (1995: 55-58).

8. This is the one example of so called "academic pork" that has been included in this research. The controversy regarding targeting funds to specific universities has been well documented in a series of articles in the Chronicle of Higher Education (see especially the citations under Cordes). The practice of academic earmarking was challenged by former House Science Committee Chairman George Brown, who issued a report (Brown, 1994) and held hearings on the subject. See also GAO (1987a); and Savage, (1992a) and (1992b).

9. On this incident, see also Munson 1993.

10. I obtained a copy of this list (entitled "Pork Projects in the FY 1997 VA/HUD Conference Report) from Neumann's office. It contains 99 earmarked projects totaling $334 million scattered throughout the committee report. Many of the earmarks are for environmental protection (this subcommittee appropriates the EPA budget as well) such as waste water treatment plants and construction or renovation of Veterans Hospitals. Some have considered this to be a shift to a more "Republican" form of pork, as the target constituencies are more likely to be important to the Republican Party. See also Freedman 1995 and Healy 1996.

11. See for example: Maass (1951); Drew (1970); Ferejohn (1974); Kirschten (1977); Reisner (1986) and Peters (1996: 83). Safire (1995) traces the term "pork barrel" to early water project bills.

12. Carter's efforts to cut Corps water projects is well chronicled by Reisner (1986: Chapter Nine).

CHAPTER FOUR

Distributive Theory and Committee Membership

> *The model is based on a set of assertions about committee operation: (a) the assignment process operates as a self-selection mechanism; (b) committees are not representative of the entire legislature but instead are composed of "preference outliers" or those who value the position most highly; and (c) most centrally, committee members receive the disproportionate share of the benefits from the programs within their jurisdiction.*
>
> *Barry Weingast and William Marshall (1988)*

> *The distributive theory is an attractive, intuitively appealing theory of geographic allocation. Yet it fails . . . to explain adequately the geographic patterns of committee membership and program expenditures . . . The distributive theory oversimplifies the politics of geographic allocation by speaking of congressmen, committees and benefits as if all congressmen share the same single goal, all committees operate in more or less identical fashion, and all benefits are so similar that differentiation between them is unnecessary.*
>
> *R. Douglas Arnold (1979)*

Although the term "distributive policy" has been in use since the nineteenth century, Theodore Lowi was the first to associate distributive policies with different patterns of congressional behavior that distinguish them from policies that are either "regulatory," "redistributive" (Lowi 1964), or "constituent" (Lowi 1972). Lowi defined distributive policies as short run policies "characterized by the ease with which they can be desegregated and dispensed unit by small unit . . . 'Patronage' in the fullest meaning of the word can be taken as a synonym for distributive" (p.690). Lowi further defined distributive policies as those that benefit some distinguishable area or class yet "if there are some who are deprived, they cannot as a class be identified" (Lowi 1964: 690).[1]

David Mayhew (1974) was one of the first to theorize about the motivation for members of Congress to pursue particularized benefits.[2] In *Congress: The Electoral Connection* Mayhew claimed that the desire to ensure reelection prompts members of Congress to seek federal benefits for their districts. According to Mayhew (p.53), " . . . it becomes necessary for each Congressman to try to peel off pieces of governmental accomplishment for which he can believably generate a sense of responsibility. For the average congressman, the staple way of doing this is to traffic in what may be called 'particularized benefits'."

Building on the theoretical foundation of Lowi, Mayhew, and the then-emerging rational choice literature, Rundquist and Ferejohn (1975) proposed (and subsequently tested) three hypotheses of congressional behavior, organization, and policy output regarding polices that were distributive. These three hypotheses, which much of the subsequent empirical literature has been devoted to testing, are: 1) the recruitment hypothesis: "members from constituencies with a pecuniary interest in a particular form of government actively seek membership on a constituency-relevant authorizing committee or appropriations subcommittee;" 2) The overrepresentation hypothesis[3]: "when the districts of committee members are compared with those of other congressmen, the committee will be found to overrepresent constituencies with a stake in their subject matter; and 3) the benefit hypothesis: "relative to other congressmen, the constituencies of committee members benefit disproportionately from the distribution of expenditures under their jurisdiction" (p.88).[4]

As the quote that begins the chapter indicates, Marshall and Weingast (1988)[5] have fully developed a theory of congressional behavior that in part rests on the empirical validity of the three hypotheses outlined by Rundquist and Ferejohn (1975). These three assertions are key aspects of the main rational choice explanation for the institutionalization and behavior of committees in the U.S. Congress and are the foundation upon which other claims—such are the relationship between pork barrel politics and deficits—are made.

According to the distributive theory, Congress is organized into committees so that members can better achieve their reelection goals because specialization and vote trading allows each member to secure those distributive benefits from the federal treasury that are perceived to be most important to each geographic electoral constituency.

The distributive theory as it applies to the structure and function of committees is built on the three assertions listed above. However, there are doubts about the empirical validity of each assertion. Brief discussions of challenges to the first two statements from within the literature are now presented. The remainder of this chapter, as well as Chapter Five, will be devoted to a discussion of the validity of the third statement.

Self-Selection

Regarding the first assertion that forms the foundation of distributive theory (self-selection or the "recruitment hypothesis"), there have been numerous accounts of the committee selection process which have documented how members pursue committee choices.[6] Shepsle's (1978) rational choice account of Democratic Committee selection supported the hypothesis that members choose committees to best meet the electoral needs of their districts. Other motives, such as individual interest and the prior professional experience of the legislator were thought to be secondary.

Recent research seems to indicate that the political parties have an important limiting function in the committee selection process. (Kiewiet and McCubbins 1991; Cox and McCubbins 1993).[7] Cox and McCubbins conclude Chapter One of their book, which is an empirical analysis of the self-selection hypothesis:

> We have uncovered little evidence that the assignment process in the House is one of pure self-selection. The interest-seeking hypothesis—that constituency concerns drive committee requests—seems reasonable, but the statistical evidence for it pertains to only a few committees . . . More than 40 percent of freshman assignment requests and nonfreshman transfer requests are denied by the Democratic CC [Committee on Committees]. More than 30 percent of entering Democratic freshmen fail to get their most-preferred committee assignment even by the end of their third Congress. Almost 10 percent of freshmen fail to get *any* of their initially

> requested committee assignments even by the end of their fifth Congress. (pp. 43- 44, emphasis in original)

Cox and McCubbins propose and test an alternative hypothesis—"the partisan selection model"—to explain committee assignments. According to the partisan selection model, self-selection only explains part of the process. Each party's committee on committees controls access to important committees, and typically rewards loyal members with appointments on the prestige committees. In addition, each party "attempt(s) to keep committees with significant external effects more or less in line with overall sentiment in the party" (p.229)." By external effects, Cox and McCubbins mean: " . . . the effects that committee decisions have on the probabilities of victory of party members not on the committee" (p.191). This finding is also contrary to the argument that committees are composed of preference outliers, which is the second important claim of distributive theory.

PREFERENCE OUTLIERS

The claim that committees are composed of "preference outliers" (Rundquist and Ferejohn's "overrepresentation hypothesis") is one that is currently being debated within the discipline. Shepsle's (1978) account of the committee selection process was widely accepted at first. According to Shepsle, members select seats on committees related to their specific reelection-oriented goals (the self-selection hypothesis). This results in a system where each committee is skewed in terms of policy preference in favor of the programs that it administers. According to this point of view committees are not broadly reflective of Congress as a whole but are stocked with high demand legislators; committees are said to be "preference outliers."

Weingast and Marshall (1988) include "evidence" in support of the claim that committees are composed of preference outliers in the form of comparisons between policy specific interest group ratings of committee members compared to ratings of the Congress as a whole. They find that committee members do indeed have higher average interest group scores from organizations favoring policies under the committees' jurisdiction than chamber means, supporting the claim that they are preference outliers. The empirical work of Krehbiel (1991) contradicts Weingast and Marshall's findings. In a more extensive study using interest group rating data, Krehbiel finds support for the preference ouliers claim for some committees (especially Armed Services), but no support in other areas, particularly and most unexpectedly in the committees that "deal most explicitly in constituency-specific benefits" (p.133). According to Krehbiel:

> As such, the absence of strong and uniform support is striking. Regardless of the policy-specific [interest group] rating employed, the quintessential pork barrel committees—Interior and Public Works—are not homogenous high demanders at all (p.133).

Additional evidence on both sides of the dispute has been provided,[8] and while the concept of preference outliers has not been discredited, it is no longer universally accepted.

Benefit Hypothesis

While both of the claims mentioned above have been disputed, it is the third claim—the "benefit hypothesis" or Weingast and Marshall's claim that "committee members receive the disproportionate share of the benefits from the programs within their jurisdiction"—which will be the focus of this chapter and of Chapter Five. The remainder of this chapter evaluates the literature on the hypothesis that committee members receive larger amounts of jurisdiction specific spending than do non-members using the framework developed in Chapter Two. The framework is useful in demonstrating that although the findings of previous studies appear to be contradictory and inconsistent, when data used in the studies are categorized according to the institutional source of the project decision process, patterns emerge that shed light on the distributive hypothesis. Chapter Five adds empirical evidence from a study of congressional appropriations earmarks, a clear example of project decisions made by Congress, to the literature-based analysis included in this chapter. This evidence will be useful in comparing the distribution of spending when Congress makes the decision, to spending decisions made by the bureaucracy and through formulas.

EMPIRICAL LITERATURE AND THE BENEFIT HYPOTHESIS

Weingast and Marshall (1988) provide "evidence" in support of their contention that committees are comprised of preference outliers who receive disproportionately large amounts of pork. The authors' evidence consists of several references to empirical studies that seem to support their claim. Empirical studies that contradict this finding are largely ignored (with the exception of Rundquist 1973, which is mentioned in passing), and no attempt is made to verify the claim with their own empirical analysis.

In fact, the empirical evidence when looked at now or at the time Weingast and Marshall were writing, is by no means in complete agreement that committee membership leads to a disproportionate share of district specific pork barrel spending.[9] Several prior studies that evaluated committee member power in obtaining district specific benefits arriving at results contrary to the theoretical expectations of Weingast and Marshall were not mentioned; these include: Rundquist and Griffin 1973; Rundquist and Ferejohn 1975; Arnold [on military installations][10] 1979; Carlton, Russell and Winter, 1980; Ray 1980a; Ray 1980b; Anagnoson 1982; Owens and Wade 1984; Gist and Hill 1984; and Wilson 1986. While it is true that some of these works suffer from methodological shortcomings, to ignore all of them is to fail to acknowledge and deal frankly with a potential threat to the theory.

The following section is a systematic analysis of the literature on empirical tests of the benefit hypothesis, using the framework developed in the previous chapter. It is clear that empirical support for the concept is clearest when Congress makes the distributive decision directly in the legislative process, and less clear when formulas and bureaucratic discretion are the methods of allocation. As direct congressional project decisions are relatively few, this has implications on the power of the benefit hypothesis in general and the distributive theory of Congress in particular.

Legislative-Project Determination[11]

Previous research concerning the politics of legislative-project expenditure programs has concentrated exclusively on water projects. In 1981, Arnold maintained that "... water projects are the only major project decisions that today's Congress makes" (p.116). Maass (1983) implicitly concurred with this evaluation (p.69):

> If the members were more project-oriented in their legislative roles, they would name individual projects in the authorizing statutes and allocate funds to them in the appropriations statutes. But they don't do this. For the vast federal programs in housing, education, health,

> welfare, environment, many of them involving the construction of projects—sewage plants, housing units, classrooms, laboratories, hospitals—the authorizing statutes contain standards and criteria for allocating funds, and the appropriations are large lump sums to be assigned by the Executive in accordance with the standards.

One of the major assumptions of the research presented here will be that this is no longer entirely the case, and that legislative earmarks have become an additional, if minor, source of congressional project decisions. However, it did accurately reflect federal spending for the period of American history (1950-1980) that Arnold describes[12], and therefore is an adequate explanation for the large quantity of research on water projects.

The literature on water projects has consistently found a measurable political effect on the geographic distribution of federal water projects. Arthur Maass (1951) was among the first to explore the relationship between congressional influence and the distribution of federal river and harbor projects in his classic work *Muddy Waters*. Relying heavily on anecdotal data, Maass found considerable evidence of congressional manipulation of Army Corps of Engineer's water policy. Ferejohn (1974), in one of the most extensive studies of distributive politics to date, found that members of the House Public Works Committee and the House Appropriations Committee were rewarded with significantly more water projects in their districts.

Rundquist and Ferejohn (1975) also examined the geographic distribution of Army Corps of Engineers Civil Works Projects. Consistent with Ferejohn's previous findings, the authors conclude: " . . . the districts and states of members of both the Public Works Committee and the Appropriations Subcommittee average significantly more new starts [new projects] than those of nonmembers" (p.97). Wilson's (1986) study of district level appropriations data for River and Harbors Committee projects from an earlier time (1889-1913) found less evidence in support of the political benefit theory. He determined that " . . . losing or gaining committee representation has little effect on a district's appropriations" (p.60). However, this does not mean that committee membership was without value. Wilson reported that "Committee representation may ensure that current levels of funding continue even after that representation is lost . . . " (p.60).

Finally, Hird (1991) examined 133 potential Army Corps of Engineers projects previously authorized and eligible for appropriations. Hird's analysis considered objective measures of a project's worth (cost-benefit analysis) as well as more political bases of distribution of projects. His results indicated that several House and Senate committees and leadership positions were especially influential in securing Corps projects in their districts or states. However, he found considerable evidence that social welfare characteristics were also a good predictor of a project's chances of being approved. Hird concludes: "the results indicate strongly that legislators are driven not only by a selfish desire for pork, but also by a regard for project attributes commonly thought to reflect the "public interest" namely efficiency and equity" (p. 449).

As a category, projects funded on the basis of legislative discretion (Army Corps of Engineers water projects) lend considerable support for the constituent benefit hypothesis. Members on the key authorizing and appropriating committees do receive benefits from committee membership. This is not surprising since water projects were the original "pork barrel" program, and have been the topic of many journalistic accounts of pork barrel spending as well.[13] However, it is important to note that, even in the program most closely associated with pork barrel politics, legislators are not solely concerned with providing benefits for their districts in the form of water projects, and do appear to take into account measures of program benefit when deciding which projects will be funded. Project decisions strongly support the benefit hypothesis; however, when complete discretion is taken out of the hands of Congress, the benefit hypothesis has less support, as is described below.

Bureaucratic-Project Determination

More programs rely on bureaucratic decision on specific projects as the method of allocation than any other method of disbursing funds to states and localities (U.S General Services Administration 1994).[14] Studies of distributive politics using evidence from programs that rely on project by project decisions of bureaucrats also outnumber studies in any other category. In some program areas, researchers have found no measurable congressional impact on the geographic distribution of benefits; in others, results have been more favorable. However, even those studies reporting evidence of political manipulation of geographic benefits typically report that committee influence is not universal, but tends to vary across committee jurisdictions, and across time. There appears then to be little support for the benefit hypothesis, the idea that committee members necessarily receive disproportionate benefits from the programs under their jurisdiction, as an overall theory of Congressional organization when evaluated using policies which rely on agency bureaucrats to make the geographic decisions. This section will begin with those studies that have failed to find evidence of a benefit hypothesis, and then move to other research where evidence is more supportive.

Although Rundquist and Ferejohn (1975) found considerable support for the benefit hypothesis when they examined Army Corps of Engineers water projects (see above); they arrived at a much different result when they studied the geographic location of prime military contracts, which are decisions that are typically made by the bureaucracy. For data that look individually at both district and state wide benefit, the authors found no significant relationship between committee membership (either authorization or appropriation) and prime military contract spending. This is a very large category of federal discretionary spending, and one that is frequently thought to be influenced by the pulls of political geography.

In an article that utilizes an interrupted time series analysis rather than the more typical method of regressing district spending using a dummy variable for committee membership among other predictors, Rundquist and Griffith (1976: 625) reported that "constituencies do not benefit from being represented on the congressional military committees . . . committee member's constituencies do not benefit relative to what they received before or after they are represented on the committees." This study also used data on military procurement (prime military contracts) expenditures.

In one of the cases studied by Arnold (1979) [his book presents three separate empirical studies], similar results were attained regarding the influence of military committees over distributive spending. According to Arnold: " . . . I have found no support for the hypothesis that members of military committees are able to affect employment at installations in their districts either by promoting their expansion or slowing their contraction" (p.120).

Anagnoson (1982) found that members of Congress influence the timing of bureaucratic grant awards, but do not play a major role in determining the geographic distribution of awards. The number of grants per district in two programs, the public works program of the Department of Commerce's Economic Development Administration

(1967-1979), and the basic water and sewer program of the U.S. Department of Housing and Urban Development (1968-1971) provided the data used in the analysis. According to Anagnoson: "The number of grants per congressional district and the processing time of projects announced during election periods indicated that agency grant announcements during election campaigns were subject to considerable political manipulation, but that these projects for the most part would have been announced anyway. Thus, agencies depoliticize grant processing by allowing the politicization of the timing of the decision" (p. 547).

Gist and Hill (1984) examined the allocation of Urban Development Action Grants (UDAGs) by bureaucratic discretion using logit and Tobit models. Gist and Hill operationalized their dependent variable as a measure of whether or not a grant application was funded. They found that bureaucratic variables were significantly related to a project being funded, that is, projects that were more likely to succeed due to greater local financial backing (an element of UDAG consideration) were more likely to be funded. Political variables, including membership on relevant committees and partisanship of communities that were grant applicants were not related to project funding decisions. According to Gist and Hill (p.167): ". . . UDAG allocations apparently have not been influenced by party or congressional committee representation."

Hird (1990) found that public interest was a better predictor of spending on Superfund toxic waste cleanup activity than were distributive considerations: "there is little committee based congressional influence over the distribution of site cleanup of funding, although evidence exists that legislators can hasten a site's transition from proposed to final status" (p.455). However, later research by Hird (1993) seems to indicate that the Superfund program is not viewed by legislators as a traditional pork barrel (distributive) program. Ideology is more important than self-interest in roll call voting on Superfund expansion.

Other scholars have achieved mixed results, with some, but not overwhelming, evidence of congressional influence in geographic distributions. These studies tend to show variations between committees; members of some relevant committees appear to receive significantly larger distributive expenditures, while others do not seem to benefit from committee position. While not disproving the benefit hypothesis, these studies do not lend the overwhelming support for the concept that is predicted by Weingast and Marshall (1988). The variance seems to be reflective of committee differences, indicating that at least some committees may be composed of high demand legislators for some programs.

For example, Goss (1972) studied defense related employment by congressional district in three categories: military, civilian and defense-related private sector. According to Goss: "The findings for the House Armed Services Committee strongly suggest that committee membership is likely to be linked to extra base employment, but not with private defense plant employment . . . The findings for the two appropriating subcommittees lend support to the hypothesis that members of military committees obtain advantages for their constituencies in the form of high employment on military bases, but not in the form of high employment in private plants . . . " (p.231). As Congress has more of a direct legislative say over decisions relating to bases[15] (military construction, force sizes) than it does over contracting, this is consistent with the theme that the benefit hypothesis only pertains to those specific areas of most import to members of Congress. It is also evidence that the premise is not universal to all benefits.

Carlton, Russell and Winters (1980) found that while congressional power did play a role skewing bureaucratic decisions during the formative years of a new distributive program, over time the effects of congressional influence were reduced. Their research on state levels of funding by the National Endowment for the Arts (NEA) concluded:

> For the early years of the National Endowment for the Arts, the distribution of state grants seems to have been related to support of the agency on the House floor by state delegations . . . The relationship declined over the first years of the agency's life . . . Our interpretation is that as the agency's appropriations became established and its need for political support lessened, it could more accurately reflect the demand for the arts in the nation (p.113).

Hamman (1993) supports Anagnoson's conclusion that congressional pressure influences the timing of bureaucratic grant announcements. Hamman studied the Urban Mass Transit Administration's (UMTA) Discretionary Capital Assistance Grants. Contrary to Anagnoson, however, Hamman reported that UMTA does reward some (but not all) congressional committee members with grants in their districts. "District representation on the appropriations and authorization subcommittees generally is beneficial, but the pattern for the other subcommittees is not consistent. Only districts of senior members on the Senate Appropriations subcommittee received larger awards, and that is only in nonelection years. Otherwise, senior members of both houses' subcommittees in election and nonelection years received smaller awards."

Arnold (1979) looked at three different examples of bureaucratic project spending: 1) Military Employment: Base Opening; Base Closing; and Reallocation. 2) Water and Sewer Facilities Grants administered by the Department of Housing and Urban Development. 3) Model Cities Grants (establishment of Program). Regarding military employment he reported: "The conclusion is inescapable; bureaucrats do take into account committee members' preferences when deciding which Army and Air Force installations should be closed" (p.114).[16] [For new installations] . . . "The evidence clearly supports the hypothesis about the value of Armed Services membership, but it is inconclusive about whether membership on Appropriations subcommittees has any value for attracting new installations" (p.117). In terms of water and sewer grants: "The evidence . . . provides strong support for the hypothesis that bureaucrats would select applications in part according to their committee representation" (p.139). "As best I can estimate, program administrators for the water and sewer program adjusted a larger proportion of their allocational decisions than did Pentagon officials" (p.162). From his research on the creation of the model cities program he found: " . . . bureaucrats allocated a disproportionate number of cities to committee members, though with the exception of [Representative] Jonas, the rewards were reserved for members who supported funding" (p.179).

Arnold is by no means convinced of the universality of the benefit hypothesis; he finds it to be subject to considerable variation. He concludes "At the stage in which specific allocational decisions are made, congressional influence, though still considerable, has less impact on a program's basic character. Depending on the program, between 10 and 30 percent of allocational decisions may be adjusted in accordance with particular congressmen's preferences . . . it is a relatively small cost for doing business in a democratic way" (p.214).

Hooton (1997) also attained results that indicate political influence on geographic spending varies over time. Hooton hypothesizes that grant distributions are more likely to favor members of subcommittees during periods of retrenchment, when, for example the administration is proposing to eliminate a grant program. His study of EDA grant distributions supports his hypothesis, as grant allocations during the Reagan administration became more favorable to subcommittee member's districts as the program was threatened with elimination. According to Hooton:

> The findings give only limited support to the "traditional" political benefits thesis, in which all members of the primary subcommittee of jurisdiction consistently receive benefits beyond those attributable to geographic merit. Notable political benefits did accrue, but only for subcommittee leaders in the period of the program retrenchment and local economic stress . . . The view that subcommittee membership is alone sufficient to win federal largess is thus incomplete as an explanation for distributive grant allocations (pp.93-94).

Once again, this finding is consistent with the notion that the benefit hypothesis is not universal, and varies with the level of discretion that bureaucrats have, the proximity of a legislative decision, as well as economic conditions.

Finally, Hamman and Cohen (1997) find conflicting evidence of committee power in a study that looks at the timing of grant announcements, and is most concerned with the relationship between proximity of presidential election, and timing of Urban Mass Transit Administration grants. Their conclusions regarding the role of congressional committee members in steering benefits to their districts are mixed. "Some committee variables also affect the time that it takes to process applications" (Hamman and Cohen 1997: 65). The relevant House authorizing subcommittee shows a statistically significant relationship, but the hypothesized relationship between Transportation Appropriations subcommittee membership and the timing of grant awards was not found. Hamman and Cohen do not examine the more central question of whether committee members influence the actual location of project awards.

The final set of studies find stronger support for the benefit hypothesis. This small subset of the research on committee influence on the geographic distribution of federal government spending are the only studies in this category that unequivocally support the relationship between committee position and benefit.

Plott (1968), using data on Urban Renewal Projects by district found that "1) Districts represented on the House Banking and

Currency Committee are favored; 2) URA [Urban Renewal Administration] changes its criteria for project approvals according to the time of year . . . " (p.320). However Plott's evidence regarding the benefit hypothesis consists of the claim that: "An examination of the 1964 banking and currency committees reveals that the 50 percent of all states which are represented on these committees receive almost 80 percent of all urban renewal expenditures" (p.307). Plott does not control for differences in state population however. According to Arnold (1979) "Later, recognizing the problem of unequal state populations, he examined it with district-level data and found somewhat weaker support for it."

When Ray (1981) limited his analysis to one government department, the Department of Defense, he did find evidence of congressional influence on the geographic distribution of expenditures by congressional district. According to Ray "once assigned to military committees, members use the influence acquired from their jurisdiction over the DOD to increase the share of the defense budget which is distributed in their districts" (p.234).

Finally, Rundquist, Lee and Rhee (1996) found a significant relationship between representation on House and Senate defense committees and the distribution of prime military contracts. Using a methodology that controlled for factors that had previously been ignored in similar studies (the district or state's industrial capacity, its history of defense contracting, member seniority, member ideology and the demand for industrial products), the authors arrived at results which contradict previous studies that used the same (or similar) data—prime military contracts during the cold war years.

Legislative-Formula Determination

Ostensibly, it would seem difficult to find political influence in the distribution of funds using formulas that rely on such "objective" criteria as population, poverty rate, age of housing stock and highway mileage.[17] However, anecdotal evidence of legislators seeking to manipulate the structure of formulas for greater local benefit is quite common.[18]

Two studies that examine programs which expend funds based on legislatively determined formulas, do so in a comparative sense, and provide empirical evidence that distribution of expenditures on the basis of standardized formulas results in even less political influence on the location of the funding than do programs with allocations based on bureaucratic discretion. Both Reid (1980) and Rich (1989) compare allocations based on statutory formulas with programs based on bureaucratic-project selection and arrive at similar results.

Reid (1980) studied the geographic distribution of five health grant programs during fiscal year 1973. According to his report: "The data . . . support the contention that formula grants are more tightly governed by programmatic criteria than are project grants" (p.48); that is they are less susceptible to political manipulation. Reid also concludes that for programs that rely on bureaucratic discretion, committee influence is variable. Congressional influence has greater distributional effects for those programs with greater political (credit claiming) value.

Rich examined the allocation patterns of six federal grant programs: Urban Renewal, Model Cities, Urban Development Action Grant, Community Development Block Grant, Title I Public Works, and Local Public Works. He found that political factors were more evident in the project grant programs than in the formula grant programs. However, "even in the project grant programs, political influence, as measured by representation on the appropriations and substantive committees with oversight responsibilities for these programs, accounted for very little in the distribution of program funds" (p.207). Rich found that district need was a better predictor of distributive benefits than the political influence of legislators.

Most recently, Svorny's (1996) analysis of the Job Training Partnership Act of 1982, a formula driven program, did not find an association between membership on relevant committees and the provision of federal funds, measured at the state level. Svorny did find congressional seniority, as measured by total years of state delegation tenure, to be a significant predictor of grant funding.

Two studies of programs with geographic distribution of funding based on legislatively derived formulas did find evidence of political manipulation of the formula. Strom's (1975) research on the Federal waste treatment construction grant program, a program that supplied each state with a dollar amount based on a legislatively determined formula, found that States represented on the House Public Works Committee (HPWC) received more policy benefits than states that were not. He also found that the party of committee members, seniority of committee members, and representation of a state by more than one committee member affected a state's distribution of grant funds.

However, there appear to be serious flaws in the design and execution of Strom's analysis which limit the validity of his results. In a critique of Strom, Arnold (1979) maintains that Strom's results are due to a high correlation between both his dependent and independent variables and state population. The formula in question allocated grants to states based on two variables, equally weighted: state population and state's per capita income. It is clear that both Strom's dependent variable (federal waste treatment construction grant funding per state) and his measure of political influence (number of statewide members of the House Public Works Committee) are strongly related to state population.

Alvarez and Saving (1997) looked at total formula outlays by congressional district and found that districts represented on some committees receive significantly greater allocations than districts lacking similar representation. However, they found that some committees traditionally thought of as pork barrel committees (Agriculture and Public Works for example) did not receive significantly greater amounts of formula spending, while other committees, especially Ways and Means, did seem to yield members greater local spending.

It is much harder for members of Congress to influence geographic spending by district when formulas are the method of allocation. Arnold (1981a) claims that Congress is more likely to establish formulas for the distribution of spending of little political value, while keeping discretion for the most valued examples of pork. Once formulas have been written, it becomes even more difficult to alter the flow of benefits, as the time for manipulation (usually only when a program is being reauthorized) and the access points (only those who have key committee spots) are limited.

While there are undoubtedly attempts to skew distributional formulas in favor of certain areas, the precision and durability of this tactic must certainly be questioned. Also, the very fact that Congress chooses to leave the distribution of funds to a general formula may say something about the pork barrel nature of the program. Formula grants don't seem to fit Lowi's original conception of a policy that is doled out on a piece by piece basis.

Studies Using Aggregate Data

Studies that combine different programs and methods of resource delivery in the same research are useful in that they can reflect any large scale geographic disparities in locality benefit. However, by combining data, these studies often lose the ability to determine which programs are more or less affected by congressional action. Frequently they are only detailed down to the agency level, which obscures differences between programs that are clearly distributive and programs that fulfill a different governmental purpose. In addition, those studies that combine expenditures based on legislative formulas with expenditures that are discretionary, are apt to conceal any legislative impact as the much larger [and according to Rich (1989) and Reid (1980) above, more objective] formula programs will dominate.

When aggregate data is used, studies have consistently failed to find much support for the benefit hypothesis. Ritt (1976) uses the amount of money spent by the federal government in each congressional district for the dependent variable in his study. Ritt found no impact of political party or seniority (tenure), and his findings regarding the influence of committee membership was limited to those of the majority party. Ritt includes formula as well as discretionary expenditures in his study which surely affects his results. More importantly, by looking at all federal funds spent in a given district, Ritt does not differentiate between expenditures that are distributive and those that are redistributive—such as Social Security and Medicare (which are considerably larger).

Ray (1980b) also looked at federal outlays by congressional district. Ray used the annual change in federal activity (outlays) as the dependent variable. Ray's study arrived at results similar to those of Ritt, probably for the same reasons. He concluded: "Successful promotional activity by powerful congressmen is an inadequate explanation of the geographic distribution of federal spending . . . No such systematic pattern was discovered. In the aggregate, those with power did little better (and often did worse) than those without influence" (p.31). In a second study Ray (1980a) once again analyzed federal outlays in congressional districts, but he limited his analysis to the following (committee) jurisdictions: Agriculture, Armed Services, Education and Labor, Banking and Currency, Interior and Insular Affairs, and Veterans Affairs. He arrived at a similar conclusion: " . . .

Congress members may not cause the location of federal projects in their districts" (p.509).

Owens and Wade (1984) used as their dependent variable total per capita government spending by Congressional district. They found little support for the benefit hypothesis: " . . . total allocations among districts bear little or no connection with the old measures of House influence or with district characteristics" (p.419). "The agricultural area provided the sole instance in which members' positions in the House emerged as an important determinant of spending" (p.412).

Ray (1980c) found that committee membership does not allow members to prevent the loss of existing federal activities in the congressional district. Gerard Gryski (1991) focused his research on the influence of committee position on federal program spending using data that included 90 percent of all domestic federal outlays. Gryski did find "modest" support for the claim that committee variables are an important predictor of outlays in those program areas where there is a strong clientele pushing for government expenditures. However, "contrary to expectations, the committee position variables for Agriculture and Banking have no significant effects" (p.450).

Finally, the recent development of the Bickers and Stein data set discussed above allows for more detailed analysis of federal spending, including differentiation by formula or project grant and by agency and program of government. Alvarez and Saving (1997) have used this data to analyze the benefit hypothesis, with results that are best described as conditional. Consistent with previous studies, they find evidence of the benefit hypothesis for some committees, but not for others. They claim they did not: " . . . find massive quantities of evidence to indicate that all important committees in the House are pure providers of pork to their members." Curiously, the authors found membership on the Ways and Means Committee to be the strongest predictor of district grant spending of any committee.

Evidence of congressional influence on geographic spending is limited in studies that look at all spending in a district. This is probably an artifact of the much larger, redistributive programs that are spent in each state regardless of the current actions of individual members of Congress. Such large expenditures (Social Security and Medicare for example) that are a function mainly of the age of the district population rather than any efforts on the part of an individual member of Congress, obscure any impact that distributive politics may have.

Evaluation of the Literature on The Benefit Hypothesis:

Much of rational choice theory of the "second generation"[19]—the distributive theory—is built on the premise that members of Congress on relevant committees receive disproportionately large benefits from the distributive programs that are authorized and appropriated by their committees. The assertion is not conditional. In order for other aspects of the distributive model to be accurate, members of committees must have some incentive to enter into logroll arrangements. All committees must be composed of high demand preference outliers who do secure gains from exchange from a committee system built on reciprocity. However, it is apparent that committee members don't always attain greater benefits from many of the programs within their jurisdiction. When allocation decisions are made by administration bureaucrats and broad-based formulas, the hypothesis is not supported across the committee system.

Of the five types of discretion outlined above, it appears that expenditures resulting from congressional project decisions show the strongest evidence of geographic manipulation. Since research to date has been limited to a single category of expenditure (public works programs of the Army Corps of Engineers), the ability to draw generalizations from this literature is limited. Also, as very few allocation decisions are in actuality made directly by Congress, the question of why the legislature has not assumed responsibility for other valuable allocation decisions, needs to be addressed by rational choice theorists.

The literature on expenditures stemming from legislatively designed formulas seems to indicate that political manipulation is limited but can occur when a program is newly established. This is probably due to the objective criteria that make up funding formulas. The area of most disagreement in the literature concerns programs that rely on bureaucratic discretion to pass out funds for specific projects. While researchers report congressional influence over some spending areas, congressional influence seems to vary between programs and over time, and may be related to the amount of credit claiming associated with the expenditure and the (perceived) need by bureaucrats to solidify weak congressional support for a new or threatened program. Empirical studies that look to congressional influence as an explanation of differences between congressional districts (or states) in total receipts of government, overlook the far more expensive redistributive programs which confound their data, and limit the value of their conclusions.

Also overlooked by this literature are the other factors that motivate bureaucratic decisions. While some public choice theorists claim that most bureaucratic decisions can be traced to the bureaucrats' desires to carry out the wishes of Congress and thereby ensure budgetary growth,[20] other scholars have shown that competing motivations (such as the wishes of the Executive and good public policy) also influence bureaucratic decisions. Therefore, research that includes programs with considerable bureaucratic discretion as models of congressional distributive policymaking inevitably encounters areas where the congressional influence on geographic decisions is less pronounced.

This chapter has shown that the empirical evidence from the many studies of the relationship between congressional committees and pork barrel benefits does not fit neatly the distributive theory predictions of preference outliers and disproportionate benefits going to committee members. The following chapter will explore this topic further using empirical data on congressional policymaking from the 102nd through 104th Congress. Additional evidence that distributive desires prompted by reelection concerns are not the guiding consideration behind the committee system will be provided.

NOTES

1. In the more than thirty years since Lowi outlined his policy distinction, many scholars have sought to clarify and redefine his categories (see for example Ripley and Franklin 1976). Lowi's original conception of the term (as described above) will be used throughout this research. See also Wilson 1973 and 1980.

2. Important prior studies of politics using a model based on economic concepts of utility maximization and rationality include Arrow (1951); Downs (1957); Olson (1965); Riker (1962) and Buchanan and Tullock (1962).

3. Following Shepsle (1978), this concept is more commonly referred to as "preference outliers" in the rational choice literature.

4. Other scholars have expanded the benefit hypothesis by theorizing that other political factors are associated with the geographic distribution of government spending. Empirical tests include the following: on seniority (Ritt 1976; Crain and Tollison 1977: Kiel and McKenzie 1983; Crain, Leavens and

Tollison 1990: Anderson and Tollison 1991), on party membership (Ferejohn 1974; Levitt and Snyder 1995).

5. The theory is developed most clearly in Weingast and Marshall (1988). See also: Shepsle (1978); Weingast (1979); Weingast, Shepsle and Johnsen (1981); Fiorina (1981b); Shepsle (1983a and 1983b); Shepsle and Weingast (1984); and Fitts and Inman (1992). For critiques see: Krehbiel (1991); and Baron (1996).

6. See for example: Goodwin (1970); Fenno (1973); Bullock (1971); Gertzog (1976); Shepsle (1978); Smith and Deering (1984); and Cox and McCubbins (1993).

7. It should be noted that the main challenge to the concept of self-selection comes from scholars who also favor the rational choice approach

8. Both Hall and Grofman (1990) and Maltzman and Smith (1994) find that committee bias is conditional and varies across committees. Londregan and Snyder (1994) use a different statistical approach to conclude "We apply our model to the House of Representatives over the period 1951 to 1984 and identify many more committee outliers than previous research" (p.233). See also: Adler and Lapinsky (1997) and Hurwitz, Moiles and Rhode (1997).

9. Stein (1981) draws a similar conclusion: "Congressional scholars . . . have long argued that representatives with key committee appointments . . . use their influence to obtain a disproportionate amount of the federal largesse for their congressional districts. In spite of the intuitive appeal of this hypothesis, supporting evidence has been lacking" (p.334). So does Ray (1980): "Recent studies have demonstrated that members of "appropriate" congressional committees are no better able to attract new federal spending within the jurisdiction of these panels to their districts than are non-members of these committees" (p.359). See also the quote from Arnold (1979: 15-16) which begins the chapter.

10. Arnold's more supportive findings from this same study are cited however, with no mention of his conclusion quoted above.

11. In addition to the works cited below, Cohen and Noll (1991) have compiled a series of case studies of research and development projects where there is apparent evidence of pork barreling. However, their research relies on analyses of roll call votes on project funding to support the benefit hypothesis, which is certainly not a very strong indicator of pork barrel politics. The conclusion that members of Congress tend to vote for funding for projects that will benefit their districts does not say much about the desire to actively seek distributive spending, nor does it help to answer the question of who gets pork.

12. The debate over the specificity of congressional appropriations is a debate that dates back to the founding of the United States. Thomas Jefferson

believed that the Constitutional power of Congress to determine all appropriations required that Congress pass very detailed appropriations laws specifying exactly what federal funds were to be used for. Alexander Hamilton argued that Congress should simply pass broad appropriations laws that allowed the administration great discretion in determining expenditures. For most of the early history of the United States, Jefferson's conception prevailed, and Congress specified appropriations down to specific line items. However, the nature of federal government involvement in domestic policy was very limited, and any geographic impacts of congressional behavior are difficult to measure (except in the area of river and harbors spending—the traditional pork barrel spending program). With the advent of program budgeting in 1950 following the great increase in government involvement in the economy and society that accompanied the New Deal, many line items were rolled into single program accounts, with an accompanying reduction of Congressional influence on specific spending. This led to the increased use of non-statutory techniques for appropriations control, especially the use of committee report language. In most of the years since 1950, Congress has not used statutory language to direct the millions of spending decisions that are required in the modern administrative state. Originally bureaucratic discretion and formulas were responsible for nearly all distributive decisions. In the period from 1950 to 1980 (the period reflected in Arnold's analysis) Congress did not exercise much direct control over geographic funding decisions. However, since 1980 Congress has dramatically increased its use of both statutory and non-statutory language to control the geographic distribution of funds. (For a historic account of appropriations politics prior to World War II see Wilmerding 1943; For an account of the use of non-statutory spending control see Kirst 1969)

13. See for example: Drew (1970); Kirschten (1977); Reid (1980) and Reisner (1986). A more detailed discussion of Army Corps of Engineers water projects is included in Chapter Three.

14. Although they make up the largest number, programs that distribute funds on the basis of bureaucratic discretion account "for only a small fraction of national intergovernmental funding." (Dilger 1989: 12).

15. In the past, members of Congress were extremely influential in preventing the closure of military bases. While this may be less so today with the creation of the Base Closure and Realignment Commission, the frequency with which Congress adds to the president's military construction request provides an opportunity to influence spending in this area. For a case that illustrates continued political involvement in base closure decisions even after the creation of the Base Closure Commission, see Bernardi (1996).

16. It should be noted that this research was undertaken prior to the establishment of a Base Closure and Realignment Commission.

17. For a complete list of legislative formulas in use in 1987, see GAO (1987b).

18. See for example Stanfield (1978) on the role of computers in enabling political manipulation of revenue sharing formulas, and Mill's (1991) account of the process by which Congress determined the formula for distributing federal highway assistance. See also Arnold (1981a: 127) for an account of the various criteria included in formulas.

19. Shepsle and Weingast (1994) use the term second generation to differentiate between early rational choice theories that were based on abstract models of legislatures (first generation); and third generation models, which have further developed the institutional aspects of second generation models (which added committees and rules) to include an emphasis on political parties and additional complexity.

20. See Niskanen (1975); Blais and Dion (1991); Fiorina (1981a).

CHAPTER FIVE

Earmarks and the Benefit Hypothesis

We may conclude that, as a general rule, the more important a policy is, the less important will be the role of self-interest in determining that policy. Self- interest does a great job explaining the location of a new federal building in Missoula. It fails with regard to the major policy upheavals in the United States of the past decades.

Steven Kelman (1987)

. . . legislators are driven not only by a selfish desire for pork but also by a regard for project attributes commonly thought to reflect "public interest," namely efficiency and equity.

John A. Hird (1991)

Pork-Barreling is of course an age-old political practice, and one which may not be all that objectionable if practiced in moderation, or for the right reasons. For example, President Lyndon Johnson used a mixture of threats and pork in order to secure the votes he needed to pass the 1964 Civil Rights Bill. Today, throughout America, there are many worthwhile dams, roads and hospitals which owe their very existence to a single YEA vote on the Civil Rights bill. This is pork for the Greater Good.

Rep. George Brown, D-CA (1993)

CONGRESSIONAL EARMARKS AND THE BENEFIT HYPOTHESIS

Previous research has consistently found that congressional districts represented on the committees responsible for authorizing and funding of Army Corps of Engineers water projects receive disproportionately large benefits from this program (for example, Ferejohn 1974; Hird 1991). There is also widespread agreement that of all the areas of geography specific spending, "Congress has managed to protect water resource spending as one of its most important 'legislative prerogatives'" (Del Rossi 1995: 287).

In defining the term "pork barrel" Safire (1993: 596) claims "the classic example of the pork barrel is the Rivers and Harbors bill, a piece of legislation that provides morsels for scores of congressmen in the form of appropriations for dams and piers . . . " Although there is considerable agreement that water resource projects have a political bias, there is also evidence that water projects often serve a legitimate policy need. Hird (1991) concludes that even in the program area most closely associated with images of politically motivated spending, legislators tend to favor projects that demonstrate characteristics of efficiency and equity. According to Hird (1991: 449):

> Given the apparent importance of project-specific economic and equity characteristics in reaching project funding decisions, even at the Army Corps of Engineers, researchers should be skeptical of models that effectively rule out the possibility of social welfare motives on the part of policy makers.

It is not surprising then to find that when earmarked Army Corps of Engineers spending is modeled for the period under examination in this study, a significant positive relationship between committee membership and the number of district specific Army Corps of Engineers water projects is found. When other programs that distribute funds through earmarks are examined, support is also found for the benefit hypothesis. However, when the spending discretion is moved outside of Congress directly, either through bureaucratic discretion or broad-based formulas, the influence of congressional committees on the distribution of funds and programs is much less apparent. Support for the benefit hypothesis is hard to come by in the vast majority of programs where Congress has delegated the decision making power.

The central thesis of this chapter is that congressional appropriations earmarks are a reflection of the project-specific decision making captured in many formal models of distributive politics, and as such should reveal a relationship between key committee membership and project location. However, most local spending is not allocated on the basis of direct congressional decision making, and does not accurately reflect the parameters of distributive models. It is therefore predicted that the benefit hypothesis—that is the claim that members of congressional committees responsible for authorizing and appropriating funds for a program will receive greater benefits from these programs—will not be supported for spending that is not allocated on the basis of congressional earmarks. In cases where the decision is delegated to the bureaucracy or made through legislatively determined formulas, the benefit hypothesis should not be accurate.

It is also asserted that in addition to the political relationship between committee membership and district benefit, measures of district need will be associated with the provision of district specific spending regardless of the method of distribution. Districts with greater policy need for federal spending will not only receive larger shares of the federal largesse when funds are allocated on the basis of formulas or bureaucratic discretion, it is also contended that earmark spending will reflect varying levels of need as well as committee membership.

OVERVIEW

Fortunately for research purposes, the presence of congressional earmarks allows us to compare congressional allocations, with delegated allocations, in several policy areas. Typically, Congress does not earmark all funds in a given spending category. In some cases (military construction for example), earmarks exist as congressional additions to a list of bureaucratically approved projects already requested in the president's budget submission. In other cases, earmarks operate alongside separately authorized programs that direct funds to specific locations either through formulas (community development, highways) or through bureaucratically administered programs that issue grants to applicants, often based on a competitive peer review process (agricultural research). Therefore, parallel tests of the same committee-based, needs-based and other political variables on the geographic distribution of earmarked projects can be performed as a test of the benefit hypothesis.

This chapter will provide empirical tests of the benefit hypothesis in several policy areas by comparing predictors of earmarked spending with non-earmarked expenditures in the same policy areas. The chapter begins with a general model of earmarked spending. Variables measuring district need as well as membership on the Appropriations Committee are shown to be significantly related to the location of earmarks. The remainder of the chapter will focus on more policy-specific examples of district specific spending.

The first specific policy to be analyzed is universally recognized as a program where considerable political influence is present—Army Corps of Engineers water resource projects. The purpose of this section is to evaluate the benefit hypothesis on the project most closely associated with pork barrel politics for the period under consideration using the same methodology that will be used in subsequent tests. Following the examination of water projects, the chapter will proceed to test the benefit hypothesis in the following areas: military construction; highway spending; community development; and agricultural research. Each of these policy areas will allow the benefit hypothesis to be tested using both earmarked and non-earmarked projects and/or expenditures to evaluate the predictive strength of the benefit hypothesis. The chapter will conclude with a discussion of how the empirical results support the findings from the previous literature described in Chapter Four.

METHODOLOGY AND HYPOTHESES

The general hypotheses to be tested in this chapter can be summarized:

H_0 = Geographic spending will be unrelated to committee membership

H_1 = Geographic spending will be positively related to committee membership

For the distributive theory and the benefit hypothesis to be supported, Hypothesis One should prevail regardless of the method by which a given program allocates resources. All committees should receive disproportionate benefits from programs under their authorization and appropriations jurisdiction. However, based on the literature review of the previous chapter, it is predicted that H_1 will only be supported for distributive programs that rely on members of Congress to make project allocations directly. It is predicted that the null hypothesis (H_0) will be supported for those programs that rely on either bureaucratic project discretion or are allocated based on statutory formulas.

Ordinary Least Squares (OLS) regression analysis will be used throughout this chapter. District (or state) specific benefits (operationalized as either the number of projects or the dollars allocated) will serve as the dependent variable. Independent variables measuring committee membership will be included in the modeled equations. Other independent variables measuring district or state need for the specific policy benefit, as well as other politically relevant factors will be described as they are encountered.

Although data are presented from the 103rd Congress, results that are virtually identical were achieved when using data from either the 102nd or 104th Congress. The level of analysis will be the congressional district except in those cases where funds are distributed to state governments rather than specific project locations. In such cases, the state will be the unit of analysis. Whenever possible, the dependent variable will be the number of district specific projects rather than the dollar amount of spending per district.[1]

GENERAL MODEL OF EARMARK SPENDING

In the seven categories where earmarks were identified for the 103rd Congress, a total of 4620 earmarks were coded as to their district and state locations. Earmarks per district ranged from a low of 0 (Eighth District of Ohio—Republican John Boehner) to a high of 88.58[2] projects (Third District of California 3—Democrat Vic Fazio). The mean number of earmarks per district was 10.62.

Before examining the individual earmark categories for a relationship between committee membership and district benefit, a general model was constructed using a dependent variable composed by pooling all seven earmark categories into a single variable. It is hypothesized that membership on the Appropriations Committee will be significantly associated with provision of total earmarks, as this is the committee responsible for determining all spending earmarks in annual legislation. Other committees are not included in the model as different legislative committees are responsible for authorizing different earmark categories. Traditional measures of political influence which may be associated with a members ability to secure earmarks—party membership and seniority—are also included in the model.[3]

It is also anticipated that measures of district need will be related to earmark locations. In the case of total earmarks, two general measures of policy need were identified. It was predicted that since many of the earmark categories involve projects that are more suited to large geographic areas (roads, parks, water projects, military construction), the land area (reported in square miles) of a district would be positively associated with the number of earmarks. In addition, it was hypothesized that the socioeconomic status of the population would be related to government earmarked spending. It was predicted that low income districts would be more likely to receive earmarks than wealthier districts, as poor districts have greater need for the economic development that can be associated with government spending. Table 5.1 reports the results of OLS analysis using total earmarks as the dependent variable.

Table 5.1: OLS Results, All Earmarks (Seven Categories), 103rd Congress by District

Variable	b	Beta	T Test
Years	.086	.051	1.109
Party	1.092	.037	.795
Appropriations Committee	4.019	.093	2.044**
Average Income	-3.091E-04	-.197	-4.199**
Land Area	1.24E-04	.274	6.043**
Constant	25.808		8.123**

$R^2 = .14$
Adjusted $R^2 = .13$
F = 14.43
SIG F = .0000
** $p < .05$
N = 435

Analysis of total earmarks in the seven studied areas supports the hypotheses. Members on the Appropriations Committee were able to secure approximately four additional earmarks than would otherwise have been received. Both measures of district need for earmarks—

average income and land area—are significant predictors of earmark location. Larger districts tend to receive more earmarks. Poorer districts likewise reap greater dividends from earmarked spending as indicated by the negatively signed variable measuring average income. Two other variables were included in the model as additional indicators of political power—political party (coded 0 for Republican and 1 for Democrat) and seniority measured in the number of years of continuous congressional service. Though positively signed, neither of these variables were of statistical significance.

Each of the following sections builds on this general model in specific policy areas using independent variables measuring political power, and measures of policy need directly related to the earmark category considered. The first case is the classic pork barrel—Army Corps of Engineers earmarked water projects—and as anticipated variables reflecting committee position are significant predictors of project location. Variables measuring district need for water project spending are likewise significant. In each of the cases that follow, earmarked spending is compared with spending in the same policy area that is not allocated by congressional earmarks.

Army Corps of Engineers Water Projects

All location specific Army Corps of Engineers water resource projects were identified from Conference Committee Reports of the Energy and Water Resources Appropriations Subcommittees for fiscal years 1994 and 1995.[4] Data locating projects by congressional district were provided to me in spreadsheet form by the Programs Management Division, Directorate of Civil Works of the Army Corps of Engineers.[5] Following the general model described above, variables related to district need and political power of members of Congress were selected. Data on district need were difficult to identify in the case of water projects, as there are a number of different types of water projects (flood control, harbor maintenance, dams etc.), each of which seems to be identified with a different geographic feature of a district. It was hypothesized that physically larger districts would have more of a need for water projects than more compact districts, and a variable measuring land area in square miles in each district was included in the equation. It was likewise hypothesized that districts with a sea coast would be more likely to need the assistance of the Army Corps of Engineers. A dummy variable was coded one if the district was located on the Atlantic, Pacific or Gulf coast and zero if the district has no direct ocean access. Finally, a variable measuring socioeconomic status of the district was included in the model (average income). It was predicted that this variable would have a negative relationship with earmark spending, as wealthier districts have less of a need for economic development spending.

Data on committee membership were included for the Energy and Water Resources Appropriations Subcommittee and the Public Works Subcommittee on Water Resources. Committee variables were coded as dummy variables (1 = member; 0 = not member). Also included in the equation were two other political variables hypothesized to have a positive affect on earmarks; seniority measured in years of continuous congressional service, and party membership, a dummy variable coded 1 for Democrat and 0 for Republican.

Table 5.2: OLS Results, Water Project Earmarks, 103rd Congress by District

Variable	b	Beta	T Test
Land Area	4.36E-05	.128	2.865**
Coastal District	8.426	.317	7.042**
Years	.096	.075	1.682
Party	-.228	-.010	-.224
Energy and Water Appropriations Sub.	10.996	.141	3.193**
Water Resources Subcommittee	4.057	0.098	2.079**
Average Income	-2.51E-04	-.212	-4.464**
Constant	17.367		7.244**

R^2= .18
Adjusted R^2 = .16
F = 13.01
Sig F = .0000
** $p < .05$
N = 435

Results of the analysis are presented in Table 5.2. As water projects are the quintessential pork barrel projects, it is not surprising that when all water projects are used as the dependent variable in the model, the benefit hypothesis is supported. Membership on both the authorizing and appropriating subcommittees are positively associated with number of water projects and the relationships are both statistically significant. According to the model, members of the Energy and Water Resources Appropriations Subcommittee receive approximately 11 additional projects, and members of the Water Resources Public Works Subcommittee reap an extra 4 water projects. Other measures of political power (seniority and party) were correctly signed, but not significant predictors. The measures of district need for water resource spending—size of the district in square miles, whether the district was on the coast, and level of income in the district— all demonstrated the hypothesized relationships. The indicator of coastal location was the strongest of these variables, leading to the provision of approximately 8.4 additional projects for those districts with a shoreline.

These results are in no way surprising. Congress has retained the ability to direct the location of water projects since it became involved in water policy in the 1820s. Although efforts to control the distributive tendency of the program have been introduced in recent years (including mandatory state cost sharing and improved cost benefit analysis procedures), water projects remain one of the (if not the) most important area where Congress stipulates spending directly in legislation (or accompanying committee reports). However, in most other cases where Congress has been involved in project decisions, these decisions merely augment the decisions of bureaucrats and statutory formulas which are responsible for the vast majority of location-specific spending decisions. The remainder of this chapter will examine how congressional committee influence affects the overall distribution of several other policy areas.

Military Construction

All location specific military construction earmarks were identified from the Conference Reports of the Military Construction Appropriations Subcommittees for the 103rd Congress; the reports include requests for funding in Fiscal Years 1994 and 1995. Data on the location and funding level of each project were recorded as were information on whether a project was requested by the administration, or was included as an add-on by Congress. Project district locations were identified using Congressional Quarterly's *Congressional Districts in the 1990s,* which contains an appendix listing the congressional district of all major military facilities in the United States. In some cases, projects were designated for locations away from an established military base; in such cases the *Congressional District Atlas, 103rd Congress* compiled by the Bureau of the Census (1993) was consulted.[6] The total number of military construction projects earmarked in a district for the two year Congress served as the dependent variable in the first equation, which is depicted in columns 1-3 of table 5.3.

As in the examples above, several variables related to district need and political power of members of Congress were identified. It is hypothesized that the number of military installations in a district would be strongly related to the number of earmarks it received, and this data was also obtained from *Congressional Districts in the 1990s.* It was again predicted that the average income of the district would be negatively associated with military construction earmarks. Political variables include dummy variables indicating membership on the pertinent appropriations subcommittee (Military Construction) and the authorizing committee (Armed Services) in the 103rd Congress. Also included in the equation were seniority and party affiliation variables.

It is hypothesized that when all military construction earmarks are considered (a variable which is heavily weighted in favor of bureaucratic decisions) political variables reflecting committee membership will be unrelated to project locations. It is also hypothesized that measures of policy need will be reflected in the geographic decisions. As can be seen in columns 1-3 of Table 5.3, analysis supports the hypothesis. When administration bureaucrats in the Department of Defense are the main decision makers, only variables measuring assumed district need for military construction spending are statistically significant, and the number of military installations in the district is a powerful predictor of earmark location. Average district income demonstrated the predicted relationship, with poorer districts receiving greater numbers of earmarks. Membership on key committees does not appear to lead to an oversupply of projects as is predicted by the distributive theory of Congress. Other measures of political factors are likewise insignificant.

Columns 4-6 of table 5.3 further supports the contention of this research. These columns represent a model predicting military construction congressional earmarks using the same independent variables as are used to predict all military construction in columns 1-3.

Table 5.3: OLS Results, Military Construction Earmarks, 103rd Congress by District

	All Projects			Congressional Earmarks		
Variable	b	Beta	T test	b	Beta	T test
Military Installations	1.874	.606	15.499**	.278	.362	8.402**
Military Construction Appropriations Subcom.	1.106	.039	1.042	1.554	.222	5.352**
Years	.026	.048	1.287	.013	.096	2.309**
Armed Services Committee	.053	.004	.096	.446	.1276**	2.98
Party	.159	.017	.444	.-.094	-.041	-.956
Average Income	-7.63E-05	-.154	-3.975**	-2.31E-05	-.188	-4.395**
Constant	2.955		3.571**	.997		4.408**

All Projects	Congressional Earmarks
$R^2 = .40$	$R^2 = .27$
Adjusted $R^2 = .39$	Adjusted $R^2 = .26$
F = 47.96	F = 26.83
SIG F = .0000	SIG F = .0000
**p<.05	**p<.05
N = 435	N = 435

Regarding the main concern of this research—the importance of committee membership variables, both membership on the Military Construction Subcommittee of the Appropriations Committee and on the Armed Services (authorizing) committee were positively related to congressional earmarks. Both variables are statistically significant at the $p < .05$ level, with the Appropriations Subcommittee being the stronger predictor of the two. Also, as was hypothesized, both predictors of district need are associated with earmark locations, with the income variable being negatively signed meaning that poor districts are more likely to receive military construction earmarks. Seniority showed a more modest, but still significant relationship with earmarks. Consistent with much of the literature, though contrary to the popular perception, the political party of the member was not related to his or her fortunes in the quest for military construction projects.

This analysis supports the claim that the benefit hypothesis is prevalent when Congress makes the geographic project decision, but is less apparent when decisions are made by bureaucrats within the executive branch. Military construction earmarked projects are fundamentally different in that members of Congress specifically add them to the projects already specified in the President's Budget. They are directly traceable to the actions of individual legislators, are often the subject of credit claiming, and represent the clearest example of political decision making. When the executive branch stipulates the location of military construction spending (the majority of military construction spending) it is not apparent that members on key committees influence the geographic distribution of projects. District specific need seems to be more important.

Highway Spending: Earmarks and Formulas

Congressionally enacted formulas have historically been the method by which the federal government has compensated state governments for the construction and repair of highways.[7] The Federal Aid Road Act of 1916 established a "somewhat complicated method of apportioning [the] federal highway subsidy" which distributed funds on the basis of one third relating to the state's relative land area, one third relating to the state's relative population, and one third relating to existing post roads (MacDonald 1928: 92-93). Over the subsequent years, other factors such as traffic density and construction costs have been incorporated into formulas. Although highway construction remains the predominant funding mechanism for highway construction, during the 1980s and 1990s the habit of earmarking specific highway projects in the form of demonstration projects has become a common practice accompanying authorizing legislation as well as appropriations reports.

This policy area will be examined with two different tests of the benefit hypothesis. Specifically: 1) are statutory spending formulas (adjusted every four to six years when highway programs are reauthorized) related to membership on key committees? and, 2) are annual appropriations earmarks related to key committee membership? It is again hypothesized that earmark spending will provide limited support for the benefit hypothesis; earmarks will be related to membership on the committee responsible for stipulating the earmark. It is further predicted that formula spending will be unrelated to measures of committee position.

Two sets of data are necessary for this policy area. Appropriations earmarks from the 103rd Congress were obtained from the Conference Reports of the Transportation Appropriations Subcommittees for fiscal years 1994 and 1995. Data on state by state allocations via the legislatively established formulas were obtained from tables included in the annual Appropriations Committee reports as well.

Analysis for highway funding was conducted initially at the state rather than the congressional district level because highway formulas disburse dollars to state governments which then have discretion over choosing which projects in their state will be funded. As Congress does not distribute formula funds to the district level, it was necessary to examine the data aggregated at the State level only. Similarly, as grants are given to states in a lump sum, and not given in discrete grants, per capita dollars rather than numbers of grants serves as the unit of analysis.

Variables that reflect statewide policy demand for highway spending include the number of cars in the state, the number of rural highway miles and the states poverty rate. This measure of economic need was included in the specified equation because highway projects are often thought of as economic development projects.[8] Committee membership is indicated by the total number of seats that each state has on the relevant Appropriations Subcommittees and full Public Works Committees in both chambers. All dependent variables were converted to a per capita basis, as one of the components of the highway formula

Table 5.4: OLS Results for Highway Spending, 103rd Congress, by State

	Appropriations Earmarks			Formula Dollars		
Variable	b	Beta	T test	b	Beta	T test
Cars Per Capita	0.362	0.015	0.106	215.190	0.299	2.095**
Rural Highway Miles	-2.7E-05	-.278	-1.618	-7.09E-03	-0.253	-1.419
State Population	-2.5E-07	-0.352	-1.113	-5.2E-07	-0.026	-0.079
Transportation Appropriation Subcommittees	3.859	0.561	3.823**	-9.717	-0.488	-0.321
Public Works Committees	0.395	0.176	0.609	-11.527	-0.178	-0.592
Poverty Rate	0.311	0.332	2.488**	-2.194	-0.081	-0.576
Constant	-1.147		-0.378	99.595		1.094

Appropriations Earmarks:
$R^2 = .32$
Adjusted $R^2 = .23$
F = 3.48
SIG F = .007
** $p < .05$
N = 50

Formula Dollars:
$R^2 = .08$
Adjusted $R^2 = .07$
F = 5.67
SIG F = .0000
** $p < .05$
N = 50

Table 5.4b: Highway Appropriations Earmarks by District

Variable	b	Beta	T test
Years	0.009	0.073	1.543
Party	0.041	0.018	0.376
Land Area	6.1E-06	0.174	3.701**
Transportation Appropriations Subcommittee	1.268	0.158	3.404**
Public Works Committee	-0.205	-0.062	-1.323
Average Income	-1.24E-05	-.103	-2.117**
Constant	1.159		4.524**

$R^2 = .08$
Adjusted $R^2 = .07$
F = 6.528
SIG F = .0000
**p < .05
N = 435

is population, therefore a relationship between formula spending and population undoubtedly exists.[9] Table 5.4 depicts the results of this analysis.

OLS regression analysis supports the predictions. Greater state membership on the Transportation Appropriations Subcommittees yields a state significantly more demonstration projects. When the identical model is used to predict the allocation of formula funds on a per capita basis, independent variables measuring committee membership are not found to be significant. The number of automobiles per capita portrays the anticipated relationship; however, all of the other predictor variables measuring statewide demand for highway money are signed incorrectly from the hypothesized direction and are not significant. The absence of a significant relationship between committee membership and formula spending supports the prediction, and further weakens the strength of a benefit hypothesis.

It is also possible to analyze appropriations earmarks at the district level, as funds are targeted to specific projects rather than as lump sum payments to states. When district specific appropriations earmarks are analyzed (table 5.4b), it appears that districts of Transportation Appropriations Subcommittee members receive more earmarks than would have been predicted by chance.[10] Membership on the Public

Works Committee is negatively signed indicating an inverse relationship (though not significant) with appropriations earmarks.[11] The area in square miles of the district, a surrogate for the need for highways, was positively related to earmarks, and statistically significant. Once again, poorer districts are oversubscribed.

Community Development: Earmarks and CDBGs

The Community Development Block Grant (CDBG) Entitlement Program was established by Title I of the Housing and Community Development Act of 1974.[12] The program allocates funds to metropolitan cities and counties and to state governments for community development activities based on the recipient area's population and need. The following characteristics are factored into the program's allocation formula: population, extent of poverty, overcrowded housing, age of housing, extent of growth lag (an indication of suburbanization/ urban flight), and 1960 population.

According to House and Senate Report language describing the Special Purpose grants section of the Department of Housing and Urban Development (HUD) appropriation,[13] projects that are funded by earmarks are to serve the same purpose as CDBGs. Specifically, "The items are targeted to address compelling local examples of important national needs in housing and community development. Provisions included generally fall within one of the broad criteria established for eligibility under the CDBG Program . . . " (Senate Report 102-356).

While the Community Development Block Grant Program and the Special Purpose earmarks have the same governmental goals, funding decisions are made by different governmental actors based on different funding criteria. Once the CDBG formula was statutorily established, it became extremely difficult for an individual member of Congress to adjust the flow of funds to his or her state or district. Only when the program is up for reauthorization are the formula criteria reevaluated by Congress, and input into this process is largely limited to a few relevant committee members. According to Rich (1991), the CDBG formula has not changed since 1978. Though the formula was not changed, program was modified somewhat in 1982 to stipulate that thirty percent of the entitlement funds would be allocated to non-urban areas.

Individual legislators do not have much discretion in determining the amount of funds allocated by the CDBG program to a given district. This limits the amount of believable credit claiming opportunities. In addition, as the program is a block grant, the decision regarding which projects are ultimately funded rests with the recipients (state and local governments). Therefore, the link between congressional action and visible result is not direct, and credit claiming opportunities are limited. I encountered few references to CDBGs in the newsletters mentioned above. Representative Harris Fawell (R-IL) made the following statement on the House floor regarding community development and credit claiming:

> . . . nobody is necessarily against the idea of communities being helped from time to time by grants of federal funds and that indeed is why we have the Community Development Block Grant (CDBG) program. But under CDBG, Federal funds are distributed to local governments back home by an established formula related to need. Local governments in turn then make grants to worthy private or public entities of their choice within general guidelines of HUD. But those kinds of Federal funds would not be acceptable here because certain members want federally funded projects which will enable them to be touted as the one who personally brought home a Federal project to his or her district. (Congressional Record September 12, 1994: H9067)

The FY 1995 Conference Report, the last fiscal year in which earmarks were disbursed in this category, contained 269 separate projects totaling $290,000,000. The CDBG entitlement allocation for 1995 was $2,536,000,000; approximately 900 communities (metropolitan cities and urban counties) were eligible for entitlements distributed according to the statutory formula.

In the following analysis, earmarks for HUD special projects from the 103rd Congress are compared with allocations from the Community Development Block Grant Entitlement Program. As in the previous example (highway funding), the state initially serves as the unit of analysis, as federal decisions for CDBGs are not disbursed at the congressional district level . The formula divides the funds among the states and local communities. OLS regression is again the method of analysis. The dependent variables are dollars spent in each program during the 103rd Congress. As the CDBG program formula is partially based on population, per capita dollars were used when analyzing CDBG allocations. The measure of committee power is the combined total of statewide seats on the relevant House and Senate committees. It is again hypothesized that measures of committee membership will be significant predictors of earmarked community development spending, but that CDBG formula spending will not be related to membership on either the authorizing or appropriating committees involved with community development programs.

Data on state allocations under the CDBG entitlement for fiscal years 1993 and 1994 were obtained from the Department of Housing and Urban Development report: "Directory of Allocations for Fiscal Years 1988-1994." Measures included as independent variables potentially related to state need for community development funds included: the states poverty rate and the density of state population. The relevant committees are the Appropriations Subcommittee on the Departments of Veterans Affairs and Housing and Urban Development and Independent Agencies, and the Banking and Urban Affairs Committees which authorize community development programs.

As can be seen from table 5.5, CDBG allocation at the state level is unrelated to committee membership. When the model is specified on a per capita basis, neither predictors of need nor predictors of political power are statistically significant, producing a model with an R Square of 0, indicating that none of the variance in the dependent variable is explained.

Table 5.5: OLS Results, Per Capita CDBG Dollars, 103rd Congress, by State

Variable	b	Beta	T test
VA/NASA/HUDAppropriations Sub.	-.517	-.023	-.130
Banking Committee	.481	.048	.284
Poverty Rate	.242	.059	.343
Population Density	.006	.087	.492
Democrats	-1.130	-.032	-.200
Constant	26.727		2.517**

$R^2 = .01$

Adjusted $R^2 = .00$

F = .08

Sig F = .99

** $p < .05$

N = 50

Table 5.5b: OLS Results for HUD Special Project Earmarks, 103rd Congress by District

Variable	b	Beta	T test
Years	0.008	0.062	1.441
Party	0.158	0.074	1.623
Construction Workers	-8.3E-06	-0.033	-0.729
Rented Dwellings	0.003	0.037	0.798
VA/NASA/HUD Appropriations Sub.	3.477	0.457	10.754**
Banking Committee	-0.072	-0.021	-0.491
Constant	0.342		1.181

$R^2 = .23$
Adjusted $R^2 = .22$
F = 21.23
Sig F = .0000
** $p < .05$
N = 435

The Community Development policy area provides an additional opportunity to test the benefit hypothesis. There is no overlap between the projects that are earmarked by the Senate Committee and projects earmarked by the House Committee during the 103rd Congress. The Senate subcommittee included earmarks in its report language, and the House committee added location specific earmarks to the Conference report. Each chamber's earmarks were included in the Conference Report; Senate projects are listed first, followed by House earmarks. Therefore, a test of the benefit hypothesis can be done for each chamber. Using the same model described above, House and Senate earmarks were considered individually. Results were supportive of the hypothesized relationship. Table 5.5b depicts House earmarks at the congressional district level. Membership on the House Appropriations Subcommittee is strongly related to receipt of district specific House earmarks. However, the variable indicating membership on the Banking (authorizing) Committee is incorrectly signed (and insignificant). None of the other variables included in the equation were statistically significant. Insignificant variables included: the two other political variables described previously (political party and seniority measured in years) as well as two new variables thought to reflect district need for community development projects. These additional variables were the percentage of dwellings occupied by renters, and the population of construction workers in the district.

Agricultural Research

The National Research Initiative Competitive Grants Program (NRI) provides project grants to colleges, universities, state agriculture experiment stations, other private and public research organizations, and individual researchers for six high priority areas relevant to agriculture, food, and the environment.[14] Grants are awarded through a competitive application process for research in the following areas: natural resources and environmental nutrition; food quality and health; animal systems; plant systems; markets, trade and policy; and processing for adding value and developing new products.[15] Peer review, using panels of scientific experts outside of the government agency evaluate the grant proposals, and make project funding decisions. In fiscal year 1994, the Department of Agriculture's Cooperative State Research, Education and Extension Service funded 833 research grants totaling $96,626,632 (USDA 1994).

In addition to the competitive project grant process described above, Congress has historically included funds for specific projects in the Agriculture Appropriations Subcommittee bill which are then detailed as earmarks in the accompanying report. For fiscal year 1994, the Agriculture Appropriations Subcommittees included funding for 134 special projects totaling $72,900,000 in their conference report. These earmarked projects fulfill virtually the same governmental mission as NRI grants, but are specific project decisions that are determined by members of Congress rather than competitive review. Once again, these earmarks have been singled out by opponents of the process as serving the political needs of Congress rather than any strict scientific or need based criteria. According to Fawell:

> These earmarks are the purest form of pork-barrel spending . . . because it completely bypasses established procedures and criteria for spending . . . In addition, a parallel $97.5 million grant program—the National Research Initiative—exists which funds agricultural research with the appropriate level of scrutiny, competitive awarding, and peer review. (Congressional Record June 30, 1992: H5567)

In objecting to Fawell's claim (and his failed amendment to strike the earmarks from the FY 1993 appropriations bill), Rep. Neal Smith responds by defending congressional discretion: "Professors should not be the only ones to sit around and decide what we need" (Congressional Record June 30, 1992: H5569).

Data on NRI grants for the 103rd Congress were obtained from the report "National Research Initiative Competitive Grants Program: Abstracts of Funded Research" for fiscal years 1993 and 1994. Earmarks were culled from appropriations subcommittee reports from the 103rd Congress. Explanatory variables potentially related to the likelihood of a state receiving agricultural research funding were initially identified. These included variables relating to the states involvement in farming (the number of farms) as well as the capability to conduct scientific research (represented by the total amount of university research spending in the state during the base year 1989).[16] The states population was also hypothesized to be related to research funding with the more populated states expected to obtain greater shares of the available funds. As funding decisions are made on an individual basis and do not rely on a formula that incorporates population, there was no need to use a per capita measure. Measures of political power were also included in the OLS regression analysis; these included combined total House and Senate membership on the authorizing (Agriculture Committee) and appropriating (Agriculture Appropriations Subcommittee) Committees. Once again, the state serves as the unit of analysis; however number of grants rather than dollar amounts was used as the dependent variable.[17]

Table 5.6 indicates that for the National Research Initiative Program, indicators of state demand for agricultural spending are predominant, while measures of congressional committee membership are signed positively, but not statistically significant. Population is the best predictor of competitively awarded grants. As one would expect, larger states have greater abilities (especially people) to compete for grants. In addition, the amount of university research conducted in a state, a measure of state research capacity, showed a significant positive relationship indicating that states with a greater academic infrastructure are better able to compete for research grants.

In contrast and as hypothesized, projects earmarked in annual appropriations reports are more closely associated with political factors, specifically membership on the Agriculture Appropriations

Table 5.6: OLS Results for Agriculture Research, 103rd Congress by State

Variable	CSREES Earmarks			NRI Grants		
	b	Beta	T test	b	Beta	T test
Number of Farms	5.1E-05	0.360	1.906	5.6E-05	0.0770	.780
Population	-3.0E-07	-0.323	-1.225	2.4E-060	493	3.590**
University Research	1.3E-09	0.167	0.705	1.3E-080	326	2.642**
Agriculture Approppriations Subcommittee	3.467	0.405	2.299**	3.0110	069	0.982
Agriculture Committee	0.183	0.047	0.275	2.4220	.121	1.368
Constant	4.379		4.238**	6.746		2.466**

CSREES Earmarks:
$R^2 = .32$
Adjusted $R^2 = .26$
F = 4.25
SIG F = .003
**p < .05
N = 50

NRI Grants:
$R^2 = .82$
Adjusted $R^2 = .80$
F = 39.45
SIG F = .0000
** p < .05
N = 50

Subcommittee. Perhaps somewhat surprisingly, state-wide population is negatively signed and has a statistically insignificant association with the location of earmarks. This is an indicator of the political nature of earmark spending. Interestingly, university research is not a significant predictor of earmark location.

Finally, when agricultural earmarks are analyzed at the district level, no statistically significant relationships could be found for committee membership. This is likely due to the lack of variance in the dependent variable. Although all congressional districts theoretically could receive agricultural research earmarks, in reality they are concentrated in the limited number of research universities that have the capacity to do this type of research. Both the number of people employed in education (a district specific measure of research capacity) and the number of people employed in farming were good predictors of the location of agricultural research earmarks.

Table 5.6b: OLS Results for CSREES Earmarks, 103rd Congress by District

Variable	b	Beta	T test
Years	0.0002	0.0007	0.015
Party	0.462	0.087	1.954
Agriculture Appropriations Subcommittee	-0.137	-0.008	-0.188
Agriculture Committee	-1.197	-0.136	-2.543
Education Employment	0.0001	0.323	7.269**
Number of Farmers	0.304	0.274	5.133**
Constant	-3.834		-6.599**

$R^2 = .16$

Adjusted $R^2 = .15$

F = 13.51

SIG F = .0000

** $p < .05$

N = 435

Conclusion

The essential point of this chapter, as well as the previous one, is that federal programs are not necessarily distributed in a way that emphasizes the electoral needs of members of congressional committees at the expense of good public policy. The provision of Army Corps of Engineers projects comes closest to a policy that is handed-out piecemeal by Congress to meet the electoral needs of its members. However, recent research into water resource distribution indicates that, even in this area, distributive needs compete with policy needs, and most of what the Army Corps does today is not wasteful (Hird 1991; Del Rossi 1995).

Leaving aside the issue of water projects, there is considerable evidence that Congress only appears to concentrate benefits upon committee members in those limited instances where the geographic decisions are actually made by Congress and contained in the legislative record. Earmarks do represent targeted spending that appears to go disproportionately to committee members, especially members of the Appropriations Committees. However, the extent of earmarking of federal expenditures pales in comparison with the much larger programs that distribute funds through formulas or bureaucratic discretion. As will be discussed in detail in Chapter Eight, the seven categories of legislative earmark identified in this research accounted for only a total of $43.2 billion ($49.4 billion if one includes highway trust fund expenditures earmarked in ISTEA) of spending during the period under study. When this is compared to the overall total of federal expenditures during the period FY 1992-FY1997[18] ($8.96 trillion), the benefit hypothesis loses much of its importance as an explanation of congressional organization and behavior.

There is no doubt that members pursue district specific projects, and that at times members on key committees are rewarded for their committee position. However, the assertion that congressional organization and policy outcomes are the result of the electoral pursuit of geographic benefits and the need to institutionalize a system that meets the needs of members of Congress is not supported by the evidence. All committees are not preference outliers, most programs do not shower relevant appropriations and authorizing committees with disproportionate expenditures in members districts, and most programs are not skewed to meet the needs of high demand legislators. Most programs appear to be targeted at district or state policy needs. The question now becomes, what does the empirical evidence say about the idea of universalism. That will be the topic of the next chapter of this study.

NOTES

1. See Bickers and Stein (1995) for a discussion of the reasons for using project numbers rather than dollars as the dependent variable. Bickers and Stein conclude that a legislator will want to maximize the number of credit claiming opportunities, and argue that ten projects may equate in monetary terms to a single alternative use for federal dollars, but legislators would prefer the ten projects rather than one project of equal or even greater cost.

2. Some projects overlap districts; in such cases projects were divided into fractions. For example, if a large National Park was located in three districts, each district was credited with .33 of an earmark.

3. The political data for this chapter were obtained from relevant editions of *Congressional Quarterly Almanac* and *Vital Statistics on Congress.*

4. Congress has in the past, included project specific water resource appropriations directly in legislation. They are currently specified in the accompanying report language.

5. I am indebted to John Micik and June Moser of the Army Corps of Engineers for providing this data.

6. Earmarks for Reserve and National Guard units are frequently for locations away from established military bases covered in the reference book. Information identifying the congressional district of a given zip-code is included in the *Congressional Staff Directory,* and this volume was at times used to supplement the other reference materials to locate projects in all policy areas considered in this project. Demographic data for this section were obtained from the Bureau of the Census 1993.

7. See MacDonald (1928) (Chapter Five) for a discussion of the development of federal involvement in highway construction. For a brief account of the history of federal highway policy see CBO (1988); for a more in-depth discussion of transportation financing, see Hoel (1990).

8. For example, although he originally threatened to veto the 1991 Highway reauthorization bill for its "pork barrel" quality, President Bush signed the law at a staged signing ceremony at a construction sight. In his signing statement Bush proclaimed: "It will enable us to build and repair roads, fix bridges, and improve mass transit; keeps Americans on the move and helps the economy in the process. But really, it is summed up by three words: jobs, jobs, jobs. And that's the priority" (Administration of George Bush 1991).

9. It is interesting to note that formula spending and state population are indeed closely linked, but when earmarks (either appropriations or authorization) are regressed using population as an independent variable, no

association was found. This is strong evidence that factors other than obvious need, especially political factors, influence the distribution of earmarked funds.

10. District specific (rather than state specific) analysis is possible for earmarks but not formula grants.

11. An ongoing dispute between appropriators and authorizers over control of highway funding is likely to be responsible for this result. (See Healy 1993a for a discussion of this dispute). This disagreement can be taken as further evidence of a lack of committee reciprocity in the modern Congress (see discussion in Chapter Six).

12. For background information on the Community Development Block Grant (CDBG) program see: U.S. HUD 1994; U.S. HUD 1993; and Rich 1991.

13. This program is under the jurisdiction of the Subcommittee on Veterans Affairs, NASA and Housing.

14. See United States Department of Agriculture 1993, 1994a and 1994b for additional detail on CSREES programs.

15. For a complete description of the application and peer review process, see CSREES 1995.

16. Statewide demographic data are from the *Statistical Abstract of the United States.*

17. Although district level analysis is possible with this data set, State level aggregations were used because analysis of the data revealed that project grants (from both programs) were concentrated in large Public Universities. Although all districts in a state are legally entitled to compete for grants or receive earmarks, in reality it appears that most funding is concentrated in one or two large research universities per state, typically ones with an agricultural focus.

18. Figure represents on and off-budget outlays for the period FY 1992—FY 1997. Outlays for FY 1997 are estimates. Source: *Economic Report of the President,* 1997

CHAPTER SIX

Universalism and Reciprocity

The necessity to spread program expenditures broadly often radically redefines the objectives of a program and thus transforms its impact. This, in turn, breaks the linkage between the program's objectives and the distribution of funds. Some districts in which the particular problem to be solved is acute end up getting fewer resources in comparison with the magnitude of the problem, while other districts obtain substantially more funds than are objectively required. The distributive tendency to spread the dollars across many districts means that too little of the program's goal is achieved relative to the amount of resources spent. In some cases, this transformation may be so complete that it is not clear whether the program's objectives are achieved at all!

Kenneth Shepsle and Barry Weingast (1984)

We do not find evidence that either individual programs or portfolios of programs are universalized. Nor do we find evidence of much of a move toward universalism. Most individual programs provide benefits to relatively small minorities of Congressional districts and never approach even a simple majority of districts over time.

Robert Stein and Kenneth Bickers (1994)

The two previous chapters cast doubts upon one of the major underlying premises of the distributive theory most closely associated with Shepsle and Weingast. While there is plenty of anecdotal evidence that individual members of committees at times receive a disproportionate share of benefits from the programs within their jurisdiction, systematic analysis of federal distributive policies reveals this affect only to be dominant in those limited areas where Congress actually specifies the location of project spending. In other areas of federal distributive policy, benefits that vary by geographic location do not appear to be influenced by the institutional structure of Congress in any meaningful way.

In this chapter a second premise of distributive theory—universalism and reciprocity—will also be examined using evidence from previous studies, an analysis of earmark spending, and three brief case studies from the contemporary Congress. Universalism is the claim that distributive benefits tend to be spread to all, or virtually all, congressional districts in legislation, and that distributive policies are supported by coalitions approaching unanimity. Reciprocity refers to a pattern of behavior characterized by committees (and individual members) deferring to the legislation of other committees (and members) in policies that contain distributive benefits.[1] The central thesis of this chapter is that universalism does occur in the U.S. Congress, and there is evidence that universalism is present when considered across the subsystem comprised of each chambers' thirteen appropriations subcommittees. Earmarks are the currency through which the system operates; they are universalized across subcommittees. However, there is less evidence of universalism and reciprocity outside of the appropriations subsystem, and universalism is especially difficult to identify when viewing the distribution of individual programs. Finally, it appears as though even within the appropriations subcommittee system these norms have become weaker in recent years.[2]

OVERVIEW

This chapter begins with a discussion of the theoretical development of the concept of universalism, and a review of the limited literature on empirical evaluations of universalism in the United States Congress. The second section of the chapter is a review of the empirical evidence derived from a study of appropriations earmarks, which provides limited support for the concepts of universalism and especially reciprocity. Following the empirical analysis are three case studies which suggest that the appropriations process demonstrates evidence of operating as a system to universalize distributive benefits, but that the power of universalism and reciprocity are confined to the annual cycle of bills produced by the thirteen appropriations subcommittees. The cases also may be seen as evidence that universalism is becoming less powerful as an explanation for distributive behavior.

The first case is a study of the failure of an amendment proposed by Senator Robert Smith (R-NH) which would have changed the way highway funds are allocated thereby disrupting a complex appropriations systemic logroll. Although the amendment would have increased highway funding in 39 states, it was defeated by a margin approaching universal in size. A second case, the defeat of an attempt by committee outsiders to reduce the spending power of the Appropriations Committee (the Penny-Kasich amendment), provides evidence that the House Appropriations Committee engages in explicit sanctions to preserve logrolls. The Penny-Kasich example also indicates that universalism does not prevail outside of the institutionalized thirteen subcommittee logroll. This second case may also indicate that the systemic power of the Appropriations Committees is declining in the modern Congress, a topic that will be considered further in Chapter Eight. The present chapter concludes with an analysis of the failed congressional attempt to enact the presidentially supported economic stimulus package of 1993, a case that suggests universalism does not hold outside of the institutionalized subsystem.

RATIONAL CHOICE THEORY AND UNIVERSALISM

Much of rational choice theory of congressional behavior is based on the inherent instability of majority-rule decisions.[3] Condorcet's classical voting paradox describes the situation in majority rule institutions where no majority is stable; there is always another group of actors that can form a new majority. Arrow's (1951) influential research introduced the concept of instability to modern political science, and his theorem forms the foundation of rational choice thought concerning the instability of majorities. As there is always another coalition of legislators that can defeat the prevailing coalition, "cycling," the movement from one majority to another was predicted in support of distributive policies. According to Riker (1980): "Disequilibrium . . . is the characteristic feature of politics."

Both Buchanan and Tullock (1962) and Riker (1962) theorized that rational legislators would form minimum winning coalitions (MWCs) on each distributive policy, in order to maximize benefits to those included in the prevailing coalition.[4] MWC's however, are inherently unstable, and new coalitions will rise to defeat previous majorities in subsequent votes. MWC supporters predict that votes on distributive policy issues will be won by majorities of just greater than 50 percent, and that benefits of distributive programs will be concentrated through the slim majority of districts made up of those included in the winning coalition.

Despite these early rational choice predictions, it is apparent that actual coalitions on distributive policies in the U.S. Congress are not characterized by MWCs. In the words of Barry Weingast (1979) "Empirical studies of Congress uniformly find that the MWC prediction is simply wrong" (p.131). In addition, rather than instability, it was noticed by observers of Congress that the institution is marked by considerable stability. Rational choice theorists subsequently increased the complexity of earlier models by including features of complex institutions which are thought to promote equilibrium and prevent cycling in the majority rule organization (Shepsle has termed this "structure induced equilibrium") (Shepsle 1986). An institutionalized committee system with rules of deference and reciprocity is seen as essential to equilibrium, preventing continual emergence of new majority coalitions.

The actual concept of universalism in support of distributive policies can be traced to Mayhew (1974:114),[5] who claimed that members of Congress must deal with each other repeatedly over time and therefore have come up with the obvious solution that avoids the instability of MWCs—universalism. According to Mayhew (88-89):

> In giving out particularized benefits where the costs are diffuse (falling on taxpayer or consumer) and where in the long run to reward one congressman is not obviously to deprive others, the members follow a policy of universalism. That is, every member regardless of party or seniority, has a right to his share of benefits. There is evidence of universalism in the distribution of *projects* on House Public Works, *projects* on House Interior, *projects* on Senate Interior, *project* money on House Appropriations, *project* money on Senate Appropriations, *tax benefits* on House Ways and Means, *tax benefits* on Senate Finance, and . . . urban renewal *projects on House Banking and Currency (emphasis added*[6]*).*

Weingast (1979) sought to provide a formal explanation of congressional behavior based on the perceived empirical predominance of universalism in distributive decisions. Weingast relies on virtually the same sources cited by Mayhew to support the empirical predominance of universalism. Weingast (p.142) defined universalism as: " . . . unanimous inclusion of representatives' projects in omnibus-type legislation produced by one committee." Weingast maintained that Congress has developed and institutionalized norms which tend to favor wide-spread provision of benefits, and coalitions in support of distributive policies that approach unanimity. His conclusions contradict those of earlier rational choice scholars mentioned above (Buchanan and Tullock 1962; Riker 1962) who concluded that self-interested legislators would form coalitions barely large enough to secure legislative victory.[7]

Uncertainty is at the center of Weingast's theory; each member is uncertain as to whether his or her projects will be included in the final legislation, and as a result the norm of universalism has been institutionalized in Congress to eliminate the fear of exclusion. If everyone abides by the norm, all will be guaranteed to receive some distributive benefits from the legislative process. Members who support the norm are rewarded with benefits for which they can claim credit which are thought to assist the recipient in getting reelected.[8] According to Weingast (1979: 135)

> The major implication of these assumptions for the analysis of distributive policy is that representatives pursuing their own interests will prefer institutional arrangements (or norms) which increase their chances of success in gaining benefits for their districts. Universalism is such an institution. Rational self-interested legislators have compelling reasons to prefer decision making by maximal rather than minimal winning coalitions.

The norm of universalism is enforced through socialization which ensures that new members will conform. This explains the presence of patterns of apprenticeship and deference to seniority that were observed by previous scholars such as Fenno (1962 and 1966) and Matthews (1960). Sanctions are imposed upon those few members who violate the norm of universalism to punish violators in order to discourage future deviations from the norm.

Fiorina (1981b) builds on Weingast's concept of universalism to provide a theoretical explanation for reciprocity. According to Fiorina, "reciprocity is merely a means to universalism in a differentiated legislature . . . given that the committees contain minorities of the legislature, within-committee agreements are not enough; agreements between committees are also necessary" (p.215). Fiorina therefore finds support for an institutionalized norm of universalism meant to enhance electoral success of all participants. Fiorina's concept of reciprocity is consistent with Matthews (1960) description of reciprocity as a folkway in the Senate.

Inman and Fitts (1990) have theorized that coalitions in the modern Congress are constrained by concerns regarding the costs associated with distributive spending. They propose a concept of coalitions larger than MWCs but less than unanimous in size. Inman and Fitts refer to these coalitions as "constrained universalism."

Empirical Investigations:

The empirical literature on universalism is much more limited than the extensive literature on the benefit hypothesis discussed in Chapter Four.[9] Collie (1988a), Krehbiel (1991) and Stein and Bickers (1994 and 1995) all point to the ambiguity surrounding how to operationalize universalism, which is a possible explanation for the limited empirical literature directly concerning universalism. Some studies that examine universalism measure the extent of geographic spread of a program or programs. Other studies examine the size of voting coalitions in favor of distributive policies. The most troubling difficulty is the level of aggregation of data. Should the research focus on individual programs, all programs within the jurisdiction of a government agency, all programs under a single subcommittees jurisdiction or even all government programs? Weingast (1994) recently gave some indication of how he believes universalism should be studied. The criteria for identifying distributive policies identified in Chapter Two (Divisibility; Omnibus; Expenditure; and Scope) must be adhered to when choosing policies to study. In addition, Weingast suggests that universalism should be tested by restricting the domain to all programs within a subcommittee's jurisdiction. To date, no study adopting Weingast's restrictive conditions has been undertaken.

In examining the literature on universalism, it is again important to recognize that different studies employ data from policy areas that allocate funds based on one of the four methods depicted in Diagram 1 (Chapter Two). The empirical literature on distributive politics and coalition size is again organized following the same format laid out above; programs are categorized on the basis of the location of the funding discretion (bureaucratic or legislative) as well as whether they are distributed on the basis of institutional discretion or standardized formulas.

Empirical Studies before Mayhew

It is important to distinguish between those studies that came before Mayhew (1974) and those which followed his work, as research done earlier and upon which Mayhew's conclusions are based does not use the term universalism, and typically treats the concepts of universalism and reciprocity only tangentially. Mayhew explicitly links the following studies with evidence of universalism: Murphy (1968); Fenno (1973); Fenno (1966); Horn (1970); Manley (1970); Surrey (1957); and Plott (1968). However, as Anagnoson (1980) points out, all of these studies discuss universalism only indirectly. They are typically case studies that refer to a wider than anticipated spread of geographic benefits or where roll call votes are nearly unanimous (or even when passage is done by unanimous consent). In none of these studies is it clear that all congressional districts benefit from the policy. Most of the studies deal more with reciprocity (especially Fenno 1966 and Horn 1970) than universalism. It is therefore more appropriate to concentrate on the more recent scholarship to see how the empirical evidence supports rational choice predictions of universalism and reciprocity.

Legislative-Project Determination

Ferejohn (1974) found that omnibus rivers and harbors legislation typically distributed projects to 350 to 400 districts (a range of 82 to 90 percent). Distribution certainly exceeds what one would expect if the minimum winning coalition is anticipated, and the amount of districts included approaches universalism. However, it is important to point out that at least 10 percent of districts receive nothing from the distributive process. Water projects are the quintessential pork barrel project, and discretion over the location of water projects rests largely with Congress, therefore one would expect to find universalism here if in any single program.

Wilson's (1986b) study of district level appropriations for river and harbor legislation (1889-1913) also lends empirical support to the concept of universalism. Wilson finds that during the time period under consideration, the proportion of districts receiving federal projects was extremely high—indicating that coalitions much larger than MWC's developed in this area of distributive politics. According to Wilson: ". . . the overwhelming number of districts sharing in this legislation points to the predictive capacity of Shepsle and Weingast's (1981) universalism model."

Del Rossi (1995) also studies Army Corps of Engineers water resource spending, and finds evidence to support Inman and Fitts' (1990) concept of "constrained universalism." She claims that, in the modern period, the requirement that all water projects be shown to have a positive cost-benefit ratio has acted as a curb on the distributive (and universalistic) desires of members of Congress by eliminating inefficient (or more likely, less efficient) projects. As in the example of the benefit hypothesis, the quintessential pork barrel program yields results anticipated by distributive theory. Water projects tend to be distributed to nearly every congressional district, and the policy area receives wide-spread support in the legislature.

Soherr-Hadwiger (1998) found that 271 congressional districts benefited from military construction spending in the 1980s.[10] Although military construction spending does not approach the universal scope anticipated by Weingast, Soherr-Hadwiger points out that voting coalitions supporting military construction spending are much greater in size, approaching unanimity. From this evidence he concludes that members of Congress are not only concerned with the provision of distributive benefits, they are even more concerned with the provision of general benefits accompanying a spending category like military construction.[11]

Bureaucratic-Project Determination

Anagnoson (1980) studied the distribution of U.S. Economic Development Administration (EDA) project data for fiscal years 1968-70 organized by congressional district. According to Anagnoson: "It seems that universalization explains the overwhelming portion of project distribution . . . EDA projects are spread out over the entire nation" (p.83). Grasso (1986) also studied EDA policy and arrived at a similar result. Grasso concludes: "The agency seems to have concentrated on achieving the goal of a wide geographic dispersal of aid, with a disproportionate share of the funds channeled to states with disproportionate representation in Congress" (p.95). However, in neither article, is the number of congressional districts receiving federal assistance discussed.

Hamman's (1993) research on Federal Mass Transportation Assistance also found evidence of universalism in this area of distributive politics. "The impetus and management of program expansion comes from administrative managers as well as from conscious agreement, tacit reciprocity, or consent among legislators. The findings presented here lend empirical support to formal models of legislative coalition building such as Shepsle and Weingast's (1981), which predict that the geographical scope of federal assistance and legislative support will expand over time"(p. 566). Hamman does, however conclude that universalization in Congress takes place over time and is not limited to single program areas, but takes place over "the broader subgovernment environment" (p.566). It is important to note, however, that mass transit funding became universalized in part through the introduction of legislatively determined formulas in 1974. Hamman concludes: " . . . an additional 130 districts benefited after the formula program was enacted" (p.561). The problems with using programs that deliver benefits on the basis of broad-based formulas as examples of distributive policy are discussed above.

Legislative—Formula Determination

Stockman (1975) identified a tendency for Congress to expand the eligibility of formula grants in a number of social welfare programs. Instead of being targeted at the areas of most need, programs become watered down because of the political pressure to universalize benefits (Stockman called this the distributive tendency). The Model Cities Program is often used as an example of a program that became too diffuse due to the political pressure to universalize. Stockman also identified universalism in federal funding of public schools. Although established as an anti-poverty program, the Elementary and Secondary Education Act (ESEA) ended up being a broadly distributed program. According to Stockman: " . . . although 56 percent of the U.S. poverty population is concentrated in the 50 largest metropolitan areas, more than 13,000, or 80 percent of the nation's school districts receive ESEA funds" (p.23). Although there is certainly political influence in many formula programs, it must again be pointed out that formulas are different than typical project programs in that they are not delivered unit by unit, spending can not be altered in one district without altering spending throughout the country, and individual credit claiming opportunities are limited.

Studies Using Data from Several Programs

Owens and Wade (1984) examined federal spending in congressional districts in four policy areas: welfare, agriculture, public works and the military. According to their findings: "If such universalizing tendencies obtain at the macro-level, they do not entirely dominate, however at the programmatic level" (p.419). Of the four areas examined by Owens and Wade, only public works policy was found to support the concept of universalism.

In a study of the distribution of federal expenditures during the period FY 1975- FY 1978, Anton, Cawley and Kramer (1980) found that only 13% of federal programs delivered benefits to every state. Likewise Gramlich (1977) determined that only a few programs deliver benefits to a majority of districts.

Finally, in the most extensive empirical study of universalism to date, Stein and Bickers (1994b)[12] found no evidence of universalism in the non-regulatory financial assistance programs that they examined. Programs that employed a project grant delivery mechanism and that contained no stated eligibility restrictions on the basis of income or unemployment were treated as distributive and were included in their data set. "Our findings show that the evidence on the extent to which benefits from distributive programs are universalized is weak." Stein and Bickers found little evidence to support universalism at either the individual program or the policy subsystem levels. They "argue that the incentive to universalize benefits is only one goal of legislators and may not always be the most fruitful strategy for enhancing their reelection prospects" (p.295).

Later, Bickers and Stein (1997) sought to explain the lack of empirical support for universalized spending in their earlier research. They examine three possible mechanisms for building support for distributive programs that provide benefits to less than a majority of districts: political parties, interest groups, and administrative agencies. They conclude that political parties could not serve the coalition building purpose in the U.S. political system, but find more support for the other two institutional mechanisms under certain circumstances.

Evaluation of Literature on Coalition Size

There appears to be some, but by no means overwhelming evidence that distributive policy making is associated with universalism. In her review of the literature on distributive policy making, Collie (1988a) found that empirical research in the area of localized spending had concentrated on the benefit hypothesis, and that the question of coalition size had been largely ignored. According to Collie: " . . . the more comprehensive empirical literature on distributive policy making is not well suited to address the question of whether all districts get something most of the time" (p.445). She calls for an increased dialogue between formal modelers and empirical researchers, including additional empirical research on coalition size in distributive policy making.

From the evidence presented above, it appears as though universalism is most common in areas where public works projects are undertaken, especially as when they are undertaken at the direct request of Congress. It is possible that although only a small number of programs deliver widespread benefits, these are the programs that are the most politically popular and have also been the subject of case studies. The failure to consider the nature of the benefit provided by a distributive policy has been common in previous studies. This study approaches the subject with the explicit understanding that not all pork is equal, and it may be that the only type of pork that is always universally in demand is spending for district specific projects that are specified during the legislative process. This research will add to the small body of empirical research on the size of coalitions in distributive politics, and specifically test the assumption that universalism varies by type of expenditure

A Study of Earmarks

Data on the geographic distribution of Congressional Appropriations earmarks provides evidence that in the policy type most closely fitting the definition of distributive policy, universalism is present in the geographic spread of benefits only when the appropriations process is viewed as a system rather than as individual earmark categories. When viewed as a systemic logroll, the appropriations process takes on more of the appearance of universalism and reciprocity. Universalism is also present in the size of supporting (voting) coalitions. When viewed by individual earmark program, however, earmarks are not universalized with the exception of water projects.

Data Analysis—House

An analysis of the data on geographic spread of appropriations earmarks to the seven areas discussed above (CSREES [Agricultural Research], FBF [Federal Building Fund] HUD [Special Projects], TRANS [Highway demonstration projects], MC [Military Construction Projects], NPS [National Park Service Construction] and CORPS [Army Corps of Engineers Water projects]) using earmark data for individual years and two year Congresses will be interpreted for the period FY1992-FY1997 for both the House and the Senate. Earmarks were identified for each fiscal year from Appropriations Conference Committee Reports. Earmarks were attributed to a congressional district or districts using the following sources: *Congressional District Atlas, Congressional Districts in the 1990s* and the *Congressional Staff Directory.*[13]

When analyzed by individual earmark category, there does not appear to be much support for the universalism thesis in terms of the spread of geographic projects. As can be seen from Table 6.1, only in the case of Army Corps of Engineers water projects does geographic spread approach anything resembling universalism. This is true not only for a given fiscal year, but also for the entire 102nd, 103rd and 104th Congresses. Aside from water projects, no other category of earmark exceeds geographic spread of fifty percent of congressional districts in a year, and only once does a spending category (military construction) exceed fifty percent of the districts for a two year Congress.

However, when all seven categories of earmark are pooled into a single variable, evidence of universalism emerges.[14] This is especially true when data are pooled across the two year periods that comprise a Congress. The geographic spread in each of the three Congresses (102nd -104th) studied approximates 100% of districts. Most members receive something to claim credit for in the Appropriations earmarking process—if it is not a new bridge, it may be funding for an agricultural research project or a new barracks for the military base in the district. This is true both when all military construction projects are considered, and when only those projects not requested in the President's budget (the strictest definition of earmark) are included in the data. This is clearly much larger than the number of districts one would predict if a minimum winning coalition was the norm.

Table 6.1: Geographic Spread of Earmarks—Percent of Congressional Districts

	1992	1993	102ND	1994	1995	103RD	1996	1997	104TH
CORPS	91.3	91.5	93.6	91.7	91.0	93.8	91.5	91.7	94.0
CSREES	14.3	15.9	17.2	14.5	13.8	16.6	12.9	12.6	13.8
FBF	7.6	12.6	16.3	12.6	16.8	16.6	11.3	16.6	22.5
HUD	27.1	36.1	43.4	0	34.5	34.5	0	0	0
MC	43.9	41.6	54.3	42.8	40.9	49.9	29.0	31.7	37.9
NPS	16.3	16.3	22.3	18.6	18.4	22.3	10.1	13.6	16.6
NRMC	22.4	26.4	38.0	16.1	26.4	34.7	14.3	16.8	22.8
TRANS	20.7	22.0	23.7	26.7	63.7	66.0	0	0	0
ALL	97.9	98.2	99.1	97.5	97.2	99.8	97.5	98.2	99.1

Table 6.2: Geographic Spread of Earmarks—Percent of States

	1992	1993	102ND	1994	1995	103RD	1996	1997	104TH
CORPS	90	96	98	73	82	90	98	100	100
CSREES	92	94	98	94	92	96	86	86	90
FBF	24	40	50	42	46	60	34	42	54
HUD	52	72	74	0	74	74	0	0	0
MC	94	98	100	74	98	98	88	96	98
NPS	70	66	78	70	70	80	46	66	70
TRANS	74	54	78	34	94	94	0	0	0
ALL	100	100	100	100	100	100	100	100	100

Data Analysis—Senate

Data on Senate Appropriations earmarks provides additional evidence of the norm of universalism, though the much less broad geographic distribution possible (50 States rather than 435 congressional districts) does not place as much statistical importance on the results from the Senate. However, it is apparent that in the Senate as in the House, a norm of universalism prevails in appropriations earmarking decisions. For example, as can be seen from Table 6.2, both military construction projects and Army Corps water projects are distributed to greater than 90% of the states in almost every fiscal year examined.

When data are pooled, the universal quality of the distributive policies is even more apparent. When each of the seven areas is combined, the resulting distribution reaches every state for all years examined. As the seven categories by no means compose all of the possible earmark areas, the appropriations earmarking process clearly provides something for everyone in the Senate.

Coalition Size, Universalism, and Appropriations Earmarks

Appropriations earmarks are best viewed as a process that extends across all thirteen subcommittees. The widespread provision of benefits is also accompanied by widespread support as reflected in voting behavior. Not only do members of Congress (during the time period under examination) tend to reject overwhelmingly any effort to strip earmarked projects from appropriations, universal coalitions also tend to form in support of final passage of appropriations bills which include earmarked projects. The following table depicts the size of supporting coalitions for the final passage of seven Appropriations Subcommittee bills containing the earmark categories for the period FY92-FY 97. Both in the House and the Senate, support for appropriations legislation typically approaches unanimity in most years. When a closer vote occurs, this is more likely the result of a policy dispute in the omnibus legislation that is unrelated to its distributive content.[15]

Large, bipartisan support of spending bills that are accompanied by report language earmarking projects that will benefit virtually every congressional district are common during the period under consideration. Additional evidence of the presence of universalism and reciprocity within the 13 subcommittees (and the seven subcommittees detailed above) will be offered in the first original case study discussed below.

Table 6.3—Percent of House Members Voting For Final Passage of Bill Containing Policy

	1992	1993	1994	1995	1996	1997
CORPS	92.5	63.1	80.4	92.0	94.4	93.0
CSREES	100	74.9	100	72.8	65.6	90.0
FBF	100	69.8	50.1	87.2	87.8	90.9
HUD	92.9	74.7	79.3	87.3.	54.4	93.9
MC	100	100	100	100	76.9	93.8
NPS	74.9	100	100	100	57.4	90.9
TRANS	88.4	100	100	100	93.1	95.4

Note: Passage by voice vote indicated by 100 percent

Table 6.4—Percent of Senators Voting For Final Passage of Bill Containing Policy

	1992	1993	1994	1995	1996	1997
CORPS	100	100	89	100	93.7	92.0
CSREES	90	100	100	100	100	100
FBF	100	100	100	100	64.3	84.8
HUD	100	100	100	90.9	55.1	93.9
MC	100	100	95	95	86	93.8
NPS	95.9	100	92	93	59.1	84.8
TRANS	96.9	100	100	90	89.7	85.8

Note: Passage by voice vote indicated by 100 percent

Case Studies

Proponents of universalism often point to the case of Senator James Buckley as evidence of the norm of universalism in Congress.[16] Buckley represented New York in the Senate from 1970 to 1976. According to the popular wisdom, Buckley violated universalism and the norm of reciprocity by actively opposing pork barrel projects, and was punished by having only the projects from his State of New York removed from an omnibus water resources bill. Krehbiel (1991) has shown, however, that the Buckley example has been overstated. Buckley himself proposed stripping the New York projects, they were later restored in Conference, Buckley again tried to strip the projects when the bill reached the Senate floor, and Buckley remained an active opponent of pork barrel spending throughout his tenure in the Senate. In addition, the assertion that Buckley was defeated in his attempt for reelection due to his refusal to pursue distributive spending is not supported by the facts of the situation.[17] It appears as though the favorite example of institutional processes designed to enforce universalism does not strongly support the concept.

Distributive theorists have recognized that legislators like Buckley (Mayhew termed them "saints") exist; however, they are always discussed as minor figures who are sanctioned for their deviant behavior. These sanctions serve to enforce the norm and prevent others (fiscal conservatives) from violating universalism. In addition to the doubts surrounding the Buckley example, Savage (1991) has argued that distributive theorists have underestimated the influence that these saints can and do have on policy. In an analysis of earmark spending for academic research and facilities, Savage shows that saints who oppose pork barrel spending can rise to positions of influence in Congress. As Appropriations subcommittee chairs (cardinals) several saints have been influential in preventing earmarking in their institutional spheres of influence. This is contrary to the predictions of universalism and reciprocity. According to Savage:

> Universalism presumes saints are always ineffective and punished. As long as they are not, and as long as they do not fear being ineffective or punished, saints are a threat to universalism's assumption of unanimity (Savage 1991: 343).

The following case studies drawn from Congress during the 102nd-104th Congress are meant to further illustrate the limitations of universalism as a generalized norm of congressional behavior. The first case describes a situation where universalism is potentially most effective—when a complex subsystem logroll is in place, and members are seeking to preserve the agreed upon arrangement (gains from exchange). In this case, projects have been specified (appropriations earmarks) and an attempt to eliminate earmarking in one area is portrayed by leaders as an attempt to unravel the whole logroll. It is defeated by a coalition much larger than a simple majority. It is important to note that debate takes place within the appropriations subsystem, on an annual piece of omnibus legislation.

The second case is an example where members of the leadership try to enforce the norm of universalism using explicit threats of sanctions and appeals to the institutionalized processes. The attack on distributive spending from outside the spending system fails; however, the very fact that a group of members challenge distributive spending, and the slim margin by which the Appropriations Committee backed-coalition holds, are evidence that universalism is not the guiding norm. The final case, the defeat of president Clinton's economic stimulus package in 1993 provides further evidence that universalism does not accurately characterize distributive spending when the decision are made outside of the established, institutionalized appropriations process. It should be noted that no cases from the 104th Congress are discussed in this chapter. The Republican electoral victory of 1994 will be discussed in the final chapter, as the implications that the election had on the behavior and organization of Congress have ramifications on all aspects of distributive theory.

Case One: Universalism and Appropriations Earmarks

During Senate debate on the Department of Transportation and Related Agencies Appropriations Act for fiscal year 1992, Freshman Senator Robert C. Smith (R-NH) offered an amendment seeking to eliminate funding for 63 highway demonstration projects from the legislation.[18] Smith's amendment would have redistributed the $387 million included in the bill for the 63 earmarked projects to each of the fifty states on the basis of a formula developed by the Environment and Public Works Committee. As the (Appropriations Committee) bill before the Senate was written, 23 states would receive no funding for highway demonstration projects; under the Smith amendment every state would receive some funding, and only 11 states would have experienced a net decrease in funding level.

Senator Smith distributed and included a chart in the Congressional Record showing that 39 states would benefit directly by receiving greater funding under the terms of his amendment (See Table 6.5).

Table 6.5 : Highway Projects in H.R. 2942 Compared with the Smith Amendment.

STATE	HR 2942	SMITH AMEND
ALABAMA	$0	$7,581,083
ALASKA	$12,000,000	$6,256,074
ARIZONA	$28,200,000	$5,294,529
ARKANSAS	$4,000,000	$4,450,916
CALIFORNIA	$0	$31,926,564
COLORADO	$0	$6,230,229
CONNECTICUT	$0	$6,727,273
DELAWARE	$0	$2,025,182
FLORIDA	$1,000,000	$14,889,555
GEORGIA	$0	$20,612,014
HAWAII	$1,500,000	$2,072,962
IDAHO	$0	$3,085,418
ILLINOIS	$0	$15,359,886
INDIANA	$0	$8,177,404
IOWA	$16,800,000	$6,197,838
KANSAS	$9,450,000	$5,664,800
KENTUCKY	$0	$6,540,717
LOUISIANA	$0	$6,482,975
MAINE	$0	$2,510,641
MARYLAND	$0	$6,185,523
MASSACHUSETTS	$0	$7,522,619
MICHIGAN	$3,000,000	$11,110,356
MINNESOTA	$0	$6,896,343
MISSISSIPPI	$2,000,000	$4,937,832
MISSOURI	$495,000	$9,673,417
MONTANA	$2,250,000	$4,368,542
NEBRASKA	$0	$4,237,850

Table 6.5 (continued)

STATE	HR 2942	SMITH AMEND
NEW HAMPSHIRE	$0	$2,431,807
NEW JERSEY	$44,650,000	$10,033,472
NEW MEXICO	$9,000,000	$4,225,667
NEW YORK	$26,000,000	$21,628,457
NEVADA	$2,000,000	$3,027,326
NORTH CAROLINA	$6,000,000	$9,629,050
NORTH DAKOTA	$1,040,000	$2,947,186
OHIO	$0	$13,712,032
OKLAHOMA	$2,800,000	$5,917,013
OREGON	$0	$4,879,079
PENNSYLVANIA	$0	$16,259,766
RHODE ISLAND	$0	$2,044,383
SOUTH CAROLINA	$0	$5,835,999
SOUTH DAKOTA	$3,240,000	$3,269,147
TENNESSEE	$350,000	$8,715,893
TEXAS	$0	$24,900,775
UTAH	$8,000,000	$3,747,483
VERMONT	$1,100,000	$2,185,047
VIRGINIA	$0	$8,257,955
WASHINGTON	$5,400,000	$6,971,292
WEST VIRGINIA	$182,200,000	$4,855,514
WISCONSIN	$8,200,000	$6,546,193
WYOMING	$6,000,000	$3,290,087

Source: Congressional Record, September 17, 1991, p. S13161

California would have been the beneficiary of almost $32 million in additional highway funds if the Smith amendment became law; Texas would have increased its share of highway demonstration money by almost $25 million. At first glance, it would appear to be an easy vote for self-interested legislators. If every Senator voted according to how his or her state would fare under either scenario (committee bill or Smith amendment) the vote would have been 78 to 22 in favor of Smith's alternative.

However, when the vote was taken on September 17, 1991, Smith's amendment failed by the overwhelming margin of 84 to14 (85.7%). Representative Harris W. Fawell (R-IL) introduced a similar amendment seeking to redistribute highway earmark project funding on the basis of a broad-based formula in the House of Representatives. Fawell's amendment also failed by the lopsided margin of 365-61 (85.7%).

During Senate debate, legislators opposed to the amendment continually reminded other Senators that the highway projects, and indeed the Transportation Appropriations bill are part of a larger process that is built upon mutual consent and encompasses other sections of the current bill, other bills, as well as even other fiscal years. This idea is perhaps best summed up by an exchange between Smith, and Senator Frank Lautenberg (D-NJ), then the chairman of the Transportation Appropriations Subcommittee:

> Senator Lautenberg: I will tell you, yes, this bill is fair. People come to the committee with projects; they articulate their needs, they remind us of our responsibility that we need to consider their requests and thusly we make our judgments. When we hear the fairness argument, I must point out that it really depends on which year and on which project, Mr. President.
>
> Senator Smith: It is not that we are passing money around under the Smith amendment. We are distributing it fairly, and using a formula, a process that is fair, rather than simply raw, political, abusive power, which is what is happening. That does not make me very popular with some of my colleagues to make comments like that, but that is a fact. That is true. So we can take on the process, and I want to see process reform. I would not mind cutting all of this out, but I know that is not going anywhere. So let me make the point: The process is wrong. If you want to change the process, then you can vote yes on the Smith amendment and help your state (Congressional Record, September 17, 1991: S 13161).

Senators also reminded Smith that he too had a stake in the process, and a veiled threat to specific projects in New Hampshire was implied.

> Senator Lautenberg: In Conway, NH, this committee provided $8 million over 3 years in 1988, 1989, 1990 for the construction of a new bridge. At that time it was fair for New Hampshire, unless the Senator wants to rescind that money. Maybe New Hampshire can pay us back the $8 million we then gave them; this year, the committee

> has provided $3.9 million for Daniel Webster College. This is a discretionary grant . . . (p.S13161).

This exchange illustrates an attempt to enforce universalism through an implied threat. The large majority that voted in favor of the status quo even though the Smith alternative would have resulted in a more favorable allocation for most, was apparently more concerned with preserving universalism (the institutionalized logroll) that exists within the committee between subcommittees and over time. When it comes to making actual geography-specific funding decisions, the Appropriations Committees in both chambers seem to have institutionalized a system that garners support much greater than majorities needed for passage by spreading earmarks throughout most congressional districts.

According to an account of this legislation (Mills 1991), Senator Lautenberg said of the bill: "[The Subcommittee] received 578 requests for special highway, transit, aviation, and other transportation projects from 85 Senators. Obviously, we were not able to provide for every request." At least eighty five Senators felt comfortable enough with the process to request something from the cardinal, and most received something in return, or anticipated that in the future they would benefit from the subcommittee's policy decisions. It is probably more than coincidental that 84 members voted to support the subcommittee's decision.

On the subject of the systemic nature of universalism across the appropriations subcommittees, the following quotes from the current chairman of the full House Appropriations Committee Robert Livingston (R-LA), and junior committee member[19] Mark Neumann (R-WI) are instructive:

> Robert Livingston (Hager 1991: 25):
>
> There are times when you just have to swallow and support a[n appropriations] bill because you've worked hard to get something in it. Suppose the chairman and the ranking member and the membership of the subcommittee have gone out of their way to really assist you in getting a particularly important project of yours in that bill . . . It makes it very difficult for you to turn around and say well thank you very much. I'll stick it in your eye and vote against the bill.

> Some members might do that, but they are not going to have anything in that bill the next time.
>
> Mark Neumann (C-SPAN Morning Journal September 1996):
>
> What happens is members of Congress write letters to these chairmen, and the chairmen then take into account their requests . . . what happens next, let's just cut through the baloney out there and say what is going on in this Congress. Once you've got one of your pork projects into one of these bills you are then obligated to make votes on other bills, because, quite frankly, they take your pork away if you don't . . . Once your project is in this bill, that then becomes a hammer for anything else they need your vote on. And I challenge you to tell me that it's not the way it works . . .

These comments are supported by Allen Schick (1995) who also describes a system of earmarking that features universalism and reciprocity. According to Schick (p.139):

> . . . the process is bipartisan; members of both parties take home some earmarks . . . members of Congress who request and receive earmarked funds are expected to vote for the appropriations bill. The basic rule is "don't ask for money if you are not going to vote for the bill."

The institutionalized earmark process described in Chapter Two and echoed by the above quotes works to enforce universalism within the thirteen annual spending bills. However, as the following two cases will illustrate, there is evidence that the norm is less strong when legislation is considered outside of the ritualized annual process, and also, the norm appears to be losing support over time even within the annual process, as distributive benefits may be becoming less important.

Case Two: Penny-Kasich—Failure of Universalism in the House

The norm of universalism is supported by the previous example. An example of legislative behavior in the distributive realm that is less supportive of the concepts of universalism and reciprocity occurred in November, 1993, with the defeat of the "Common Cents Deficit Reduction Act of 1993" better known as the Penny-Kasich amendment after the co-authors of the legislative proposal.[20] Penny-Kasich represented an attack on the jurisdiction and expertise of the House Appropriations Committee, and the arguments and events surrounding the proposed legislation offer insight into the congressional process. Not only does this example fail to support the predictions of universalism and reciprocity, this example may also be taken as symbolic of the wave of anti-spending behavior that has influenced many members of Congress in recent years.

Representatives Timothy Penny (D-MN) and John Kasich (R-OH) proposed a rescission to the fiscal year 1993 budget, seeking to reduce federal spending by $90 billion over five years. Their plan specified over eighty different money saving measures, including reductions in domestic discretionary spending,[21] and was offered as a substitute to a Clinton administration backed rescission package (which was also supported by the Appropriations Committee leadership) to reduce spending by $37 billion over the same time period. The Penny-Kasich proposal was ultimately defeated by a vote of 213-219.

In his recent memoir, former Representative Penny (1995) details how pressure was applied by Appropriations Committee elders to preserve the committee's jurisdiction over spending decisions and ensure reciprocity. According to Penny: "The leaders of the House Appropriations Committee, the power center that doles out all the federal dough, sent letters to dozens of lawmakers saying that a vote for Penny-Kasich would jeopardize projects in their home district . . . these letters were signed by the Democrats who ran these committees and by the highest ranking committee Republicans" (emphasis in original, pp.30-31). These "Dear Colleague" letters apparently singled out specific projects in the recipient's district that could be threatened by Penny-Kasich. A letter sent by Energy and Water Resources Appropriations Subcommittee Chairman Tom Bevill (D-AL) said: "I know you would want to be made aware that the Penny-Kasich amendment would jeopardize many projects of the Corps of Engineers, including: [the name of a specific project in the member's district]" (Mills 1993: 3255). One recipient of a letter, Republican Freshman Rod Grams (R-MN) told Congressional Quarterly "I know this stuff goes on, but I'm shocked to see them being so cavalier as to put it in writing" (Ibid.: 3255).

Many senior members of Congress stressed the need to maintain the system or process that gave the Appropriations Committee jurisdiction in such matters during debate on the Penny-Kasich amendment on the House floor. For example Dan Rostenkowski (D-IL), at the time the Chairman of the House Ways and Means Committee spoke out against the proposal and in favor of committee reciprocity:

> . . . I have learned during my years here that we disregard regular order at our peril. And this legislation totally ignores regular order. This bill may initially smell like deficit reduction, but it will leave a bitter aftertaste. We do not know enough about this bill to make a reasoned decision about whether it is good policy . . . I object strenuously to the procedural shortcuts that we are using to bring up a measure that few of us have seen before and even fewer can understand. It reminds me of the 1981 reconciliation bill that was debated in this House that contained take-out pizza orders on the margin of the text. In 1981 we legislated in haste—and then spent a decade trying to undo the damage. Let us not repeat that sad exercise (Congressional Record: H 10821-10822).

Other powerful Committee Chairs spoke out against the amendment on the floor (John Dingell, Martin Olav Sabo, George Brown, William Natcher). All used terms decrying the violation of the established process. Natcher, at the time the chairman of the House Appropriations Committee concluded his remarks: "Resist this approach. Let's continue to develop budget resolutions and appropriations bills the right way and vote this amendment down" (Congressional Record: H10824).

Supporters of distributive spending were able to defeat the Penny-Kasich amendment, but not by anything close to a universal margin. The proposal was defeated by a slim margin of six votes. Distributive theory predicts that opponents of spending will be small in number and lacking in power. Yet Penny and Kasich and their supporters nearly eliminated $90 billion in federal spending over five years, much of it district specific in nature. Many members openly defied the wishes of the Appropriations Cardinals who threatened retribution. According to Penny (1995: 32), "To our surprise and delight, many of the intimidating letters from the appropriators seemed to backfire. Many members sided with us just to teach the power brokers a lesson." This is contrary to the expectations of universalism and reciprocity. Rather than deferring to the wishes of others in order to ensure that their own distributive needs would be met, members openly defied the Appropriations leadership without fear of retribution. Members risked retaliation in order to reduce discretionary spending. Many did not defer to the expertise of the Appropriations Committee on matters of distributive spending. The Penny-Kasich example does not fit nicely with the picture of distributive policy portrayed by Shepsle and Weingast.

Case Three: The Failed Stimulus and the Failure of Reciprocity

One of the early priorities of the newly elected Clinton administration in 1993 was to get Congress to pass a short term economic stimulus of approximately $16.3 billion in discretionary spending.[22] The package of programs included such favorite distributive projects as Army Corps of Engineers Water Projects, Highway construction, funding for National Parks, Federal Building Funds, Community Development dollars and state Wastewater treatment programs. The proposal's intent was to provide a jobs package to stimulate the economy that was just beginning to recover from recession.

Distributive theory would predict that such an omnibus bill would be universally supported, and provide benefits to all congressional districts. This is just the kind of policy Mayhew (1974: 128) predicted from reelection motivated legislators: "Thus in time of recession congressmen reach for 'accelerated public works' bills listing projects in various districts . . . " Yet the bill died; after passing the House by a slim margin (235-190), it was defeated in the Senate by a filibuster, a parliamentary technique that requires at least 41 faithful adherents to a point of view, in this case, opponents of the distributive spending package. In the previous two examples, members of the Appropriations Committee coalesced around the side in favor of distributive spending. In this case, division was along party lines, with Republican appropriators in both chambers opposed to the spending bill.

Why would Congress defeat an omnibus spending bill that contained a wide variety of distributive benefits? Certainly partisan considerations and the desire to teach a newly elected president a lesson in the need to work with the minority party played a role. The explicit reason given by most who opposed the bill in both the House and the Senate was that it was an inefficient pork barrel bill that the country could not afford at a time of high deficits. Two quotes from Republican opponents of the stimulus package, one each from the House and Senate, summarize opposition to the proposal. It is important to note that both of these quotes are drawn from legislators who are members of their chamber's Appropriations Committee, and not outsiders or in Mayhew's terms "saints."

Senator Connie Mack's (R-FL) comments refer not only to his opposition of the bill, but also to the parliamentary tactics of floor manager and Appropriations Committee Chairman Robert Byrd, who attempted to limit amendments to the proposal by constructing an "amendment tree."[23] Representative Joseph McDade's (R-PA, of Steamtown fame) comments likewise refer to restrictive procedures that accompanied the House legislation; this was the first urgent supplemental not to allow amendments since 1977 (CQ Almanac, 1993: 708).[24]

> Senator Mack: I am delighted to have the opportunity to tell the people in this country what is going on. By allowing us to continue to talk and not allowing us to offer amendments, we still can inform the people that this bill is about more spending, more spending, more spending, and more pork, more pork, more pork. The more people around the country hear this simple fact, the more they are inclined not to support the President's so-called economic plan (Congressional Record, April 3, 1993: S 4470).

> Rep. McDade: My colleagues, there are no shortages of dubious spending in this bill. We cannot change it. They are in the bill, going to create fish atlases, going to study large river populations of sickelfin chub . . . There is money in here from arts education, to Olympic white water canoeing.

In this example from the 103rd Congress, we see the development of partisanship on a spending package, rather than the bipartisanship predicted by universalism. It is apparent that although the annual spending bills within the Appropriations Committee's jurisdiction were treated in a bipartisan way during this same session of Congress (wide geographic spread of benefits and large supporting coalitions), when the issue of distributive spending was removed from the institutionalized system, universalism was not present. In fact a filibuster, the most drastic tool available to minorities in Congress was exercised to stop distributive spending. This example is in no way anticipated by rational choice predictions of universalism. The extreme level of divisiveness on this issue can be seen as evidence that a change in legislative behavior towards spending in general is occurring in the

Congress. This topic, and its ramifications on distributive theory, will be explored in Chapters Seven and Eight.

Conclusion

Universalism appears to be an accurate description of the way that the Appropriations Committees of Congress ensure passage of the annual funding bills that keep the government operating. There are institutionalized procedures for requesting earmarks, expected norms of behavior once an earmark (or earmarks) is bestowed, and sanctions that can be used against members who violate the norms (with enforcement enhanced through repeat play conditions). When policymaking is removed from the annual appropriations process, there is less evidence of the presence of universalism, in either the operation of the process or its results. The only real evidence of the very wide-spread provision of distributive benefits by Congress appears in areas where tangible benefits are specified in the legislative process—often through earmarking.

A final point on universalism concerns the different models of distributive policy that separate Weingast (1994) from Stein and Bickers (1994). Weingast's motivation for universalism rests on uncertainty —benefits are universalized because members fear exclusion from the winning coalition. By voting for a bill that includes something for everyone, members are certain to receive something. Stein and Bickers model involves provision of benefits by the bureaucracy. Bills therefore contain standards (often vague) about how to distribute funds. There is no question of certainty or uncertainty as members are not themselves deciding on the coalition of districts that will receive program benefits. Universalism as modeled by Weingast (and others) may be an accurate reflection of what happens when Congress makes the distributive decision. However, as is argued in several places in this research, only a small minority of distributive decisions are determined directly by Congress, most notably earmarks.

NOTES

1. See Matthews (1960) for an earlier description of reciprocity as a sociological norm in the Senate. See also Fenno (1962 and 1966) and Horn (1970).

2. See Chapter Eight for a discussion of the dynamic perception of distributive spending.

3. Many summaries of the "classical voting paradox" and the instability of majority rule coalitions exist. These explanations range considerably in technical sophistication. The standard statement is Arrow, 1951. Two brief but clear summaries are: McCubbins and Sullivan (1987: 309-317) and Green and Shapiro (1994: 98-114).

4. Buchanan and Tullock (1962) theorized that minimum winning coalitions (MWCs), that is coalitions barely exceeding the majority required for success, would form when organized groups were deciding on the provision of geographic benefits. Using the example of a group of one hundred farmers voting on the provision of roads in a given area, Buchanan and Tullock claimed that a MWC of fifty one farmers would form and approve the maintenance of only the roads passing their farms. The coalition would reject any maintenance for other local roads.

5. See also Shepsle and Weingast 1981, and Weingast, Shepsle and Johnsen 1981. Actually, Mayhew attributes the concept of universalism to Polsby (1968); however, Soherr-Hadwiger (1993) provides evidence that Polsby's idea of universalism did not mean unanimous or near unanimous support of a policy. Polsby instead was referring to the universal application of congressional norms in the institutionalized Congress.

6. Note that all of the studies that Mayhew cites are examples where Congress makes the distributive decision on a project basis (i.e. not bureaucrats or formulas).

7. Other rational choice scholars have modeled distributive coalition size using different assumptions and have arrived at conclusions different from Shepsle and Weingast. Baron (1989 and 1991) has modeled coalitions much smaller than universal. Groseclose and Synder (1996) also find supermajorities that are smaller than universalistic. They explain the absence of universalism in the following language: "If legislators who do not receive projects are not indifferent to the bill's passage but instead are slightly opposed, say because they care (only slightly) about the fact that the bill adds to the tax burden of their constituents, then the optimal coalition size will typically not be universalistic" (p.305).

8. Other scholars from the rational choice perspective (Niou and Ordershook 1985) have disputed Weingast's model as he does not account for the predominance of inefficient projects in pork barrel legislation. They have produced a model that, unlike Weingast's, can accommodate inefficient legislation directly, without additional ad hoc assumptions. See also Shepsle and Weingast 1981. The inefficiency argument is tangential to the research presented here. The main point of concern is the prediction that coalitions are

universal, which is supported by rational choice scholars who don't necessarily agree with the exact model specified by Weingast.

9. On this point see Collie 1988a.

10. Soherr-Hadwiger looks at the location of military bases rather than location of spending. While this allows him to identify military bases near district boundaries, it does not include military spending that is not directly targeted to a base (national guard construction, for example).

11. See also Arnold (1990) on the concept of general benefits.

12. See Weingast (1994) for a critique of Stein and Bickers' work which proposes some reasons for their failure to support universalism.

13. Other resources that were useful in this task were Frome (1995); and Hearings of both the Agriculture and Energy and Water Appropriations subcommittees.

14. As the seven earmark categories studied in this research do not exhaust the universe of earmark categories, it is likely that the presence of universalism is greater than shown.

15. For example, many of the Appropriations bills during the first year of the 104th Congress included controversial policy proposals that delayed some, and caused votes on others to be along party lines (i.e. not universal). According to Shear (1996: 875.): " . . . the failure to enact five of this fiscal year's spending measures can be traced in large part to the House's propensity to use appropriations measures to achieve policy goals. The Labor-Health and Human Services bill, for example, was bottled up in the Senate because of a striker replacement provision that the House added to it. And the Treasury, Postal Service and General Government bill was hung up by an amendment, pushed by freshman Rep. Ernest Jim Istook, R-Okla., to cut federal funds to advocacy organizations that lobbied Congress."

16. See for example, Mayhew 1974; Ferejohn 1974, Weingast 1979, and Shepsle and Weingast 1987.

17. Buckley was originally elected in a three-way election in which he received only 39 percent of the vote. He was defeated on the same ballot that elected Jimmy Carter President; His opponent (Daniel Patrick Moynihan) received 54 percent of the vote, close to the 52 percent received by Carter in New York (See Krehbiel 1991: 52).

18. For an account of this case, see Mills 1991.

19. Neumann has been an outspoken critic of the appropriations process and earmarks in particular. Additional discussion of Neumann is included in Chapter Seven.

20. For accounts of the Penny-Kasich defeat, see: Mills 1993; Pianin 1993, Penny 1995 and Congressional Record, November 22, 1993: H10795-H10860.

21. The proposal would have done a number of things to reduce spending in the short and long term including placing a moratorium on new federal building construction and rescinding spending in a number of discretionary programs favored by appropriators.

22. See Administration of William J. Clinton, 1993: 215-224.

23. Byrd's tactics are described in Congressional Quarterly Almanac 1993: 708-709. On Byrd's tactical attempts to guide the stimulus package through the Senate without amendment, see also Woodward 1994: 153-154.

24. A single amendment, to be proposed by Appropriations Committee Chairman Natcher, was the only amendment allowed under the rule.

CHAPTER SEVEN

Distributive Theory and the Electoral Connection

Congressmen consider new dams, federal buildings, sewage treatments plants, urban renewal projects, etc. as sweet plums to be plucked. Federal projects are highly visible, their economic impact is easily detected by constituents, and sometimes they even produce something of value to the district. The average constituent may have some trouble translating his congressman's vote on some civil rights issue into a change in his personal welfare. But the workers hired and supplies purchased in connection with a big federal project provide benefits that are widely appreciated.

Morris Fiorina (1989)

Investigation into the question of whether congressmen must vote for higher spending in order to get reelected comes up with a negative conclusion: Legislators may think so but their perceptions are mistaken. (Of course, were this relationship held uniformly, no fiscal conservative could ever get elected). Every test so far devised suggests that spending in general or within the district does not help an officeholder. High spenders, even if they occupy marginal seats, fare no better at the polls than low spenders. Congressmen who announce their retirement do not change their pattern of voting or vote differently than those who continue to run for office. Members from safe districts do not systematically vote for lower spending.

Aaron Wildavsky (1992)

> *Virtually all recent models of distributive policy making in the legislature assume that the reelection instinct inspires legislators to provide constituencies' benefits. Yet the literature does not establish that the provision of tangible benefits is the engine behind electoral success, as each model suggests it is. The few studies that have tested directly for some linkage between electoral returns and district benefits have so far produced somewhat mixed if not unsupportive evidence though admittedly the methodological problems are severe.*
>
> *Melissa Collie (1988a)*

Distributive theory is based on the premise that rational legislators seek to maximize district specific benefits in order to pursue the central goal of reelection. It is taken for granted in much of the literature on distributive politics that members pursue pork barrel benefits aggressively in their quest for reelection. It is likewise taken for granted that there must be some electoral payoff, otherwise why would legislators devote scarce resources to providing projects to their districts and states? One representation of the distributive theory being critiqued in this study, which is based on the assumption that "policies are the by-product of the legislator's pursuit of election and power" (Shepsle and Weingast 1984) concludes: " . . . we have emphasized a legislative predilection in favor of expenditure programs. Legislators like money to be targeted to their constituents almost independent of program purposes . . . the norm is for legislators to seek dollars and to claim credit for the economic stimulus it provides" (p.365).

Despite the apparent certainty of the connection between the desire to be reelected and the pursuit of distributive policies, and the corresponding assumption that members are rewarded for pork barrel spending with votes, empirical support for both of the assertions is scarce and both are confronted with serious barriers to definitive empirical analysis. Regarding the motivations for member pursuit of pork barrel projects, assessing the actual geographic distribution of federal expenditures is not an accurate reflection of members pork barrel desires, as there is not necessarily a correlation between how hard a member pursues pork and how much he or she receives. Asking members why and how hard they pursue district specific projects may be problematic, as legislators may wish to avoid being labeled a free spender. When Feldman and Jondrow (1984) asked congressional staffers and lobbyists about the impact of pork barrel projects, "they denied that election outcomes are sensitive to changes in spending" (p.148).

As distributive theorists are quick to point out, however, there is no way to tell whether this is how decision makers actually behave, or whether this is how they wish us to think they behave. It is therefore extremely difficult to ascertain the motivations of members.[1] Certainly, many members do seek pork barrel benefits as part of their electoral strategy. However, from the evidence that will be presented in this chapter, the claim that this is universal appears to be an exaggeration. The statement first attributed to David Stockman (1975) and subsequently echoed by Kenneth Shepsle (1984) and Kiewiet and McCubbins (1985) that "there is no such thing as a fiscal conservative when it comes to his district or his subcommittee" is likely an exaggeration of reality.

OVERVIEW

The purpose of this chapter is to suggest that the electoral connection between pork and votes is not as universal, static or as certain as distributive theorists have claimed. The existing literature on the electoral connection will first be analyzed and the conclusions of both Wildavsky and Collie quoted at the start of this chapter will be supported. The subsequent section is an analysis of earmarked projects as a reflection of pork barrel behavior which likewise does not support an association between pork barrel spending and electoral margins. Next, descriptions of the behavior of four contemporary legislators will be presented as evidence that the electoral connection is neither as strong nor as universal as is assumed by distributive theory. This chapter concludes with the suggestion, to be developed further in Chapter Eight, that to the extent that there is an electoral connection, it is dynamic and has lessened as the public has become more aware of wasteful government spending and large annual deficits and debt.

PREVIOUS STUDIES OF PORK BARREL POLITICS AND ELECTIONS

The connection between localized spending and political considerations has long been recognized by observers of Congress.[2] In Charles Warren's 1932 book *Congress as Santa Claus*, the author discusses the then-recent passage of several federal laws to provide federal funding for programs at the state level. Objecting to this tendency, Warren claims:

> All of these statutes take money from the National Treasury and spread it among the States for an ostensible National purpose, but in reality for local purposes, often controlled by political reasons. They inevitably tend towards State extravagance (pp.100-101).

The political nature of providing local benefits from the federal Treasury has been the subject of discussion since the earliest federal efforts in the states and localities.

David Mayhew's *Congress: The Electoral Connection* remains one of the most widely accepted depictions of congressional behavior. According to Mayhew, members of Congress actively seek to secure federal spending in the districts that they represent. Members then claim credit (through press releases and other media and direct voter contacts) for each project and dollar that is spent by the federal government in their district, because voters are thought to value local spending and associated benefits such as jobs, improved infrastructure and economic development. In addition to voters, and perhaps more important, crucial sources of campaign financing (interest groups and elites) are thought to respond to pork barrel spending by rewarding the incumbent with financial support. Mayhew did not test whether there was a real connection between distributive benefits and reelection; it is sufficient for his analysis to assert that members believe that there is a connection, and act accordingly. According to Mayhew:

> How much particularized benefits count for at the polls is particularly difficult to say. But it would be hard to find a congressman who thinks he can afford to wait around until precise information is available. The lore is that they count—furthermore, given home expectations, that they must be supplied in regular quantities for a member to stay electorally even with the board.

Morris Fiorina (1977 and 1989) takes Mayhew's thesis further along a normative path by claiming that not only do members of Congress engage in pork barreling (and the equally important casework) but they also pursue these reelection oriented activities at the expense of good public policy. For Mayhew, so-called institutional maintainers, such as an economy minded Appropriations Committee and political parties act to ensure that Congress as a whole keeps the public interest as an important goal. For Fiorina, and many scholars who follow in the distributive theory tradition, there are no institutional maintainers; the single minded pursuit of reelection works against the interests of good policy and in favor of government growth and inefficiency.

EMPIRICAL INVESTIGATIONS

Empirical evidence connecting the provision of pork with improved electoral fortunes is hard to come by. The two major studies to examine the relationship between local spending and electoral outcomes (Feldman and Jondrow 1984 and Stein and Bickers 1994a and 1995) find no direct relationship between district specific spending and electoral margins in congressional elections, and analyses of attitudes and opinions of both the public and legislators lead to results that fail to support the connection.

Kiewiet and McCubbins (1985a) tested the hypothesis that Congress as a whole is sensitive to reelection considerations and increases gross appropriations levels in election years. Using spending data from the period 1948-1979, Kiewiet and McCubbins concluded that Congress appropriated more dollars to the thirty seven agencies that they studied during election years than during off years. However, empirical evidence did not support their hypothesis that " . . . the tendency for Congress to treat agency requests more generously in election years is stronger for those agencies which supply divisible, constituency oriented benefits—especially public works—than for agencies which supply largely indivisible benefits" (p.75). Their research supports a general increase in spending during election years, but the type of spending tied to questions of geography—distributive spending—did not seem to be affected by timing of elections. Kiewiet and McCubbins do not investigate whether increased distributive benefits improves a member's chances of reelection.

Feldman and Jondrow (1984) used change in federal construction since the last election and change in federal civilian employment in the same time period as the dependent variables in their analysis of the electoral connection. To account for districts of different sizes, they divide each change by total employment in the district. Feldman and Jondrow found no evidence that those legislators who are more successful in securing contracts and employment are any more successful at election time. The authors conclude: "While variables reflecting party affiliation, the incumbent's vote in the last election, and scandal associated with incumbents are important determinants of the vote [the author's control variables], changes in both local federal spending on construction and federal civilian employment in the incumbent's district are shown to have no effect on the share of votes going to the incumbents" (p.147).

Payne (1991a) tested for the electoral connection in two ways using a spending score developed by the author to determine each members' support of congressional spending.[3] Initially, Payne hypothesized that support for spending would be a function of the member's degree of electoral insecurity measured by vote in the previous election. Payne finds that "the electoral effect is statistically insignificant" (p.496). There was no relationship between member's marginality and their support for selected spending bills. Payne's second attempt to test for the electoral connection involved testing for the effect of impending retirement on support for spending. Although Payne's analysis is based on only a small number of cases, he did find that " . . . retirees are, if anything, more in favor of spending programs than other members" (p.502).[4]

In a study of split-ticket voting, Alvarez and Schousen (1993) did find a positive relationship between the amount of pork barrel spending and an indirect measure of electoral gains by incumbents. The authors report that: " . . . the greater the amount of federal money flowing to the district, the greater the probability that a [survey] respondent would recognize the incumbent's name and report at least one thing they liked about the incumbent" (p.426). However, Alvarez and Schousen rely on a measure of pork barrel spending that is problematic. Their research relies on contract expenditures by county which are then divided into congressional districts based on "assumptions about the proportion of certain counties in different districts." Not only are these assumptions subject to certain inaccuracies, but the data set also excludes the major metropolitan areas of the United States.

Morris Fiorina has written or co-written several pieces (Fiorina 1981b and 1989; Cain, Ferejohn and Fiorina 1987 and Rivers and Fiorina 1989) that are critical of empirical attempts to test aspects of the electoral connection especially as they relate to the relationship between casework, pork barrel spending and electoral margins. He is especially critical of the work of Johannes and McAdams on casework (1981 and 1986) but he also finds Feldman and Jondrow (1984) guilty of some of the same errors. Johannes and McAdams have found a negative relationship between electoral margin and efforts by legislators to increase their margins through a number of factors including increased casework and pork. Fiorina, along with his co-authors, has observed in these four works that the failure of Johannes and McAdams, Feldman and Jondrow and others to find empirical evidence in support of the electoral connection is likely due to problems in their methods and analyses, especially related to problems of simultaneous causation.[5]

Stein and Bickers[6] (1994b; 1995) analyzed the provision of domestic assistance awards to congressional districts (discretionary programs of either the bureaucracy or Congress). The key independent variable in their analysis is measured as the change in the proportion of new discretionary awards to the total number of discretionary awards from one Congress to the next (99th and 100th Congress). Stein and Bickers test the conventional electoral connection hypothesis—that pork barrel spending is rewarded with large reelection margins—and achieve results virtually identical to those of Feldman and Jondrow. There does not appear to be a relationship between greater amounts of pork and larger margins of victory.

Stein and Bickers (1994b and 1995)[7] also proposed and tested an alternative theory of the electoral connection based in part on the findings of Jacobson (1978) regarding campaign spending, that gets around some of the criticisms that have been made by Fiorina and others on empirical models of the electoral connection. Stein and Bickers have hypothesized that not all legislators have the same incentives to seek localized benefits from the federal treasury. Specifically, they note that Jacobson found an inverse relationship between campaign spending and reelection margins which is attributable to the fact that vulnerable incumbents are the ones who are most in need of campaign spending to secure victory. Candidates in safe seats have less need to spend heavily. Applying this idea to the issue of pork barrel spending, Stein and Bickers conjectured that vulnerable incumbents have the greatest incentive to pursue aggressively distributive benefits for their districts. Therefore, one would expect to find an inverse relationship between electoral margins and subsequent pork barrel spending. Stein and Bickers find modest support for their alternative hypothesis. They conclude that "Only some incumbents, namely those who are most vulnerable, are likely to seek increases in new awards . . . "(p.394).

Alvarez and Saving (1997b) employed the data base developed by Bickers and Stein in testing this alternative view of the electoral connection based on differences in legislator needs. Relying on empirical data from the 101st Congress, Alvarez and Saving (p.828) concluded " . . . distributive benefits help some but not all legislators and, given that Democrats reap substantial electoral benefit from pork barreling but Republicans do not, the identity of the majority party can affect the structure of the legislative organization . . . "

Sellers (1997) likewise relies on Bickers and Stein's data set to test electoral connection hypotheses, and does not find evidence that pork influences electoral margins. However, Sellers proposes and tests an alternative hypothesis. He suggests that electoral outcomes are related to what he calls "fiscal consistency." Fiscal consistency suggests that fiscal liberals will be rewarded for high pork delivered to districts, and fiscal conservatives will be rewarded for limiting pork. Sellers (p.1024) reports that "Fiscally conservative legislators receive more votes than fiscally inconsistent legislators."

Levitt and Snyder (1997) address the estimation problem identified by Fiorina and others by using instrumental variables. Specifically, they use spending outside the district but inside the same state as an instrument for spending in the district. Using the Bickers and Stein data set for their empirical analysis Levitt and Snyder (p.52) find: "strong evidence that increased federal spending in congressional districts helps incumbents win votes."

Three studies that use survey research methods to explore the electoral connection hypothesis also find evidence that challenges the simple conception of electoral connection. These studies indicate that members of Congress are typically concerned more with national than local issues when forming opinions on fiscal policy issues (Schier 1992); that citizens prefer that their legislators adopt a national rather than local outlook on policies that involve government spending (Hibbing and Theiss-Morse 1995); and that when evaluating individual spending programs, people base their support on their belief in the legitimacy of the client or program, rather than pure self-interest (Sanders, 1988).

Schier conducted interviews with members of Congress to determine their opinions and behavior towards issues of fiscal policy. Schier found that:

> Locally oriented legislators are particularly inclined to operate to "maintain their programs" or "defend the home turf" as they sometimes put it. They see resolution and particularly reconciliation and appropriations votes as opportunities to help the local economy by preserving particular spending programs. By the mid-1980s, relatively few remained uniformly locally-oriented in their approach to budget votes; most at least discussed resolution votes in "big-picture" terms, probably because large deficits required a more broad-based conception in order [to] find a solution. Only a small percentage of those I interviewed discussed budget voting solely in local terms. As a House Republican leader put it: "you really have to think nationally if you're going to solve this problem."

Hibbing and Theiss-Morse (1995) conducted a national opinion survey and also carried out in-depth focus groups with ordinary individuals to ascertain their opinions on a number of issues relating to their feelings towards Congress. Hibbing and Theiss-Morse (1995, p.66.) found that the public "clearly want their member to act on behalf of the country (85 percent), not the district (9 percent)." They also arrived at some specific conclusions regarding pork barrel spending (p.66):

> Many members devote significant energy to bringing home the pork. While constituents undoubtedly appreciate these efforts, pork is not nearly as important to them as might be imagined or at least this is what they claim. When we asked respondents a series of questions on what they believed was the most important part of a representative's job, they mentioned two tasks most often: passing laws on important national problems and helping people deal with the governmental bureaucracy. Dead last in the list was bringing money or projects back to the district. We also asked, "To help balance the budget, would you encourage your representative to quit trying to bring federal projects back to your district even if other representatives around the country did not quit?" We thought this to be a stern test since the public was being asked if they were willing to give up unilaterally the race for pork. Even so, the answer was usually yes (55 percent). Constituents may be less parochial than is usually believed.

Finally Sanders (1988) explored public support for different types of federal government spending in 1982 and 1984. Sanders concluded: "The underlying attitudes people have, not whether they receive government aid, is what leads people to support particular programs" (p.323).

Evaluation of the Literature on Distributive Politics and the Electoral Connection

Although the belief in a connection between the provision of distributive benefits and reelection is widespread, there is little empirical evidence supporting the existence of such a direct connection. The two major studies to test the direct relationship between distributive spending and electoral margins (Feldman and Jondrow, 1984 and Stein and Bickers 1994) found no relationship between pork and electoral margins, however, and studies of both the attitudes of legislators and of voters confirmed these findings. The limited amount of empirical research, as well as the difficulties in operationalizing the connection between distributive benefits and electoral success outlined especially by Fiorina, limits the conclusiveness of this result, however.

Stein and Bickers (1995) do provide one very important piece of evidence for why this might be so. They include in their study an analysis of voter awareness of pork and determine that voters who are aware of new projects in the district are more likely to vote for the incumbent. However, they also find that only the most politically active voters tend to be aware of new awards for the district. According to Stein and Bickers: "Most members of the general public remain indifferent to alterations in the flow of new awards" (p. 377). This is a very problematic finding for the electoral connection hypothesis. If people do not know about spending in the district, they cannot reward pork barrel spending with votes.

The electoral connection between pork barrel spending is certainly more complex than has been assumed by many scholars. Different legislators have different needs, voters have differing levels of awareness and differing views as to what the role of government should be, and the electorate may have different attitudes towards government spending depending on the state of the economy and prevailing ideological forces. The next section will begin to delve into that complexity by modeling the electoral connection using data on congressional appropriations earmarks in the seven program areas described in Chapter Three.

Earmarks and the Electoral Connection

Data on congressional appropriations earmarks can be used to examine further the electoral connection hypothesis. Although earmarks represent only a small fraction of district specific spending, the seven categories included in this study do include the most highly visible and sought after projects. These are the projects for which legislators are most likely to claim credit. Mayhew (1974: 54-57) explicitly linked the provision of particularistic benefits with large and highly visible projects where the legislator's claim of credit is believable. Therefore one can test the following alternative hypotheses:

> H_0 = Incumbent electoral margin in an election is unrelated to the provision of earmarks during the previous Congress.
>
> H_1 = Incumbent electoral margin in an election is positively related to the provision of earmarks during the previous Congress.

Analysis was conducted for the results of the 1994 election based on earmarking during the 103rd Congress. Following Stein and Bickers (1994), ordinary least square (OLS) regression analysis was used to assess the relationship between a candidate's reelection margin in 1994, (the dependent variable) and the total amount of pork in the district (as measured by the number of congressional appropriations earmarks in the seven previously discussed areas). Other independent variables with known and suspected relationships to reelection margin were also included in the model as control variables. These variables were: incumbent's years of seniority, incumbent's political party, the incumbent's share of total district specific campaign expenditures for the electoral period[8], the incumbent's margin of victory in the previous (1992) election. Only incumbents who sought reelection to the same office were included in the analysis; this resulted in an N of 378 cases. The results of the regression analysis are included in Table 7.1.

The analysis supports the null hypothesis. Consistent with the findings of Feldman and Jondrow (1984) and Stein and Bickers (1994), the amount of pork barrel spending during a Congress (in this case measured as the number of earmarks) is not positively related to the subsequent election margin (1994). Also consistent with previous analyses, variables capturing the members relative advantage in campaign expenditures and the members track record (previous margin) were positively related to electoral margin in 1994. The variable

Table 7.1: Electoral Margin in the 1994 Election

Variable	b	Beta	T test
Electoral Margin '92	.4113	.3319	8.413**
Party	-18.5400	-.3319	-9.195**
Incumbent Share of Campaign Spending	72.7784	.450911	.375**
Years	-.2469	-.0716	-2.040**
Total Earmarks 103rd Congress	-.0667	-.0339	-.979
Constant	-22.7270		-4.213**

$R^2 = .57$
Adjusted $R^2 = .57$
F = 97.99
Sig F = .0000
** $p < .05$
N = 378

capturing party membership showed unusually strong predictive capacity, which can be explained by the nature of the 1994 election. The strong negative relationship for the dummy variable coded 1 for Democrat is reflective of the strong Republican showing in the 1994 election which gave the Republicans a congressional majority for the first time in forty years. The final variable, seniority measured in years also demonstrated a significant relationship with the dependent variable which was unanticipated. The negative relationship between seniority and margin of victory may also be reflective of the unusual nature of the 1994 election, as many long-time members (mostly Democrats) lost their seats or received less secure margins than in the past.

As is discussed above, Fiorina and others have been especially critical of previous models that failed to show the relationship predicted by his and other rational choice distributive models. One specific criticism is described in Cain, Ferejohn and Fiorina (1987). It is possible that the earmark variable is better considered as a dichotomous variable sorting members into two classes—those who are high demanders of pork and those who are not. The data as presented above is only reflective of seven categories of spending and might be only an indicator of which members receive greater amounts of pork rather than a statistically precise variable. To test for this possibility, I recoded the measure of all earmarks in the 103rd Congress into a dichotomous variable coded 1 for high demander (earmarks > 30 projects) and 0 for not high demand member. The results for this second analysis are included in Table 7.2.

Table 7.2: Electoral Margin in the 1994 Election

Variable	b	Beta	T test
Electoral Margin '92	.4136	.3338	8.491**
Incumbent Share of Campaign Spending	72.2830	.4478	11.289**
Years	-.2499	-.0724	-2.078**
Party	-18.6222	-.3334	-9.259**
High Pork District	-3.5082	-.0470	-1.367
Constant	-22.8606		-4.299**

$R^2 = .58$
Adjusted $R^2 = .57$
F = 98.41
Sig F = .0000
** $p < .05$
N = 378

As table 7.2 demonstrates, results using the recoded variable are virtually the same as are reported in table 7.1. There is no indication that pork leads to increased margins.

One final alteration was made to the model. As is discussed above, Stein and Bickers (1994a and 1995) have proposed an alternative understanding of the electoral connection hypothesis based on the suspicion that it is the most vulnerable members of Congress who are the most likely to pursue distributive spending. Jacobson (1978) has found that, paradoxically, there is an inverse relationship between incumbent campaign spending and resulting electoral margins. This conclusion that is at first surprising, is understandable when one considers that the most vulnerable incumbents face well funded challengers who may in turn force incumbents to spend aggressively to retain their seats. Stein and Bickers have hypothesized that pork barrel spending may be similar in that the incentive to engage in pork barreling increases with incumbent vulnerability. According to their hypothesis, members who are elected with slim margins are most likely to pursue distributive spending. They have tested this hypothesis using data on grant allocation, yielding results that while modest, are supportive. These hypotheses can be summarized as:

H_0 = Vulnerable incumbents (those elected with low margins) will not receive greater amounts of pork (earmarks)

H_1 = Vulnerable incumbents (those elected with low margins) will receive greater amounts of pork (earmarks).

Table 7.3 is a replication of Stein and Bickers analysis using the number of earmarks in the 103rd Congress as the dependent variable and including the electoral margin from the previous (1992) election as a predictor. According to Stein and Bickers' hypothesis, weaker incumbents, that is those who are elected by smaller margins in the previous election, have a greater incentive to pursue district spending in the subsequent session of Congress. The model was tested using data on congressional earmarks. It is apparent from Table 7.3 that their hypothesis is not supported, as there is not a statistically significant relationship between the number of earmarks and prior weakness as reflected by electoral margin. The weak predictive strength of the model (R-Square = .01) makes any conclusions drawn suspect. Seniority, measured in years of service was, however, positively associated with the number of earmarks. This is contrary to the expectations of the hypothesis, and it may be explained by the different measure of pork barrel spending used in this study when compared to Stein and Bickers.

Table 7.3: All Earmarks (seven categories) in the 103rd Congress

Variable	b	Beta	T test
Electoral Margin '92	-.0194	-.0314	-.530
Party	1.5083	.0520	.961
Incumbent Share of Campaign Spending	.2588	.0031	.052
Years	.1950	.1079	2.067**
Constant	15.3566		3.735**

R^2 = .014
Adjusted R^2 = .003
F = 1.352
Sig F = .2501
** $p < .05$
N = 378

Using congressional earmarks as the measure of pork barrel spending, I was unable to find any relationship between distributive spending and reelection margins when the relationship is operationalized as a direct model of causation where pork barrel spending is assumed to lead to greater success at the ballot box. However, when the relationship is modeled according to the Stein and Bickers hypothesis, the use of earmark data yielded results that are different from their results in a way that is intuitively logical. It may be that senior members are better able to tap one form of pork barrel (earmarks), while more vulnerable (and often first term) members rely instead on stimulating grant proposals from within the district.

These results not only indicate the difficulties of operationalizing the electoral connection, they also reveal some of the complexity of evaluating distributive politics. It is apparent that not all members have the same incentive to seek distributive spending, and not all members have the same access to project spending. Factors in addition to those already mentioned are also likely to affect how strongly a member pursues benefits for his or her district. Other explanations, such as constituency view of the deficit, presence of a fiscally conservative challenger and of course member view of good public policy may be important predictors.

Case Studies

As formulated by supporters of distributive theory, the electoral connection is static; legislators should always pursue more pork and voters should always reward legislators who provide pork with reelection. The exceptions to the model are few. Mayhew and others allow for the existence of so called "saints" (members who do engage in actions that may jeopardize their reelection prospects) but saints are typically sanctioned internally and often suffer by losing in their bids for reelection. The following section will provide evidence that the electoral connection between members and their desire for pork, and reelection is not as simple as the theory suggests. Certainly many legislators earn reputations for providing pork, and some may win reelection on this factor. However, there is evidence that legislators who provide large amounts of pork are sometimes defeated in their quest for reelection, and there is also evidence that some members who vehemently oppose pork barrel spending for all districts (including their own) are given institutional positions overseeing the distribution of government funds and are rewarded with reelection to Congress. Two examples of each of these scenarios will be described in the following section. Although four cases do not necessarily rule out the existence of the electoral connection as a strong, general rule, when combined with the limited empirical support given the electoral connection hypothesis, these cases do suggest that the claim may be somewhat overstated.

Neal Smith

Neal Smith (D-IA) was first elected to Congress in 1958.[9] Smith served eighteen terms in Congress, rising to become chairman of the influential House Appropriations Subcommittee on Commerce, Justice and State and subsequently chairman of the Labor, Health and Human Services, and Education Subcommittee. In 1994, Smith lost his bid for a nineteenth term in Congress to Republican Greg Ganske, a plastic surgeon with no previous political experience. Smith was defeated despite his claims that he used his seat to shower his district with millions of dollars in federal projects and grants.

Ganske positioned himself in the race as a fiscal conservative, and used Smith's claims of credit to portray Smith as a traditional free spending Democrat. Ganske specifically attacked Smith's pork barrel propensity. He was quoted in Congressional Quarterly as stating: "Pork is like taking one of the nice lean Iowa pigs [and] shipping it to Washington [to have] Neal as the Butcher [send back] two pieces of bacon" (Greunwald 1994: 2533).

Smith meanwhile, defended his record pointing out that he had secured more than $200 million in federal projects and grants for Iowa. He ran radio ads claiming credit for bestowing projects upon his district and state. In a newsletter dated June 28, 1994,[10] Smith lists nine separate earmarks that he had included in appropriations language:

> Recent funding requests of interest to Central and Southwest Iowa approved by the House for the year beginning October 1 include: (1) $400,000 for the Hungry Canyons soil project; (2) another year of funding for the Mosquito Creek projects in Western Iowa; (3) $6.5 million for the Swine Research building at Ames; (4) $6 million for the Walnut Creek Wildlife Refuge; (5) adequate operation and maintenance funding for the Desoto Bend Wildlife Refuge; (6) $4 million for Des Moines River Greenbelt Projects, including more trails; (7) $6.5 million to operate Red Rock and Saylorville next year;

> (8) $4 million for Highway 5 relocation portion of the loop south of the Des Moines Airport; and (9) an amount to be determined for telemedicine projects (Smith 1994).

Contrary to conventional wisdom, Smith's success in bringing home federal largesse did not translate into an electoral victory. In fact, criticism of Smith's propensity to earmark federal funds for Iowa's fourth district probably played a role in defeating a veteran legislator, and electing a new-comer who pledged to avoid wasteful, pork barrel spending.

Mark Andrews

The story of former Senator Mark Andrews (R-ND) has been chronicled by Richard Fenno (1992) in *When Incumbency Fails: The Senate Career of Mark Andrews.*[11] According to Fenno's account, Andrews developed and perpetuated a reputation as someone who could deliver benefits to his state. From his seat as Chairman of the Senate Appropriations Subcommittee on Transportation, Andrews was especially fond of earmarking funds to his and other states, and also for using his institutional position to push for earmarks from other Appropriations Subcommittees throughout North Dakota. Richard Fenno, one of the keenest observers of the modern Congress, made the following assertion about Andrews: "Surely he was the most dedicated, most single-minded, most successful procurer of grants, projects, and protective legislative language I have ever encountered" (Fenno: 278). Andrews was well known for his penchant for the pork barrel; Time magazine proclaimed him "King of Pork."

Andrews believed that his pork barrel behavior would be rewarded at the polls. According to Fenno (1992: 281):

> His pork barrel performance was what he thought would reelect him; that was what he campaigned on; that is what he emphasized when it was over; and that was what he wanted to be remembered by.

Despite Andrews' obvious success pork barrel spending, he was defeated in his quest for reelection by Democrat Kent Conrad in 1986. Conrad ran as an opponent of deficits, and pledged not to run for reelection if he was unsuccessful in reducing the federal deficit by eighty percent during his first term.[12]

Fenno attributes Andrews' loss, at least in part, to his failure to pay attention to broad issues of national policy. Fiorina predicted just the opposite; that reelection depends on ignoring national interests in favor of district specific concerns. Both Smith and Andrews were appropriators (in fact both were cardinals) who despite their best efforts, were defeated by opponents who stressed national rather than local issues. For both Smith and Andrews, the assumption that members pursue pork to win reelection holds. However, for two of the most successful pork-barrelers in recent times, their spending proclivities probably played some part in their electoral defeat. This prediction is not supported by distributive theory. The following two cases are examples of members who despite being in the best institutional positions to help their constituents through earmarking projects, publicly opposed the practice, yet were successful when judged by the voters.

William Natcher

William Natcher (D-KY) represented Kentucky in the House for over forty years prior to his death in 1994. Natcher was able to rise to the position of Chairman of the House Appropriations Committee, certainly one of the most influential positions for obtaining distributive projects in the entire Congress.[13] Yet Natcher was well known for his opposition to congressional influence on the specific location of government spending. On taking over leadership of the full committee at age 83 from the ailing Jamie Whitten (D-MS), Natcher stated: "This is the best method and the method I hope we follow through our 13 subcommittees—no earmarking" (Starobin 1993). Natcher had earned a reputation as an opponent of earmarking during his tenure as chairman of the Subcommittee on Labor, Health and Human Services and Education and Related Agencies, a position that he retained after becoming full Committee chair (Munson 1993: 218). Savage's account of "saints" in the appropriations process singles out Natcher; he is referred to as a "champion against earmarking," and his efforts to limit earmarking in his subcommittee apparently resulted in only 11 identifiable earmarks in an important part of domestic discretionary spending for the period FY 1987- FY 1990.[14] According to one Appropriations Committee staff member interviewed by Savage, the issue of pork barrel spending gets right to the "chairman's fundamental view of right or wrong. [Natcher's] whole life is devoted to a system of merit versus politics."

Natcher was chosen by the Democratic caucus to head the Appropriations Committee despite his well-known objection to the practice of earmarking. When Natcher became too ill to continue as Appropriations Chairman in March, 1994, Neal Smith was next in line of Committee seniority to assume the leadership position. David Obey (D-WI), a member third on the list of Committee seniority challenged and defeated Smith by a 152-106 vote of the House Democratic caucus (Hook 1994). Unlike Smith, Obey was also an opponent of earmarking, and Obey received the support of the more fiscally conservative members of the caucus, including Representative Penny and three-quarters of the freshmen class (Pianin 1994). If distributive benefits were as important as distributive theorists claim, its is odd that House Democrats would twice choose a member to head the panel most responsible for distributive spending who was opposed to the practice of earmarking spending. It is especially perplexing that the seniority system would be violated to place a member who opposed earmarking ahead of a member who was well known for his distributive behavior.

Mark Neumann

Freshmen Representative Mark Neumann (R-WI) was probably the most vocal opponent of pork barrel spending in the 104th Congress, a Congress that was characterized by its opposition of government spending in general and pork barrel spending in particular. Neumann attained a seat on the Appropriations Committee, rare for a freshmen, even though he had campaigned as an opponent of pork barrel projects (Willen 1994). As a member of the committee, Neumann refused to engage in earmarking (Hager 1996). Neumann also proposed amendments to strip earmarks from several appropriations bills and reports at both the committee and House floor stages during his first year in Congress (Appel 1995). At one point he proposed to eliminate several military construction earmarks from a committee bill, including funds earmarked for Nellis Air Force base which is located in the district of fellow Republican Barbara Vucanovich (R-NV) who at the time was chair of the Military Construction Appropriations Subcommittee.

Not only did Neumann oppose pork barrel spending in other districts, he also refused to use his position on the Appropriations

Committee to deliver earmarks to his own district. Neumann refused to bow to pressure from constituents to earmark funds for a sewer system in his district, although his seat on the Departments of Veterans Affairs, and Housing and Urban Development and Independent Agencies Subcommittee likely would have allowed him to include report language for the project (Hager 1996 and C-Span 1996). When asked whether he was jeopardizing his reelection prospects by refusing to deliver projects to his district Neumann responded: "I find it morally and ethically unacceptable to suggest that I have to spend my children's money to get elected" (Hager 1996: 2171). Not only was Neumann reelected in a district that had previously been held by Democrat Peter Barca (the seat once held by former Defense Secretary Les Aspin), he increased his electoral margin from 49.4% to over 51%.

Changing Perceptions of Pork

> "I'm getting no mileage out of it, said Rep. Peter J. Visclosky, D-Ind., an appropriator of his efforts to bring projects to his district. I don't even talk about it anymore."[15]

It is uncertain if an electoral connection ever existed to the extent believed by distributive theory modelers. Empirical evidence is not conclusive, but seems to suggest that the strong association between pork barrel spending and reelection that forms the foundation of the distributive theory of Congress has been overstated. It is clear that some members cultivate reputations for their ability to win federal projects for their districts. It is also clear that other members do not use federal expenditures to further their reelection goals and that some may even cultivate reputations as opponents of pork barrel spending.[16] However, it is also apparent that a change has occurred in the way that many members of Congress view pork barrel spending. As the quote from Representative Visclosky seems to indicate, pork barrel spending appears to have lost some of its appeal in recent Congresses. This change and the reasons behind it, as well as the influence of the national debt and annual deficits on the behavior of Congress will be discussed in the following chapters.

NOTES

1. For example, Fiorina (1989) points out that "Motivation is a thorny issue. Individuals may not fully appreciate their own motives, and even when

they do there is a human tendency to sugarcoat motivation, especially among politicians, a class of people whose stock-in-trade is the claim to higher motivation" (pp.89-90).

2. One only has to think of Frank Capra's 1939 film *Mr. Smith Goes to Washington* to realize that the provision of localized government spending for political purposes likely has been widely recognized in this country for quite some time.

3. In addition to the inability to use this index to determine which members actually benefit from the spending policies, this measure is also problematic in that all votes that received 80 percent support or greater were removed from consideration for the index. By removing universal votes, some might argue, Payne may not be measuring support or opposition to spending (which may be universal, see Chapter Six), but other, more partisan issues that may be involved in some or all of his 36 indexed votes.

4. There is anecdotal evidence to support this. Witness, for example, the behavior of Senator Mark Hatfield (R-OR) in the 104th Congress (Taylor 1996b).

5. Simultaneous causation refers to a situation such as the example from Jacobson (1978) cited below where the observed phenomena is paradoxical because other variables more important than the one in question are acting on the dependent variable in the opposite direction. In Jacobson's example, incumbent spending is negatively related to electoral margins because a simultaneous occurrence—a strong well funded challenger is causing the incumbent to spend more and is drawing votes from the incumbent. For discussions of simultaneity see especially: Fiorina 1981b; Fiorina 1989: 94-97; and Cain, Ferejohn and Fiorina: 128-130.

6. The problems with using Stein and Bicker's (1995) data and analyses as representative of pork barrel spending are discussed in Chapter Two.

7. See also Stein and Bickers (1996) for an extension of this hypothesis that introduces the quality of the challenger as another factor that may be influenced by level of district specific spending.

8. Data on campaign expenditures were obtained from Makinson (1995). The variable is constructed as: Incumbent expenditures in 1994/(Incumbent expenditures in 1994 + major party opponent expenditures in 1994).

9. Information on the Smith case was derived from Gruenwald 1994; Congressional Quarterly's Politics in America 1993, and Babson and Rapp 1993: 649.

10. I believe this to be Smith's last newsletter prior to his electoral defeat.

11. On Senator Mark Andrews see also: Brownstein 1986.

12. Conrad kept his promise and did not run for reelection in 1992. He did however, run for, and win, the other Senate seat from North Dakota when it became vacant upon the death of Senator Quentin Burdick.

13. The three most recent Chairmen of the Senate Appropriations Committee by contrast did use their institutional position to secure federal spending for their states. Stories regarding the abilities of Robert Byrd (D-WV), Mark Hatfield (R-WA) and Ted Stevens (R-AK) to secure projects for their states are legendary. In 1996, all three were selected to the list of the top ten pork-barrelers in Congress by George magazine (Zaroya 1996). All three were in the top five.

14. Savage (1991) described the behavior of other cardinals who opposed earmarking. They included: Jake Garn (R-UT); William Proxmire (D-WI); Edward Boland (D-MA) and Lawton Chiles (D-FL).

15. See Taylor 1996b page 2173.

16. Witness the development of a congressional "Porkbusters" coalition.

CHAPTER EIGHT

Distributive Politics and Deficits

No reasonable observer would argue that pork barrel spending has always been employed as a force for good or that there are no pork projects that would have been better left unbuilt. But singling out pork as the culprit for our fiscal troubles directs attention away from the largest sources of budgetary growth and contributes to the illusion that the budget can be balanced simply by eliminating waste and abuse. While proposals to achieve a pork-free budget are not without superficial appeal, they risk depriving leaders trying to enact real deficit-reduction measures of one of the most effective coalition-building tools at their disposal.

John Ellwood and Eric Patashink (1993)

With little more than a fragmentary knowledge of the relative sizes of various components of the budget, most citizens think there must be some relatively painless way of achieving balance. The steady diet of stories of waste, fraud, and abuse in government programs that politicians and the media feed the public has created the impression that tens of billions can be saved through improving government efficiency and eliminating pork and low-priority activities, and thus that the budget can be balanced without seriously affecting popular programs or ones with powerful constituencies. Political leaders have not disabused the public of this misapprehension, for "sacrifice" has become a four-letter word in the world of politics.

Robert D. Reischauer (1997)

. . . the big increases in government spending since the 1950s have not been in grants to localities, which provide particularistic

> ***constituency benefits, but in various general transfer programs that do not allow members to demonstrate they have gotten something special for the district.***
>
> *Steven Kelman (1987)*

There is widespread consensus among academicians as well as politicians that the federal deficit and national debt are among the most important issues in American politics. In the words of Donald Kettl: "The federal deficit has become the most prominent issue of American domestic politics—indeed, perhaps of all American politics" (Kettl 1992: 15).[1] Deficits and debts have become the focus of congressional behavior; virtually every policy issue is framed in the context of its effect on fiscal policy. According to Makin and Ornstein (1994: 281): "For most of the 1980s, dealing with the deficit became the overwhelming preoccupation of the president, House and Senate." The late Aaron Wildavsky (1992: 462) claimed, " . . . the deficit has become the leading issue of our time." Regardless of the economic importance of deficits and debt, their importance as a political issue is beyond dispute.

Despite the apparent importance of the deficit as a political issue, the academic political science literature on the relationship between budget deficits and congressional distributive behavior is limited in scope and tends to be descriptive (and often prescriptive) rather than theoretical or empirically based. However, the rapid growth of deficits and debt in the 1980's and early 1990's has stimulated several recent efforts to explore individual and collective behavior in Congress regarding deficit, and especially spending, policy.[2]

OVERVIEW

This chapter will examine the deficit and distributive politics in the 1980's and 1990's. The first section is a discussion of the thesis promoted most heavily by Shepsle and Weingast, that congressional behavior and the pulls of geography are the cause of inefficient government spending, and are a major contributor to deficit spending. The second section is a review of the literature on deficits in the 1980's and 1990's. These works, mainly from scholars who study budgeting rather than congressional behavior, universally refute the claim that distributive spending drives the deficit. The literature review will be followed by an empirical analysis of the small size of total congressional earmarking relative to the size of federal expenditures and deficits. The earmark evidence does not support the claim that members of Congress pursue unlimited amounts of pork at the expense of the federal treasury and the common good. The subsequent section will present some evidence that distributive spending has become less important to members of Congress, as the demand for pork competes with the demand to lower deficits. Although pork does not cause deficits, it appears as though the presence of deficits combined with the media's focus on government waste and inefficiency, work to limit the scope of distributive spending. Here the electoral consideration may motivate members to behave in ways contrary to the predictions of Shepsle and Weingast.

DISTRIBUTIVE THEORY AND DEFICITS

Although Mayhew (1974) offered a model that was explicitly based on the reelection motivation, he did not portray a Congress sacrificing the public good for the sake of expensive particularistic benefits. Following Fenno (1966), Mayhew portrayed the House Appropriations Committee as the "guardian of the federal Treasury." More specifically, Mayhew (referring to the House Appropriations Committee) claims (p.152):

> By cutting budgets, they work against the diffuse and primal danger that Congress will spend more money than it takes in. They lean against particularism and also against servicing of the organized.

Although individual members may have an incentive to pursue pork barrel spending according to Mayhew's model, institutional controls limit the overall affects of too much pork, which would reflect negatively on the institution.

The distributive theory of Congress, which describes a legislature organized around the need to preserve gains from exchange, associates inefficiencies and deficit spending with the reelection motive. Kenneth Shepsle and Barry Weingast's[3] 1984 work "Legislative Politics and Budget Outcomes" will be used in this chapter to represent this school of thought. Shepsle and Weingast claim that the desire to seek reelection causes members of Congress to pursue inefficient policies that lead to deficits. Specifically, members of Congress seek ever increasing amounts of localized federal spending (distributive benefits) and are unwilling to raise taxes to compensate for increased expenditures. Distributive spending often results in inefficient, wasteful projects as the tendency to universalize benefits often leads to projects being located in places without a policy need, and a distributive tendency causes increased demand for more and more particularized spending. Shepsle and Weingast (1984) conclude that "legislator motivations" and "institutional practices" cause there to be ". . . little incentive to employ an efficient mix of program inputs and that the scale of expenditure projects is too large" (p.367).[4] According to Shepsle and Weingast (1984):

> So long as the ties that bind legislators to the electoral constituencies remain strong, and so long as legislative institutions like the committee system enable legislators to serve parochial interests, simple solutions aimed at ameliorating the biases in policy . . . are likely to be superficial. Add to this the adaptability and ingenuity of legislators in dealing with constraints imposed on them and one is almost prepared to accept John Adams's aphorism (in the play "1776") that the opposite of *pro*gress is *Con*gress" (p.367, emphasis in original).

Shepsle and Weingast maintain that the institutional structure of the contemporary Congress plays a key role in the failure of Congress to restrain localized spending policies. The authors place much of the blame for what they see as Congress' fiscal failure on the evolution of committee and subcommittee autonomy.[5] Throughout much of this century[6], the parochial desires of individual members were checked by institutional structures including strong political parties, a powerful Rules Committee and an Appropriations Committee that served to control expenditures. Shepsle and Weingast argue that in the post-reform Congress committees and subcommittees have usurped the power of the central control committees, and these committees no longer act as a check on distributive behavior. Because committees and subcommittees are autonomous, "Congress can no longer check the narrow, provincial impulses of its subunits as it once could" (Shepsle and Weingast 1984, p.347).

Elsewhere Shepsle (1983a) likens fiscal policy to the problem of the commons; the benefits of grazing on the budgetary commons (through parochial spending) are detached from the costs of such grazing.[7] Shepsle argues that the main cause of deficits in the American political system is the propensity of members of Congress to engage in distributive politics. According to Shepsle: " . . . current nominal deficits are a political (if not an economic) problem of major proportions. The reason that they have become a serious problem is that governmental revenues and debt financing opportunities, like the proverbial commons, are a common pool" (p.211).

DEFICIT LITERATURE

Much of the recent literature on federal government deficits has been devoted to explaining the dramatic increase in the size of nominal deficits that has been the norm since the Reagan era.[8] In contrast to the theoretical conclusions of Shepsle and Weingast[9] there is virtual agreement in the more empirically based budgeting literature that congressional distributive spending is not the source of the growth of deficits. Despite the extensive literature refuting the claim that deficits are caused by waste and pork barrel spending, much of the public still believes that wasteful government spending is at the root of the deficit (Reischauer 1997).[10] Although there are certainly examples of distributive spending that would not meet an objective test of efficiency, it is clear from the literature on deficits in the modern United States that pork is dwarfed by other programs that spend government funds based not on geography, but on some other redistributive criteria (mainly entitlements). It is also clear that changes to the revenue side of the equation enacted during Ronald Reagan's first year in office, as well as patterns of slow economic growth that may be immune to congressional manipulation, were integral to the creation of large deficits that plagued the economy during the 1980s and early 1990s.[11]

Criticism of Shepsle and Weingast's thesis from scholars more closely associated with the budgeting subfield was immediate. Ellwood's (1984) comments, included in the same volume with Shepsle and Weingast (1984) rely heavily on the work of Arnold (1979 and 1981) in framing the criticism. Ellwood contends:

> . . . I believe that the thrust of Shepsle's and Weingast's basic contention—that when it comes to public dissatisfaction with federal budget policy the problem is Congress—is overdrawn, shows a misunderstanding of the forces currently driving federal budget policy, and underestimates the ability of the system to correct the

> excesses of the pull of geography and power of subcommittees (p.368).

Ellwood supports his conclusion by examining the composition of federal expenditures over the period 1950 to 1980. The data (derived from Arnold 1981) indicate that the budget accounts that fund programs with the greatest distributive benefits (geographic pull) have accounted for continually decreasing shares of federal expenditures throughout the period examined. Far from being the driver of government growth and by extension inefficiency and deficits, distributive programs such as water projects and intergovernmental grants declined by 42 percent and 26 percent respectively (when measured in constant dollars) over the period.

Also commenting directly on Shepsle and Weingast (1984) was Schultze (1984). Schultze acknowledges that Shepsle and Weingast identify some important aspects of congressional budgetary behavior. However, he claims that they are "insufficiently precise and too all-encompassing in describing the kind of situation to which their analyses apply" (p.381). Schultze agrees with Ellwood that " . . . insofar as the nondefense part of the budget is concerned, the evidence is quite strong that in recent years the discretionary programs were not the real cause of the upward trend in federal spending (relative to the gross national product—GNP)" (p.380).

Peterson (1985) compared presidential budget requests with what Congress appropriated for each fiscal year during the post war period. Peterson uses this data to argue that the President, and not Congress is responsible for setting overall spending targets. He concludes that Shepsle and Weingast underestimate the incentives that work against wasteful spending by Congress. According to Peterson (p.377): "The data . . . not only put in question popular conceptions of Congress's spending predispositions but contradict recent scholarly interpretations [i.e. Shepsle and Weingast] as well."

Peterson and Rom (1989) build on Peterson's previous (1985) findings to show that Congressional appropriations have historically been remarkably close to the totals requested by presidents. Congress, according to this line of reasoning, is not responsible for government growth and deficits, but merely responds to presidential requests as both Congress and the President share the common goal of long-term economic growth. Peterson and Rom explain the appearance of pork barrel spending as:

> Legislators are unlikely to want to make local sacrifices to accomplish national fiscal goals and so will strongly resist any presidential attempts to shortchange programs dear to their hearts. They do this not so much by changing the president's fiscal policy as by rearranging spending within its overall limits (p.167).

Pork does not stimulate deficits. Pork simply represents a slight redistribution of presidential spending priorities by a Congress that must appeal to a more local constituency.

Arnold (1990) theorized that legislators' decisions tend to be more fiscally conservative than presidents' recommendations. According to Arnold, "the electoral quest inspires both a concern with group and geographic benefits, which when pursued to excess can produce deficits and a concern with some of the general costs and benefits associated with governmental spending" (p.191). He concludes that these conflicting desires cancel each other out, and the resulting policy is more fiscally responsible than that of presidents. According to Arnold, by structuring votes in terms of explicit economic policy (for example an across the board spending reduction, or deficit reduction packages) rather than in terms of individual expenditure programs (geography specific cuts), coalition leaders can and do achieve results consistent with national (rather than parochial) interest. Congress will enact policies that contain tax increases and expenditure cuts, but in order for this to occur, policies must be structured in a way where there is no apparent geographic bias. Arnold also relies on the empirical evidence of Peterson (1985) who found that during the early 1980s, a period of rapidly increasing deficits, Congress typically reduced presidential spending requests.

Ippolito (1990) analyzed the levels of domestic discretionary spending from the presidency of Franklin Roosevelt through Ronald Reagan's tenure. Ippolito finds that in the early years of deficit growth during the Reagan administration, there was a relative decline in domestic spending. His analysis provides evidence contradicting the theories of Shepsle and Weingast as well. He concludes that "The spending patterns of the Reagan years, however, do not conform very well to the prospending bias theories [i.e. Shepsle and Weingast] . . . Domestic program outlays were, in the aggregate, at almost the same level at the end of the Reagan presidency as at the beginning. In real terms, this stasis represented a significant decline" (p.194). According to Ippolito, the budget share of domestic outlays in the 1980's was roughly the same as that of the 1950's, providing evidence that the deficits of the Reagan era were not the result of uncontrolled distributive spending. He concludes: "Moreover, the "old" [i.e. appropriations] budget process can cut spending for domestic programs, despite the credit-claiming and congressional policy decentralization hypotheses" (p.226).

There is considerable agreement that the economic policies of the administration of Ronald Reagan were an attempt to alter the configuration of fiscal policy by reducing taxes, reducing spending on domestic discretionary programs and social programs that benefit the poor rather than the middle class and increasing spending on national defense. Although Reagan was confronted with congressional opposition that became more hostile to his intentions after his first year in office, he was successful to some extent in each of these areas. Wildavsky (1992) is one of the many analysts who point out that pork barrel spending did not play a role in the complex policy changes of the early 1980's which contributed to the increase in structural deficits. According to Wildavsky (1992, p.464):

> Spending growth from 1979-1985, roughly 2.4 percent of GNP, can be entirely explained by increases in defense, social security, Medicare and debt interest. The real growth in social spending was entirely a product of the bad economy; it disguised the significant reductions made in domestic discretionary programs and in means-tested entitlements during the period.

Ellwood and Patashink (1993) make the case that distributive outcomes in Congress (pork) are not responsible for deficits and in fact can play a role in reducing deficits. They argue that " . . . pork doled out strategically, can help to sweeten an otherwise unpalatable piece of legislation" (p.21). In other words, distributive politics are not seen as driving the federal deficit, and true cuts in the size the deficits can be achieved if legislators are still provided with opportunities to credit claim for district specific expenditures. Evans (1994 and 1995) has shown that legislators use pork barrel projects to secure passage of politically unpopular legislation that they view to be in the public good, but she does not explicitly link pork with facilitation of deficit reduction.

Makin and Ornstein (1995) also refute the assertion that deficits are the result of reelection driven legislators and their desire to overspend on wasteful pork barrel projects. They defend this conclusion with data that demonstrates the growth of programs that are non-distributive at a time when domestic discretionary spending was decreasing as a share of the federal budget. "The most rapid growth in federal spending has come through programs no longer controlled by politicians; the areas of spending that can be targeted and controlled, where politicians can claim credit to win individual support from voters have actually shrunk as a share of the budget" (p.279).

Stein and Bickers (1995) also found that the growth of the deficit in the 1980s was not due to distributive behavior of Congress. On the contrary, "a very small number of domestic programs account for virtually all of the growth in domestic spending . . . three programs—Social Security, Medicare and Medicaid—are responsible for the vast majority of the growth in domestic spending in the 1980s" (p.139.).

Schick (1995) explicitly discussed earmarks as the embodiment of pork, as well as the impact of earmarks on the deficit. Consistent with other scholars, and the interpretation in this research, Schick concludes that claims linking deficits with pork barrel spending are inaccurate. In discussing the "political arithmetic" of earmarks, Schick demonstrates that even in a hypothetical situation where each member of Congress earmarked $1 million to her district, "the total would be a bit more than $500 million, or barely one-thirtieth of 1 percent of total federal spending" (p.141). According to Schick (p.141):

> The truth is that most earmarks are relatively cheap; many can be crammed into tight budgets . . . To say that earmarking is cheap is not to justify the practice or to claim that all the money is well spent. But neither should one believe that the financial crisis in federal budgeting is due to pork. It is not.

Finally, former Congressional Budget Office Director Robert Reischauer (1997) has shown that real nondefense discretionary spending has increased only six percent since 1980. It has been the other spending categories, particularly entitlements that have driven the deficit. As a percentage of Gross Domestic Product (GDP), nondefense discretionary spending actually peaked at 5.2 in 1980, prior to the beginning of the huge Reagan era deficits. According to Reischauer: "This ratio fell gradually back to 3.4 percent in 1989, then rose to 3.8 percent in 1995, and edged down to 3.6 percent in 1996" (p.135). During the years of maximum deficit growth, nondefense discretionary spending, the limited portion of the budget that is available for distributive spending, was actually shrinking when measured as a percentage of GDP.

Earmarks and the Deficit

From the data presented in Chapter Three, it should be apparent that the amount of spending on district specific projects for the seven most popular earmark categories is extremely small compared to the overall budget of the federal government or even to total domestic discretionary outlays. Table 8.1 compares the amount spent on earmarks in these categories with outlay totals.[12] As the seven categories are only a sample of spending that is earmarked, total pork barrel spending is certainly somewhat larger than depicted in the spending totals for each year.

Table 8.1: Total Earmarks in Seven Categories

	Total Earmarks		Outlays		
FY	Number	$'s Billions	$'s Billions	% Earmarked	Deficit ($'s B)
1992	2484	8.2	1381.7	0.6	-290.4
1993	2299	6.9	1409.4	0.5	-255.0
1994	2243	8.4	1461.7	0.6	-203.1
1995	2377	7.2	1515.7	0.5	-163.9
1996	1897	6.0	1560.3	0.4	-107.5
1997	2032	6.5	1631.0	0.4	-21.9

Not only are earmarks a very minor portion of federal spending, it is also apparent that the pattern of earmark spending did not increase dramatically at the same time that large deficits began, and although earmarks have been reduced since the Republicans won control of Congress in 1994, earmarks continue to be included in spending bills and reports, and some shift in the categories of earmarked spending has been witnessed. Interestingly, after a dramatic downturn in total earmarks in the categories examined in the first year following the Republican capture of both chambers of Congress, total earmarks increased in the fiscal year 1997 appropriations reports.[13]

The findings of this research regarding the relationship between pork barrel spending and deficits are consistent with those of scholars

Table 8.2: Earmarks by Category FY 1982—FY 1997[14]

Year	CORPS	CSREES	FBF	HUD	MC	NPS	TRANS	TOTAL	DEFICIT
1982	487	27	30	0	716	29	1	1790	-128.0
1983	1060	30	30	0	716	48	0	1884	-207.8
1984	1088	36	30	0	804	139	2	2099	-185.4
1985	1084	43	30	0	979	102	6	2244	-212.3
1986	1067	44	30	0	850	78	6	2075	-221.2
1987	1099	49	28	0	920	68	13	2177	-149.8
1988	1139	53	78	0	809	50	16	2145	-155.2
1989	510	106	96	10	828	76	29	1655	-152.5
1990	1217	138	63	45	799	142	53	2457	-221.2
1991	1306	153	88	61	736	166	87	2597	-269.4
1992	1239	183	23	78	713	121	127	2484	-290.4
1993	1182	175	34	214	504	135	55	2299	-255.0
1994	1253	173	32	0	692	70	13	2243	-203.1
1995	1223	157	52	266	418	135	127	2377	-163.9
1996	1263	138	27	0	425	44	0	1897	-107.5
1997	1407	132	39	0	389	65	0	2032	-21.9

from the budgeting subfield discussed above. Pork barrel politics are not a significant factor in overall spending, and increases in pork barrel spending are not responsible for the deficits of the 1980s and 1990s. Eliminating all earmarks from the seven most popular categories would only reduce annual deficits by very small amounts. In 1992 for example, eliminating all earmarks in the categories covered by this research would have reduced the annual deficit by a mere 2.8 percent. Clearly, earmarked spending is not responsible for budget deficits.

Table 8.2 tracks the inclusion of earmarks in the seven major categories throughout the period FY 1982 to FY 1997. Total earmarks have remained relatively stable from year to year despite changes in the size of nominal deficits.

Deficit Reduction

Congress has enacted several politically painful deficit reduction packages, most notably the Omnibus Budget Reconciliation Act of 1990 (OBRA90) and the Omnibus Budget Reconciliation Act of 1993 (OBRA93) which are not consistent with Shepsle and Weingast's model of Congress as responsible for deficits. Both major Budget Reconciliation Acts increased taxes and put limitations on future levels of domestic discretionary spending. It is likely that economic considerations outside of the control of Congress (especially the decline in U.S. economic growth rate and the rapid decrease in inflation that accompanied the monetary policies of the Volcker Federal Reserve) and the fiscal policies proposed by Ronald Reagan as well as the explosion in entitlement spending that are most responsible for long-term structural deficits. In contrast to the opinions of Shepsle and Weingast, Congress can be viewed as enacting a number of politically difficult policy changes to reduce the size of the deficit. Aaron Wildavsky (1992: 476) claimed that:

> As Rodney Dangerfield gets no respect, politicians neither get nor give themselves credit. From 1982 on, Congress has gored a series of special interests, ranging from doctors to defense contractors. You don't take on the AMA (freezing physician payments on Medicare) or Wall Street (many of the provisions of the 1984 tax bill), or the armed services and arms makers (cutting defense in the past six years), unless you really care about the deficit. Through 1986, according to the most careful analysis of policy changes, the politicians had

> reduced the fiscal year 1986 deficit by an estimated $162 billion, or 3.9 percent of gross national product, from what it would have been if past policies had been left in place.

Wildavsky was writing prior to OBRA93 which, according to the 1997 Economic Report of the President, resulted in more that $100 billion in deficit reduction in fiscal year 1996 alone through a combination of tax increases and spending cuts.[15]

From the perspective of this research, probably the most important elements of OBRA90 and OBRA93 were the mandated caps on discretionary spending.[16] In the budget deal of 1990, congressional negotiators accepted dollar limits on future discretionary domestic spending. Despite presidential efforts to remove the caps in the 1993 deal (see Woodward, 1994), Congress tightened the caps and extended them through fiscal 1998 (Schick 1995). Instead of Congress being the instigator of additional domestic discretionary spending, Congress acted to prevent the president from implementing his plan to invest in infrastructure as a way to increase long term economic growth. Clinton had campaigned on an economic policy that emphasized increasing economic growth through increased investment in infrastructure, rather than on a platform that stressed deficit reduction. Woodward (1994: 163.) summarized administration attempts to increase spending by altering the spending caps and congressional resistance in the following passage:

> 'If you could feel the mood on the Hill, Mr. President,' [former Budget Director Leon] Panetta said to Clinton later, trying to explain what had happened. They all had grossly underestimated the forces coming out of the November election and the power of Perot's deficit reduction message. In the economic plan, Panetta had proposed an increase in the spending caps so Clinton would get his investments. But then they had hit a brick wall: deficit mania. The leadership and key members of Congress were determined to take the administration package and do it one better. Panetta explained how his successor as House Budget Committee Chairman, Martin Sabo, the Minnesota Democrat, had said that the only conceivable way to keep the conservative Democrats on board was to obey the old caps . . . The Senate was stacking up the same way only worse.

At the same time Congress was enacting politically painful deficit reduction (that increased taxes and curtailed discretionary spending) Congress continued to provide earmarks. Pork appears to be unrelated to fundamental decisions driving fiscal policy. OBRA90 and OBRA93 contained spending caps on discretionary spending, the 35 percent of the budget that is susceptible to earmarking. Congress willingly curtailed the one area of the budget capable of manipulation for location specific electoral benefits, while at the same time refusing to do much to reduce the long term growth of redistributive entitlements, the largest and fastest growing portion of federal spending.

Deficit Mania

As the quote from Bob Woodward indicates, there is evidence, much of it anecdotal, that the 103rd Congress marked a turning point in congressional attitudes and behavior towards the deficit. It appears as though the discussion of the deficit during and subsequent to the 1992 Presidential election altered the salience of the issue.[17] Former Senator Paul Tsongas made the deficit and national debt the theme of his campaign for the Democratic nomination for the presidency in 1992, and garnered a surprising amount of support (especially from the media and elite segments of society). Businessman H. Ross Perot launched an independent campaign for the White House which was largely centered around the deficit issue. Perot spent millions of his personal fortune on television "infomercials" in which he explained the deficit issue and decried its supposed economic impact. Perot received nineteen percent of the popular vote in November, 1992, and several opinion polls had him leading in a three way race, when he abruptly withdrew his candidacy during the summer of 1992 (only to later enter the race with considerably less support).

Public opinion polling indicates an increase in the salience of the issue at this time as well. In November, 1991 (one year before the election), only four percent of the population felt that the deficit was the most important issue facing the country. By January, 1993 (when the 103rd Congress convened), the percentage of respondents citing the deficit as the number one issue had increased to thirteen percent (see Gallup Poll Annual, 1991-1993.). An additional piece of evidence supporting the claim that the 1992 election made the deficit a more visible political issue involves an analysis of the Washington Post yearly indices. In preparing their year end volume for 1992, the editors felt the need to establish a new category, "The Federal Budget" to deal with the volume of articles published concerning the deficit and the budget process during that year.

If the 103rd Congress is not considered to be more fiscally conservative than its predecessors, certainly the Republican controlled 104th Congress must be recognized for its focus and success in cutting the federal budget. The central element of the Republican program was a balanced budget proposal that necessitated large reductions in domestic discretionary spending. Although the Republicans were unable to enact their multi-year deficit reduction plan, they were successful in reducing domestic discretionary spending below previous year totals in each of the sessions of the 104th Congress. A 1996 report by the National Taxpayers Union claimed that 236 Representatives and 70 Senators sponsored bills that would result in reductions of annual spending. In 1991, the group reported that only 16 members of Congress supported legislation calling for reduced spending.

Rather than claiming credit for bringing home the bacon, it now appears to be more common to claim credit for reducing the deficit. In the study of newsletters from the 103rd Congress discussed in Chapter Two, it was more common for a member to claim credit for working to balance the budget, than it was for a member to claim credit for a distributive benefit. The following quotes seem to suggest the declining importance of pork barrel spending and the increased importance of deficit reduction to the reelection calculus:[18]

> Today, public opinion is an overwhelming force to bring the deficit down.
>
> Rep. Barney Frank, D-MA, 1997

> At least in my state, they're going to applaud you for cutting a lot more than for spending the money.
>
> Rep. Jim Ross Lightfoot, R-IA, 1996

> We don't even think along those lines. It will never be cut out of politics, but the more people who come in here with our approach, the less [earmarking] you're going to see.
>
> Rep. Robert L. Ehrlich, Jr. R-MD, 1996

> We can't just say, 'I'm going to bring back all these lovely projects.' It's more important to deal with the deficit.

Former Rep. Marjorie Margolies-Mezvinski, D-PA, 1993

> The most noticeable difference between the newer members and their elders is the newcomers' willingness to cut spending . . . Freshmen from both parties provided big majorities for the most important votes to cut spending in 1993 and 1994.
>
> Former Rep. Timothy Penny, 1995

> The days when members of the Appropriations Committee could use its power to the benefit of their districts have passed . . . People are not going to keep voting for appropriations bills with wasteful projects.
>
> Rep. Robert Torricelli, D-NJ, 1996

> Now if there is any Member here that has been to a townhall meeting and not found themselves recently berated by people in their community whom they represent, for pork barrel politics and pork barrel projects, they certainly must not have spent much time in their district.
>
> Rep. Dick Armey, R-TX, 1993

NOTES

1. This sentiment is echoed by Wildavsky and White (1989: 3), Schier (1992), and Jacobson (1994) in the academic community and by countless floor statements of members of congress including this one by Senator Kent Conrad (D-ND): " . . . this issue concerns me perhaps more than any other. I am personally persuaded that one of the most important things we can do is reduce this budget deficit" (Congressional Record, February 23, 1994: S1721).

2. A parallel literature has developed on the tendency of bureaucrats to maximize budgets (see for example Wildavsky 1964, Niskanen 1971, 1975 and 1991, and Blais and Dion 1991). While there is substantial empirical evidence that bureaucrats seek larger budgets, it is less clear how successful they are in receiving larger budgets (Blais and Dion: 360). Bureaucrat's information advantage over the level of information possessed by politicians does seem to provide bureaucrats with some additional influence in the process.

3. See also Fiorina 1981, Shepsle and Weingast 1985, Shepsle 1983a, 1983b, 1984, Rabushka 1983 Inman and Fitts 1990, and Fitts and Inman 1992. This argument can be traced in part to Stockman (1975 and 1986) and Fiorina

(1977) in political science and Buchanan (1984 and Buchanan and Wagner 1977) in economics. Stockman focused on distributive as well as redistributive programs to argue that deficits were inevitable because government (Congress) has created a "social pork barrel" which bestows benefits on segments of the population at the expense of all taxpayers. Although Fiorina was writing at a time when deficits were not the major political issue, his depiction of Congress as the "keystone" of a growing Washington establishment foreshadowed the development of deficit spending. James Buchanan also wrote that the political desire to distribute benefits to constituents will lead to deficits. However, unlike Shepsle and Weingast who attribute the growth in deficits to institutional factors in Congress, Buchanan believes that the increase in deficits in modern times is attributable to the lack of moral constraints against deficit financing caused by the acceptance of Keynesian theory. For a treatment which attributes deficits to uncontrolled Congressional spending that is not electorally motivated, see Payne (1991).

4. An alternative rational choice explanation attributes responsibility for increased deficits to divided government rather than to the executive or legislative branches individually. Mathew McCubbins (1991) claims that " . . . divided partisan control of Congress in the 1980s was the principle cause of the rapid growth in budget deficits during the decade" (p.114). McCubbins' argument does not seem to have won many adherents. It appears as though his conclusions, while applicable to the 1980s, are not generalizable for other periods of American history when divided control of the government was common, including the 104th Congress, when the deficit decreased for two consecutive years despite divided government (see Fiorina 1992: 94 and Green and Shapiro 1994: 43.). In addition Mayhew (1991) did not find significant differences between policy outcomes under unified government compared to outcomes under divided government.

5. See in particular Shepsle and Weingast 1985. This point refers to the claim that members of relevant committees receive greater benefits in the policy areas under the jurisdiction of the committee (Chapters Four and Five) and that universalism and reciprocity are characteristic of the congressional system (Chapter Six).

6. Prior to this century, members of Congress were less likely to be professional legislators with reelection as their overriding motivation. See Polsby (1968) for a discussion of the differences in behavior of 19th and 20th century members of congress. See Fenno (1966) for a discussion of the institutional norm of economy that characterized the House Appropriations Committee.

7. For a more in-depth explanation of the tragedy of the commons analogy see Hardin 1968.

8. It should be noted that deficits decreased during each of the first six years of the Clinton Presidency.

9. Shepsle and Weingast do not limit their discussion to the world of theory. Three works of these authors in particular are meant for an applied audience (Shepsle and Weingast 1985 and Shepsle 1983b and 1984). The authors propose a number of institutional remedies to the distributive problems that they have identified.

10. Reischauer (1997) attributes the public belief that deficits are the result of wasteful government spending in part to the media which tends to favor stories of government waste (see also Cohn 1996) and in part to politicians who make this claim. Savage (1988) indicates that Ronald Reagan espoused the point of view in his campaign against Jimmy Carter (p.203). Another more recent example comes from Rep. Mark Neumann who claimed: ". . . it's pork barrel spending that has led to $5 trillion in [national] debt."

11. Scholars are of differing opinions concerning how much (if at all) deficits act as a drag on the economy. Although this is a question best left to the economists, there is currently a fairly broad consensus that deficits in times of full employment at the very least crowd out some level of investment by diverting resources to government rather than the private sector. For a brief representation of the opposing views of the economic impact of the deficit see Wildavsky (1992, Chapter 11). See also the panel discussion between Robert Eisner and William Niskanen included in Savage 1994: 19-28.

12. Discretionary programs now account for only about 35 percent of total outlays, down from 70 percent in the early 1960s (Schick 1995: 7)

13. This is consistent with the findings of Cordes (1997) who found that academic earmarks increased by 49 percent between FY 1996 and FY 1997. Codres also found a dramatic decrease between FY 1995 and 1996.

14. During this period, Congress relied on Continuing Resolutions to fund all or part of government activities on several occasions. In cases where no Conference Committee Report was produced for a given fiscal year, the House Appropriations Committee Report was used to determine the number of earmarks. Also, note that in fiscal years 1982 and 1989, Committee Reports failed to itemize (earmark) spending for the operations and maintenance account for the Army Corps of Engineers water projects. This is the reason for the low earmark totals for these years.

15. It should be emphasized that these are baseline savings, which report as savings anything less than the totals anticipated under previously enacted policy. Baselines typically assume increased spending; any reduction in the

anticipated increase (even if the program still receives more funds than in previous years) is scored as deficit reduction (savings).

16. Discretionary spending caps were originally contained in Title XIII of OBRA90, known commonly as the Budget Enforcement Act.

17. See for example Cohen (1993) and Schneider (1993) on the increased fiscal conservatism of the 103rd Congress.

18. Sources of the quotes are as follows: Frank (Congressional Record February 14, 1997); Lightfoot, Ehrlich (Taylor, 1996); Margolies-Mezvinsky (Congressional Quarterly, 10/23/93: 2869); Penny (Penny and Garrett 1995); Torricelli (Shear 1996); and Armey (Congressional Record 1993).

CHAPTER NINE

Conclusion

During World War II, Franklin Roosevelt summoned the congressional leadership for a top-secret meeting on the need for an atomic bomb. All the members voted to put aside petty concerns. Then Tennessee Sen. Kenneth McKellar, Chairman of the Appropriations Committee, spoke up: "Mr. President, I agree that the future of civilization may depend on the success of this project. Where in Tennessee are we going to build it?" So Oak Ridge Laboratory was created. Fifty years later, Oak Ridge remains open, one of the crown jewels of our complex of national laboratories.

Rep. George Brown, D-CA (1993)

Distributional concerns—whether in the classical sense of who gets what, when and how, or in the contemporary sense of how legislators capture gains from trade—are undeniably a part of legislative politics. However, the current distributive theories mischaracterize the key components of legislative politics in theoretically and empirically significant ways.

Keith Krehbiel (1991)

CONCLUSION

In Chapters One and Two, the distributive theory of Congress, which models the United States Congress as an institution designed to promote member reelection through exchange of geographic based benefits was introduced, and five key premises were outlined. The first four premises have been the subject of most of this research, and each has been evaluated based on the previous literature as well as through an empirical analysis of congressional earmarks. Each of these premises will now be discussed based on the findings presented in previous chapters.

Premise 1: Legislatures are composed of committees comprised of self-selected preference outliers. Members of committees reap disproportionate benefits from the programs within the jurisdiction of their committees.

Chapters Four and Five rely on different types of evidence to reach the same conclusion regarding the first premise. There is evidence that when Congress directly stipulates the location of project spending, committee members responsible for a given policy do receive greater benefits from that policy than do non-committee members. This finding appears to support the first premise of distributive theory. However, the vast majority of project location decisions are not made directly by Congress. Bureaucratic discretion (often constrained by peer review), and previously determined formulas determine the location of most district specific federal spending, and in policy areas where these methods predominate, there is little evidence that committee members are favored over other members in the provision of distributive benefits. In addition, factors associated with the policy needs of specific districts are also associated with the geographic spread of benefits. Therefore, although formal models of distributive politics may accurately capture policies such as water resources and federal building construction, these models do not appear to be valuable predictors of the vast majority of federal spending and grant policy.

This finding is not what was anticipated by distributive theory. Distributive theory portrays a Congress organized to best provide particularistic benefits to legislators. If only a small fraction of federal spending is decided in this manner, the claim that Congress is organized specifically for distributive purposes appears to be overstated. As distributive theory models congressional behavior based on the assumption that members choose between sets of competing projects offered by members, it is likely that this assumption leads to conclusions that are only applicable to the relatively minor programs that rely on congressional discretion for funding decisions—mainly policies that are funded through earmarks in either appropriations laws or, more commonly, committee reports.

Premise 2: Legislatures are organized into committees and subcommittees that provide pork barrel benefits to all members (In the language of formal modeling, they institutionalize norms of universalism and reciprocity to secure gains from exchange).

Through a review of the previous literature, original case studies, as well as data on congressional earmarks, Chapter Six of this study has concluded that universalism (provision of benefits to all or virtually all districts) and reciprocity (committee and individual deference to those committees responsible for a policy) accurately describe the annual appropriations process and earmarked spending included in annual appropriations. When all types of earmarked programs included in this analysis are considered, virtually all congressional districts benefit in some way. Large voting coalitions approaching unanimity are common in both the House and the Senate on annual spending bills reported by the Appropriations Subcommittees. Congressional observers and members of Congress frequently speak of an appropriations system that provides benefits for all those who support the process, and punishes those who oppose it.

However, there is much less evidence of universalism in congressional behavior outside of the annual appropriations process. Once again the extremely limited scope of earmarked spending needs to be stressed. Most of the location specific spending decisions are made through programs that are designed by the authorizing committees, and are not lumped together in omnibus laws. The appropriations process currently funds about 35 percent of total federal spending, and only a small fraction of this amount is delivered to specific locations through earmarks,.

In recent years there appears to be evidence that universalism and reciprocity within the earmarked spending process are declining. Members may willingly oppose distributive spending without retribution, which is not predicted by the universalism model. Large coalitions have formed in opposition to increased distributive spending, and in favor of reducing discretionary expenditures. In addition, it appears as though the increasing fiscal conservatism of Congress, as well as the Republican assumption of congressional leadership following the 1994 election, has reduced the influence of universalism and reciprocity.

Premise 3: All legislators seek pork barrel spending to help secure reelection.

Chapter Seven is a discussion of thc electoral connection between pork barrel spending and reelection which does not support the premise put forth by distributive theorists. Although the relationship between local spending and reelection is often taken for granted, there is little empirical evidence supporting such a connection. While there are serious methodological difficulties involved with testing the electoral connection empirically, at the very least it must be concluded that the relationship between pork barrel spending and reelection is more complex than has been recognized by many previous models.

Rather than there being a direct, unalterable relationship between pork barrel spending and votes, it is more likely that the influence of pork barrel spending varies considerably from district to district, and that the ability of legislators to secure pork and the desire to increase federal spending in the district varies as well. Quite simply, the electoral connection is more complicated than the one suggested by Mayhew and adopted by formal modelers. The assumption of a direct and universally shared electoral connection often results in an oversimplification by formal modelers which again lessens the generalizablity of the distributive theory.

Premise 4: Universalism of benefits is directly associated with government growth, inefficiency, and deficit spending that plague the modern Congress.

Government growth and deficit spending are not the result of pork barrel spending. As many students of budgeting have shown, deficits are the result of other large scale fiscal policy and economic factors such as growth in entitlements, decreased economic growth rates (and slower growth of revenues) and Reagan era tax cuts and military spending increases which were not offset elsewhere in the budget. This research supports this finding by showing that all of the most popular pork barrel spending taken together account for only a small fraction of spending, and this portion has not changed considerably during the period of large nominal deficits under consideration.

This research has shown that at times Congress can even be seen to act as a curb on the spending desires of presidents. It was Congress that insisted upon the continued imposition of caps on domestic discretionary spending in OBRA93, even though the President wanted to lift the caps in order to increase government spending on infrastructure. Likewise, it was Congress that prevented President Clinton from implementing a short term economic stimulus package in 1993. Distributive theory claims that Congress is responsible for recent fiscal policy problems; evidence from recent Congresses however, indicates that the legislature has been more fiscally conservative than the executive branch.

Premise 5: Legislators are single minded seekers of reelection.

Each one of the four premises already described has become part of the distributive portrayal of Congress. There are doubts about the universal applicability of each aspect of the theory. Taken together, these doubts lessen the application of a general theory of the distributive Congress. Formal models that portray Congress as engaged in direct specification of project locations may accurately capture spending that is earmarked. When Congress does not directly specify the location of projects, the models do not appear to be very relevant. As the vast majority of federal spending is decided by entities other than congressional committees, the success that formal distributive models have in reflecting overall policymaking is not great.

This is likely to be the result of the oversimplification that is the fifth premise. Certainly, most members of Congress are keenly aware that their actions will have an effect on their electoral fortunes. But to conclude that one can understand not only the behavior of individuals but the entire structure of Congress on the basis of this assumption is not supported. Competing motivations, including the desire for good public policy are frequently in conflict with the electoral desire, and sometimes prove to be more important. In addition, the electoral connection means different things to different members, and is subject to change as the salience of the deficit issue, and a link between deficits and pork barrel spending is presented by the media and politicians.

Formal models that rely on the simplifying assumption that congressional behavior, policy outcomes and organization can be understood by depicting members as single-minded seekers of reelection do not lead to a complete and accurate picture of Congress. Pork barrel politics do play a role in the modern Congress; however, that role is often constrained. Differing motivations and attitudes limit the generalizability of distributive theory and the formal models upon which it is based.

> *As I am fond of saying, if the Congress had a vote on whether to build a cheese factory on the moon, I would oppose it based on what I know now, and I cannot imagine the circumstance under which I would support it. But on the other hand, if Congress in its lack of wisdom decided to start a cheese factory on the Moon, I would want a Texas firm to do the engineering, I would want a Texas construction firm to do the construction, I would want the milk to come from Texas cows, and I would want the celestial distribution center to be in Dallas, TX or College Station, TX or somewhere else in my State.*
>
> *Senator Phil Gramm (R-TX)*

The quote from Texas Republican Senator (and Public Choice Economist) Phil Gramm sums up this conclusion quite nicely. It is not inconsistent for members individually and Congress as an institution to value both the public good and district specific spending. When done in moderation, district spending can be used to entice legislators to support big picture policies that are efficient, economical and prudent. Most of the discretion for determining the location of federal spending is delegated by Congress to agency bureaucrats or is determined by broad-based formulas. Congress uses broad authorizing statutes to limit its own ability to target spending geographically.

However, Congress has kept for itself decisions regarding the spending location of a small amount of especially favorable projects that are doled out annually as appropriations earmarks. These earmarks are frequently used to guarantee support for the overall Congressional budget and spending process. The pork barrel segment of the budget exists, and will probably continue to exist to some extent regardless of which political party controls the White House and Congress.

Pork barrel spending does not lead to deficits. The popular conception, fed by the media and even by many politicians is inaccurate. Eliminating all earmarks—the purest form of pork and the spending most frequently criticized by opponents of wasteful spending—would not dramatically reduce the size of annual deficits. In fact, pork may be used to compensate members for making politically dangerous votes for deficit reduction.

References

Aberbach, Joel D. and Bert A. Rockman. 1988. "Mandates or Mandarins? Control and Discretion in the Modern Administrative State." *Public Administration Review* 48:606-612.

Adler, E. Scott and John S. Lapinski. 1997. "Demand-Side Theory and Congressional Committee Composition: A Constituency Characteristics Approach." *American Journal of Political Science* 41,3:895-918.

Administration of George H. Bush. 1991. "Remarks on Signing the Intermodal Surface Transportation Efficiency Act of 1991." *Weekly Compilation of Presidential Documents*. 18 December 1991.

Administration of William J. Clinton. 1993. "Address before a Joint Session of Congress on Administration Goals." *Weekly Compilation of Presidential Documents*. 17 February 1993. pp.215-224.

Alvarez, R. Michael and Matthew M. Schousen. 1993. "Policy Moderation or Conflicting Expectations? Testing the Intentional Models of Split-Ticket Voting." *American Politics Quarterly* 21,4:410-438.

Alvarez, R. Michael and Jaon L. Saving. 1997a. "Congressional Committees and the Political Economy of Federal Outlays." *Public Choice* 92: 55-73.

Alvarez, R. Michael and Jason L. Saving. 1997b. "Deficits, Democrats, and Distributive Benefits: Congressional Elections and the Pork Barrel in the 1980s." *Political Research Quarterly* 50,4:809-831.

Anagnoson, J. Theodore. 1980a. "Politics in the Distribution of Federal Grants: The Case of the Economic Development Agency." in Rundquist, Barry (ed.) *Political Benefits*. (Lexington, MA: Heath).

Anagnoson, J. Theodore. 1980b. "Targeting Federal Categorical Grants: An Impossible Dream?" in Ingram, Helen M. and Dean E. Mann (eds.) *Why Policies Succeed or Fail*. (Beverly Hills: Sage).

Anagnoson, J. Theodore. 1982. "Federal Grant Agencies and Congressional Election Campaigns." *American Journal of Political Science* 26,3:545-561.

Anagnoson, J. Theodore. 1983. "Bureaucratic Reactions to Political Pressures: Can a Grant Agency 'Manage' Its Political Environment?" *Administration and Society*.

Anderson, Gary M. and Robert D. Tollison. 1991. "Congressional Influence and Patterns of New Deal Spending, 1933-1939." *Journal of Law and Economics* 34:161-175.

Andres, Gary J. 1995. "Pork Barrel Spending—On the Wane?" *PS Political Science & Politics* 28 207-211.

Anton, Thomas J. Jerry P. Cawley and Kevin L. Kramer. 1980. *Moving Money: An Empirical Analysis of Federal Expenditure Patterns*. (Cambridge, MA: Oelgeschlager, Gunn and Hain, Publishers, Inc.)

Appel, Adrianne. 1995. "Pet Projects Usually Involve Pork, Says Spending Foe Ed Royce." *Los Angeles Times (Orange County Edition)*. 7 August 1995. p.B4.

Arnold, R. Douglas. 1979. *Congress and the Bureaucracy: A Theory of Influence*. (New Haven: Yale University Press).

Arnold, R. Douglas. 1981a. "Legislators, Bureaucrats, and Locational Decisions." *Public Choice* 37:107-132.

Arnold, R. Douglas. 1981b. "The Local Roots of Domestic Policy." in Thomas Mann and Norman J. Ornstein (eds.) *The New Congress*. (Washington, D.C.: American Enterprise Institution).

Arnold, R. Douglas. 1990. *The Logic of Congressional Action*. (New Haven: Yale University Press).

Arrow, Kenneth J. 1951. *Social Choice and Individual Values*. (New Haven: Yale University Press).

Arvidson, Cheryl. 1993. "As the Reagan Era Fades, It's Discretion Vs. Earmarking in the Struggle Over Funds." in Laurence J. O'Toole, Jr. *American Intergovernmental Relations: Foundations, Perspectives, and Issues* (Second Edition). (Washington: CQ Press).

Atlas, Cary M., Robert J. Hendershott, and Mark Zupan. 1997. "Optimal Effort Allocation by U.S. Senators: The Role of Constituency Size." *Public Choice* 92:221-229.

Babson, Jennifer and David Rapp. 1994. "Stubborn Power: Neal Smith, D-Iowa." *Congressional Quarterly Weekly Report* 19 March 1994. p.649.

Baron, David P. 1989. "A Noncooperative Theory of Legislative Coalitions." *American Journal of Political Science* 33:1048-1084.

Baron, David P. 1990. "Distributive Politics and the Persistence of Amtrak." *Journal of Politics* 52,3: 883-913.

Baron, David P. 1991. "Majoritarian Incentives, Pork Barrel Programs, and Procedural Control." *American Journal of Political Science* 35,1:57-90.

Baron, David P. 1996. "A dynamic Theory of Collective Goods Programs." *American Political Science Review* 90,2:316-330.

Baron, David P. and Ferejohn, John. 1989. "Bargaining in Legislatures" *American Political Science Review* 83:1181-1206.

Benenson, Bob. 1993. "Perennials Hard to Uproot." *Congressional Quarterly Special Report: Where the Money Goes.* 11 December 1993. p.29.

Bernardi, Richard A. 1996. "The Base Closure Commission: A Rational or Political Decision Process?" *Public Budgeting & Finance.* Spring 1996.

Bessette, Joseph A. 1994. *The Mild Voice of Reason: Deliberative Democracy and American Government.* (Chicago: University of Chicago Press).

Bickers, Kenneth N. and Robert M. Stein. 1996. "The Electoral Dynamics of the Federal Pork Barrel." *American Journal of Political Science* 40,4:1300-1326.

Bickers, Kenneth N. and Robert M. Stein. 1997. "Building Majority Coalitions for Sub-Majority Benefit Distributions." *Public Choice* 91:229-249.

Blais, Andre, and Stephane Dion. 1991. *The Budget Maximizing Bureaucrat.* (Pittsburgh, PA: The University of Pittsburgh Press).

Bowens, Gregory J. 1993. "Building a Military." *Congressional Quarterly Special Report: Where the Money Goes.* 11 December 1993. pp.118-122.

Bratton, Kathleen A. 1994. "Retrospective Voting and Future Expectations: The Case of the Budget Deficit in the 1988 Election." *American Politics Quarterly* 22,3:277-296.

Break, George F. 1993. "The Economics of Intergovernmental Grants." in Laurence J. O'Toole, Jr. *American Intergovernmental Relations: Foundations, Perspectives, and Issues* (Second Edition). (Washington: CQ Press).

Brown, George E. Jr. 1993. "Academic Earmarks: An Interim Report by the Chairman of the Committee on Science, Space and Technology." Mimeo.

Brown, Ronald 1986. "Mark Andrews." *National Journal.* 12 April 1986.

Buchanan, James M. and Gordon Tullock. 1962. *The Calculus of Consent.* (Ann Arbor: University of Michigan Press).

Buchanan, James M. and Richard E. Wagner. 1977. *Democracy in Deficit: The Political Legacy of Lord Keynes* (New York: Academic Press).

Buchanan, James M. 1984. *The Deficit and American Democracy.* (Memphis, TN: P.K. Seidman Foundation).

Burd, Stephen. 1994. "Agriculture Department Releases $150-Million in Grants." *The Chronicle of Higher Education.* 5 October 1994. p.A29.

Business Executives for National Security 1995. "The FY 1996 Military Construction Budget: Business as Usual?" [Press Release]. 28 July 1995

Cain, Bruce, John Ferejohn and Morris Fiorina. 1987. *The Personal Vote: Constituency Service and Electoral Independence.* (Cambridge: Harvard University Press).

Calleo, David P. 1992. *The Bankrupting of America: How the Federal Budget is Impoverishing the Nation.* (New York: Avon Books).

Calvert, Randall L., Mark Moran, and Barry R. Weingast. 1987. "Congressional Influence over Policy Making: The Case of the FTC." in Mathew D. McCubbins and Terry Sullivan (eds.) *Congress: Structure and Policy.* (Cambridge: Cambridge University Press).

Carlton, Ralph, Timothy Russell, and Richard Winters. 1980. "Distributive Benefits, Congressional Support and Agency Growth: The Cases of the National Endowment for the Arts and Humanities." in Rundquist, Barry (ed.) *Political Benefits.* (Lexington, MA: Heath).

Cogan, John F., Timothy J. Muris, and Allen Schick. 1994. *The Budget Puzzle: Understanding Federal Spending.* (Stanford, CA: Stanford University Press).

Cohen, Linda R. and Roger G. Noll. 1991. *The Technology Pork Barrel.* (Washington, D.C.: The Brookings Institutions).

Cohen. Richard E. 1993. "How 535 Big Spenders Became Misers." *National Journal.* 24 July 1993; 1883.

Cohn, Jonathan. 1996. "The Fleece Police." *The American Prospect* 26: 12-14.

Collie, Melissa P. 1988a. "The Legislature and Distributive Policy Making in Formal Perspective." *Legislative Studies Quarterly* 13,4:427-458.

Collie, Melissa P. 1988b. "Universalism and Parties in the U.S. House of Representatives, 1921-1980." *American Journal of Political Science* 32:865-883.

Congressional Budget Office. 1988. "New Directions for the Nations Public Works." (Washington, D.C.: GPO).

Congressional Budget Office. 1998. "CBO Memorandum: The Line Item Veto Act After One Year." April.

Congressional Record (Various Dates).

Congressional Quarterly Almanac (Washington, D.C.: CQ Press) (1988-1996).

Cook, Timothy E. 1989. *Making Laws and Making News: Media Strategies in the U.S. House of Representatives.* (Washington, D.C.:The Brookings Institution).

Cordes, Colleen. 1994. "Opponent of Earmarks Threatens to Join His Foes at the Pork Barrel." *The Chronicle of Higher Education* 28 September 1994. p.A40.

Cordes, Colleen.1994. "King of the Earmarks." *The Chronicle of Higher Education.* 2 November 1994. pp. A49-A51.

Cordes, Colleen. 1997. "Congressional earmarks for Colleges increased by 49% for Fiscal 1997." *The Chronicle of Higher Education* 28 March 1997. pp. A36-A41.

Cordes, Colleen and Dylan Rivera. 1995. "Trimming Academic Pork." *The Chronicle of Higher Education* 8 September 1995. pp. A36-A43.

Council of Economic Advisors. 1997. *Economic Report of the President, 1997* (Washington, D.C.).

Cover, Albert D. 1980. "Contacting Congressional Constituents: Some Patterns of Perquisite Use." *American Journal of Political Science* 24,1:125-135.

Cox, Gary W. and Mathew D. McCubbins. 1993. Legislative Leviathan (Berkeley: University of California Press).

Crain, W. Mark, Donald R. Leavans and Robert D. Tollison. 1990. "Pork Barrel Paradox." in W. Mark Crain, Robert D. Tollison (eds.) *Predicting Politics: Essays in Empirical Public Choice.* (Ann Arbor: The University of Michigan Press).

Crain, W. Mark and Robert D. Tollison. 1977. "The Influence of Representation on Public Policy." *Journal of Legal Studies* 6:355-366.

Curran, Tim. 1993. "Senators Franked Mass Mail Very Light" *Roll Call* 29 March 1993.

Davidson, Roger H. and Walter J. Oleszek. 1995. *Congress and Its Members.* (Washington: CQ Press).

Del Rossi, Alison F. 1995. "The Politics and Economics of Pork Barrel Spending: The Case of Federal Financing of Water Resources Development." *Public Choice* 85:285-305.

Dilger, Robert Jay. 1989. *National Intergovernmental Programs* (Englewood Cliffs, NJ: Prentice Hall).

Dimaggio, Paul J. 1991. "Decentralization of Arts Funding from the Federal Government to the States." in Stephen Benedict (ed.) *Public Money and the Muse: Essays on Government Funding for the Arts.* (New York: W.W. Norton and Company).

Downs, Anthony. 1957. *An Economic Theory of Democracy* (New York: Harper).

Drew, Elizabeth. 1970. "Dam Outrage: The Story of the Army Engineers." *The Atlantic* April 1970.

Ellwood, John W. 1983. "Budget Control in a Redistributive Environment." in Allen Schick (ed.) *Making Economic Policy in Congress.* (Washington, D.C.:The American Enterprise).

Ellwood, John W. 1984. "Comments." in Mills, Gregory B. and John L. Palmer (eds.) *Federal Budget Policy in the 1980s.* (Washington, D.C.: The Urban Institute).

Ellwood, John W. and Eric M. Patashink. 1993. "In Praise of Pork." *The Public Interest* 110:19-33.

Evans, Diana M. 1991. "Lobbying the Committee: Interest Groups and the House Public Works and Transportation Committee." in Allan J. Cigler and Burdett Loomis (eds.) *Interest Group Politics* (third edition) (Washington, D.C.: CQ Press).

Evans, Diana. 1994. "Policy and Pork: The Use of Pork Barrel Projects to Build Policy Coalitions in the House of Representatives." *American Journal of Political Science* 38,4: 894-917.

Evans, Diana. 1995. "Who's Calling the Shots? Vote-Buying and the Control of Pork" Paper prepared for presentation at the annual meetings of the American Political Science Association, Chicago, IL, August 31-September 3, 1995.

Feldman, Paul and James Jondrow. 1984. "Congressional Elections and Local Federal Spending." *American Journal of Political Science*. 28:147-164.

Fenno, Richard F. Jr. 1962 . "The House Appropriations Committee as a Political System: The Problem of Integration." *American Political Science Review* 56:310-324.

Fenno, Richard F. Jr. 1966. *The Power of the Purse: Appropriations Politics in Congress.* (Boston: Little Brown and Company).

Fenno, Richard F. Jr. 1973. *Congressmen in Committees.* (Boston: Little, Brown and Company).

Fenno, Richard F. Jr. 1978. *Homestyle.* (Boston: Little, Brown and Company).

Fenno, Richard F. Jr. 1991a. *Learning to Legislate: The Senate Education of Arlen Specter.* (Washington, D.C.: CQ Press).

Fenno, Richard F. Jr. 1991b. *The Emergence of a Senate Leader: Peter Domenici and the Reagan Budget.* (Washington, D.C.: Congressional Quarterly Press).

Fenno, Richard F. Jr. 1992. *When Incumbency Fails: The Senate Career of Mark Andrews.* (Washington, D.C.: CQ Press).

Ferejohn, John. 1974. *Pork Barrel Politics.* (Stanford: Stanford University Press).

Ferejohn, John. 1986."Logrolling in an Institutional Context: A Case Study of Food Stamp Legislation." In Gerald C. Wright, Leroy N. Reiselbach, and

Lawrence C. Dodd (eds.) *Congress and Policy Change.* (New York: Agathon Press).

Ferejohn, John, Morris Fiorina and Richard D. McKelvey. 1987. "Sophisticated Voting and Agenda Independence in the Distributive Politics Setting." *American Journal of Political Science* 31:167-193.

Fiorina, Morris P. 1977. *Congress: Keystone of the Washington Establishment.* (New Haven: Yale University Press).

Fiorina, Morris P. 1981a. "Congressional Control of the Bureaucracy: A Mismatch of Incentives and Capabilities." in Dodd, Lawrence C. and Bruce I. Oppenheimer (eds.) *Congress Reconsidered* (Second edition) (Washington, D.C.: Congressional Quarterly Press.

Fiorina, Morris P. 1981b. "Universalism, Reciprocity, And Distributive Policymaking in Majority Rule Institutions." *Research in Public Policy Analysis and Management.* 1:197-221.

Fiorina, Morris P. 1981c. "Some Problems in Studying the Effects of Resource Allocation in Congressional Elections." *American Journal of Political Science* 25,3:543-567.

Fiorina, Morris P. 1989. *Congress: Keystone of the Washington Establishment.* (New Haven: Yale University Press).

Fiorina, Morris P. 1992. *Divided Government.* (New York: Macmillian Publishing Company).

Fisher, Louis. 1989. "Micromanagement by Congress: Reality and Mythology." in L. Gordon Crovitz and Jeremy A. Rabkin (eds.) *The Fettered Presidency.* (Washington, D.C.: American Enterprise Institute for Public Policy Research).

Fitts, Michael and Robert Inman. 1992. "Controlling Congress: Presidential Influence in Domestic Fiscal Policy." *The Georgetown Law Journal* 80:1737-1785.

Fitzgerald, Randall and Gerald Lipson. 1984. *Porkbarrel: The Unexpurgated Grace Commission Story of Congressional Profligacy.* (Washington, D.C.: The Cato Institute)

Forgette, Richard G and James V. Saturno. 1994. "302(b) or Not 302(b): Congressional Floor Procedures and House Appropriators." *Legislative Studies Quarterly* 19,3:385-396.

Franklin, Daniel P. 1993. *Making Ends Meet: Congressional Budgeting in the Age of Deficits.* (Washington, D.C.: CQ Press).

Freedman, Allan. 1995. "Members' Pet Projects Survive Despite Tight Fiscal Limits." *Congressional Quarterly Weekly Report.* 8 July 1995. pp.1990-1992.

Friedman, Jeffrey ed. 1996. *The Rational Choice Controversy: Economic Models of Politics Reconsidered.* (New Haven: The Yale University Press).

Froman, Lewis A. 1967. *The Congressional Process.* (Boston: Little Brown and Company).

Frome, Michael. 1995. *National Park Guide* (New York: Simon and Shuster, Inc.).

General Accounting Office. 1987a. University Funding: Patterns of Federal Research Funds to Universities. Resources, Community, and Economic Development Division, February 1987.

General Accounting Office. 1987b. Grant Formulas: A Catalog of Federal Aid to States and Localities. Human Resources Division, March 1987.

Gertzog, Irwin N. 1976. "The Routinization of Committee Assignments in the U.S. House of Representatives." *American Journal of Political Science* 20:693-712.

Gilmour, John B. 1990. *Reconcilable Differences? Congress, the Budget Process and the Deficit.* (Berkeley, CA: University of California Press).

Gist, John R. and R. Carter Hill. 1984. "Political and Economic Influences on the Bureaucratic Allocation of Federal Funds: The Case of Urban Development Action Grants." *Journal of Urban Economics* 16:158-172.

Goodsell, Charles. 1983. *The Case For Bureaucracy.* (Chatham, NJ: Chatham House Publishers).

Goodwin, George. 1970. *The Little Legislatures.* (Amherst, MA: University of Massachusetts Press).

Goss, Carol F. 1972. "Military Committee Membership and Defense Related Benefits in the House of Representatives." *Western Political Quarterly* 25:215-233.

Grasso, Patrick G. 1986. "Distributive Policies and the Politics of Economic Development" in F. Stevens Redburn, Tery F. Bus and Larry C. Ledebur (eds.) *Revitalizing the U.S. Economy* (NY: Greenwood Press).

Green, Donald P. and Ian Shapiro. 1994. *Pathologies of Rational Choice Theory: A Critique of Applications in Political Science.* (New Haven: Yale University Press)

Green, Mark J., James M. Fallows and David R. Zwick. 1972. *Who Runs Congress?: The President, Big Business, or You?* (New York: Bantam Books).

Greene, Kenneth V. and Vincent G. Munley. 1980. "The Productivity of Legislators' Tenure: A Case of Lacking Evidence." *Journal of Legal Studies* 10:207-219.

Grofman, Bernard. 1993. "On the Gentle Art of Rational Choice Bashing." In Bernard Grofman (ed.) *Information, Participation, and Choice.* (Ann Arbor: University of Michigan Press).

Groseclose, Tim and James M. Snyder, Jr. 1996. "Buying Supermajorities." *American Political Science Review* 90,2:303-315.

Gross, Martin L. 1993. *The Government Racket: Washington Waste From A to Z.* (New York: Bantam Books).

Gryski, Gerard S. 1991. "The Influence of Committee Position on Federal Program Spending." *Polity* 23,3:443-459.

Hager, George. 1996. "Two Incumbents, Two Views . . . On Bringing Home the Bacon." *Congressional Quarterly Weekly Report.* 3 August, 1996. pp. 2170-2171.

Hall, Richard and Bernard Grofman. 1990. "The Committee Assignment Process and the Conditional Nature of Committee Bias." *American Political Science Review* 84:1149-1166.

Hamilton, Alexander, James Madison, and John Jay. 1961. *The Federalist Papers.* (Clinton Rossitor, ed.) (New York: New American Library).

Hamm, Keith E. 1983. "Patterns of Influence Among Committees, Agencies, and Interest Groups." *Legislative Studies Quarterly* 8,3:379-426.

Hamman, John A. 1993a. "Universalism, Program Development, and the Distribution of Federal Assistance." *Legislative Studies Quarterly* 18,4:553-568.

Hamman, John A. 1993b. "Bureaucratic Accommodation of Congress and the President: Elections and the Distribution of Federal Assistance." *Western Political Quarterly* 46,4:863-879.

Hamman, John A. and Jeffrey E. Cohen. 1997. "Reelection and Congressional Support: Presidential Motives in Distributive Politics." *American Politics Quarterly* 25,1:56-74.

Hardin, Garrett. 1968. "The Tragedy of the Commons." *Science* 162:1243-1248.

Harris, Joseph P. 1969. *Congressional Control of Administration.* (Washington, D.C.: Brookings Institution).

Hartzog, George B. Jr. 1988. *Battling for the National Parks* (Mt. Kisco, New York: Moyer Bell Limited).

Healy, Jon. 1993a. "House Hands Mineta a Victory Killing Carr's Road Projects." *Congressional Quarterly Weekly Report.* 25 September 1993. pp.2535-2538.

Healy, Jon. 1993b. "Where the Money Goes: Transportation." *Congressional Quarterly Special Report: Where the Money Goes.* 11 December 1993. pp.124-135.

Healy, Jon. 1996. "Bond Draws Line on VA Hospital." *Congressional Quarterly Weekly Report.* 28 September, 1996. p.2763.

Hird, John A. 1990. "Superfund Expenditures and Cleanup Priorities: Distributive Politics or the Public Interest?" *Journal of Policy Analysis and Management* 9,4: 455-483.

Hird, John A. 1991. "The Political Economy of Pork: Project Selection at the U.S. Army Corps of Engineers." *American Political Science Review* 85,2:429-456.

Hird, John A. 1993. "Congressional Voting on Superfund: Self Interest or Ideology?" *Public Choice* 77:333-357.

Hoel, Lester A. 1990. "Financing Transportation." *Transportation Research* (General) Special Issue, 1990.

Holcombe, Randall G. and Asghar Zardkoohi. 1981. "The Determinants of Federal Grants." *Southern Economic Journal* 48:393-399.

Hook, Janet 1994a. "Seniority System Tested by Smith-Obey Face-Off." *Congressional Quarterly Weekly Report.* 5 March 1994. pp.518-521.

Hook, Janet. 1994b. "Appropriations Under Obey Will Have a Harder Edge." *Congressional Quarterly Weekly Report.* 26 March 1994. pp.713-716,

Hook, Janet. 1996. "GOP Freshmen Keep Pork on Reelection Menu." *Los Angeles Times. 1* July 1996. p.A1.

Hooton, Cornell G. 1997. "Politics Versus Policy In Public Works Grants: A Critical Test of the Simple Model." *American Politics Quarterly* 25,1:75-103.

Horn, Stephen. 1970. *Unused Power: The Work of the Senate Committee on Appropriations.* (Washington, D.C.:The Brookings Institution).

Hosansky, David. 1997. "Lawmakers Brace for Battle Over Highway Funding." *Congressional Quarterly Weekly Report.* 1 February 1997. pp.294-297.

Hurwitz, Marks S., Roger J. Moiles and David W. Rhode. 1997. "Distributive and Partisan Issues in Agriculture Policy in the 104th House." Paper prepared for delivery at the 1997 Annual Meeting of the American Political Science Association, Washington, D.C.

Inman, Robert P. 1993. *Presidential Leadership and the Reform of Fiscal Policy: Learning From Reagan's Role in TRA 86.* (Cambridge, MA: National Bureau of Economic Research).

Inman, R.P. and Fitts, M.A. 1990. "Political Institutions and Fiscal Policy: Evidence from the U.S. Historical Record." *Journal of Law, Economics and Organization* 6 (Special Issue) 79-132.

Ippolito, Dennis, 1990. *Uncertain Legacies: Federal Budget Policy from Roosevelt to Reagan.* (Charlottesville: University of Virginia Press).

Jackley, John L. 1992. *Hill Rat: Blowing the Lid Off Congress.* (Washington: Regnery Gateway).

Jacobson, Gary C. 1978. "The Effects of Campaign Spending in Congressional Elections." *American Political Science Review* 72:469-491.

Jacobson, Gary C. 1993. "Deficit-Cutting Politics and Congressional Elections." *Political Science Quarterly* 108,3:375-402.

Johannes, John R. and John C. McAdams. 1981. "The Congressional Incumbency Effect: Is It Casework, Policy Compatibility, or Something Else? An Examination of the 1978 Election." *American Journal of Political Science* 25,3:512-542.

Johannes, John R. and John C. McAdams 1987. "Entrepreneur or Agent: Congressmen and the Distribution of Casework, 1977-1978." *Western Political Quarterly* 535-553.

Kalas, John W. 1987. *The Grant System.* (Albany, NY: State University of New York Press).

Kau, James B. and Paul H. Rubin. 1979. "Self-Interest, Ideology, and Logrolling in Congressional Voting." *Journal of Law and Economics* 22:365-384.

Kay, Alan F., Hazel Henderson, Fredrick T. Steeper, Stanley B. Greenberg, and Christopher Blunt. 1995. *Who Will Reconnect with the People: Republicans, Democrats, or . . . None of the Above?* (St. Augustine, FL: Americans Talk Issues Foundation).

Kelman, Steven. 1987. *Making Public Policy: A Hopeful View of American Government.* (New York: Basic Books).

Kettl, Donald F. 1992. *Deficit Politics: Public Budgeting in its Institutional and Historical Context* (New York: Macmillian Publishing Company)

Kiel, Lisa J. and Richard B. McKenzie. 1983. "The Impact of Tenure on the Flow of Federal Benefits to SMSA's." *Public Choice* 41:285-293.

Kiewiet, D. Roderick and Mathew D. McCubbins. 1985a. "Congressional Appropriations and the Electoral Connection." *The Journal of Politics* 47:59-82.

Kiewiet, D. Roderick, and Mathew D. McCubbins. 1985b. "Appropriations Decisions as a Bilateral Bargaining Game between President and Congress." *Legislative Studies Quarterly* 10,2:181-201.

Kiewiet, D. Roderick, and Mathew D. McCubbins. 1991. *The Logic of Delegation.* (Chicago: The University of Chicago Press).

Kirschten, J. Dicken. 1977. "Draining the Water Projects Out of the Pork Barrel." *National Journal*. 4 April 1977. pp.540-548.

Kirst, Michael W. 1969. *Government Without Passing Laws.* (Chapel Hill: University of North Carolina Press).

Krehbiel, Keith. 1991. *Information and Legislative Organization.* (Ann Arbor: University of Michigan Press).

Kriz, Margaret. 1995. "Land Wars." *National Journal.* 2 September 1995. pp.2146-2151.

Levitt, Steven D. and James M. Poterba. 1994. "Congressional Distributive Politics and State Economic Performance." National Bureau of Economic Research Working Paper No. 4721. (Cambridge, MA: NBER).

Levitt, Steven D. and James M. Snyder, Jr. 1995. "Political Parties and the Distribution of Federal Outlays." *American Journal of Political Science* 39,4:958-980.

Lineberry, Robert L., George C. Edwards, and Martin P. Wattenberg. 1994. *Government in America: People, Politics, and Policy.* (New York: HarperCollins College Publishers).

Lipinski, Daniel. 1995 "Running 'With' Congress: Institutional Support in Congressional Newsletters." Paper prepared for the 1995. Annual Meeting of the American Political Science Association, Chicago IL.

Londregan, John and James M. Snyder, Jr. 1994. "Comparing Committee and Floor Preferences." *Legislative Studies Quarterly* 19,2:233-266.

Lowi, Theodore J. 1964. "American Politics, Public Policy, Case Studies, and Political Theory." *World Politics* 16:667-715.

Lowi, Theodore J. 1972 ."Four Systems of Policy, Politics, and Choice." *Public Administration Review* 32:298-310.

Lowi, Theodore J. and Benjamin Ginsberg. 1996. *American Government: Freedom and Power* (4th Edition). (New York: W.W. Norton & Company).

Lowry, William R. 1994a. "Paved with Political Intentions: The Impact of Structure on the National Park Services of Canada and the United States." *Policy Studies Journal* 22,1:44-58.

Lowry, William R. 1994b. The Capacity for Wonder: Preserving National Parks. (Washington, D.C.: The Brookings Institution).

Maass, Arthur. 1951. *Muddy Waters.* (Cambridge: Harvard University Press).

Maass, Arthur. 1983. *Congress and the Common Good.* (New York: Basic Books).

MacDonald, Austin F. 1928. *Federal Aid: A Study of the American Subsidy System.* (New York: Thomas Y. Crowell Company).

McCubbins, Mathew D. 1991. "Government on Lay-Away: Federal Spending and Deficits Under Divided Party Control." in Gary W. Cox and Samuel Kernell (eds.) *The Politics of Divided Government* (Boulder, CO: Westview Press).

Makin, John H. and Norman J. Ornstein. 1994. *Debt and Taxes*. (New York: Times Books).

Makinson, Larry and Joshua Goldstein. 1994. *Open Secrets: The Encyclopedia of Congressional Money & Politics* (Third Edition) (Washington, D.C.:CQ Press).

Makinson, Larry and Joshua Goldstein. 1996. *Open Secrets: The Encyclopedia of Congressional Money & Politics* (Fourth Edition). (Washington, D.C.:CQ Press).

Maltzman, Forrest and Steven S. Smith. 1994. "Principals, Goals, Dimensionality, and Congressional Committees." *Legislative Studies Quarterly* 19,4:457-477.

Manley, John F. 1970. *The Politics of Finance: The House Committee on Ways and Means.* (Boston: Little, Brown and Company).

Mansbridge, Jane J.(ed.) 1990. *Beyond Self-Interest.* (Chicago: The University of Chicago Press).

Marshall, Bryan W. Brandon Prins, and David W. Rhode. 1997. "The Senate Purse: A Longitudinal Study of the Senate Appropriations Committee in the Postreform Era." Paper prepared for the Annual Meeting of the American Political Science Association, Washington, D.C., August 28-31, 1997.

Martin, Janet M. 1994. *Lessons from the Hill: The Legislative Journey of an Education Program.* (New York: St. Martin's Press)

Matthews, Donald R. 1960. *U.S. Senators and Their World.* (New York: Vintage Books)

Mayer, Kenneth R. 1991. *The Political Economy of Defense Contracting.* (New Haven and London: Yale University Press).

Mayer, Kenneth R. 1995. "Electoral Cycles in Federal Government Prime Contract Awards: State-Level Evidence from the 1988 and 1992 Presidential Elections." *American Journal of Political Science.* 39,1:162-185.

Mayhew, David R. 1974. *Congress: The Electoral Connection.* (New Haven: Yale University Press).

Mayhew, David R. 1974b. "Congressional Elections: The Case of the Vanishing Marginals." *Polity* 6:295-317.

Mayhew, David R. 1991. *Divided We Govern.* (New Haven: Yale University Press).

Merry, Robert W. (ed.) 1993. "Where the Money Goes." *Congressional Quarterly Special Report.* 11 December 1993.

Miller, James C. III. 1994. *Fix the U.S. Budget!* (Stanford California: Hoover Institution Press).

Mills, Mike. 1991. "Highway Formulas Give Way to Old-Style Horse Trades." *Congressional Quarterly Weekly Report.* 23 November 1991, pp.3447-3448.

Mills, Mike. 1993."Ambitious Set of Deficit Cuts Narrowly Fails in the House." *Congressional Quarterly Weekly Report.* 27 November 1993, pp.3254-3256.

Moe, Terry M. 1987. "An Assessment of the Positive Theory of 'Congressional Dominance'." *Legislative Studies Quarterly* 12,4:475-519.

Moneypenny, Phillip. 1993. "Federal Grants-In-Aid To State Governments: A Political Analysis." in Laurence J. O'Toole, Jr. *American Intergovernmental Relations: Foundations, Perspectives, and Issues* (Second Edition). (Washington: CQ Press).

Monroe, Kristen Renwick. 1991. *The Economic Approach to Politics: A Critical Reassessment of the Theory of Rational Action.* (New York: HarperCollins Publishers)

Moore, Michael K. and John R. Hibbing. 1996. "Length of Congressional Tenure and Federal Spending: Were the Voters in Washington State Correct?" *American Politics Quarterly* 24,2:131-149.

Morgan, Dan. 1996. "Redrawing the Spending Lines." *The Washington Post National Weekly Edition.* 29 July—4 august, 1996.

Munson, Richard. 1993. *The Cardinals of Capitol Hill: The Men and Women who Control Government Spending.* (New York: Grove Press).

Murphy, James T. 1971. *Science, Geopolitics and Federal Spending.* (Lexington, MA: D.C. Heath).

Murphy, James T. 1974. "Political Parties and the Pork barrel: Party Conflict and Cooperation in House Public Works Committee Decision Making." *American Political Science Review* 68:169-185.

Nathan, Richard P. 1993. "The Politics of Printouts: The Use of Official Numbers to Allocate Federal Grants-In-Aid." in Laurence J. O'Toole, Jr. *American Intergovernmental Relations: Foundations, Perspectives, and Issues* (Second Edition). (Washington: CQ Press).

National Science Foundation Panel on NSF Decisionmaking for Major Awards. 1994. Major Award Decisionmaking of the National Science Foundation (Washington, D.C.: National Academy Press).

National Taxpayers Union (NTU). Congressional Ratings 1987-1994.

Neustadt, Richard E. 1964. "Politicians and Bureaucrats." in David B. Truman (ed.) *The Congress and America's Future.* (Englewood Cliffs, NJ: Prentice-Hall Inc.).

Niou, Emerson M.S. and Peter C. Ordeshook. 1985. "Universalism in Congress." *American Journal of Political Science* 29:246-258.

Niskanen, William A. 1971. *Bureaucracy and Representative Government.* (Chicago: Aldine Atherton).

Niskanen, William A. 1975. "Bureaucrats and Politicians." *Journal of Law and Economics* 18,3:617-644.

Niskanen, William A. 1991. "A Reflection on Bureaucracy and Representative Government." in Andre Blais and Stephane Dion (eds.) *The Budget Maximizing Bureaucrat.* (Pittsburgh, PA: University of Pittsburgh Press).

Noll, Roger. 1983. "The Case Against the Balanced Budget Amendment." in Lawrence H. Meyer (ed.) *The Economic Consequences of Government Deficits.* (Boston: Kluwer-Nijhoff) pp.201-210.

Olson, Mancur. 1965. *The Logic of Collective Action.* (Cambridge, MA: Harvard University Press).

Ornstein, Norman, Thomas E. Mann and Michael J. Malbin. 1996. *Vital Statistics on Congress 1995-1996.* (Washington, D.C.: Congressional Quarterly, Inc.).

Owens, John R. and Larry L. Wade. 1984. "Federal Spending in Congressional Districts." *Western Political Quarterly* 37:404-423.

Parker, Glen R. 1986. *Homeward Bound: Explaining Changes on Congressional Behavior.* (Pittsburgh: University of Pittsburgh Press).

Parker, Glen R. 1992. *Institutional Change, Discretion, and the Making of the Modern Congress: An Economic Interpretation.* (Ann Arbor: The University of Michigan Press).

Payne, James L. 1990. "The Congressional Brainwashing Machine." *The Public Interest.*

Payne, James L. 1991a. "Why Government Spending Grows: The 'Socialization' Hypothesis." *Western Political Quarterly* 44,2:487-508.

Payne, James L. 1991. *The Culture of Spending: Why Congress Lives Beyond Our Means* (San Francisco: ICS Press).

Penny, Timothy J. and Major Garret. 1995. *Common Cents.* (New York: Avon Books).

Perot, Ross. 1993. *Not for Sale at any Price.* (New York: Hyperion).

Peterson, Paul E. 1985. "The New Politics of Deficits." in John Chubb and Paul Peterson (eds.) *New Directions in American Politics.* (Washington, D.C.: The Brookings Institution).

Peterson, Paul E. and Mark Rom. 1989. "Macroeconomic Policymaking: Who is in Control? in John Chubb and Paul Peterson (eds.) *Can the Government Govern?* (Washington, D.C.: The Brookings Institution).

Peterson, Peter G. 1994. *Facing Up: Paying Our Nation's Debt and Saving Our Children's Future.* (New York: Simon and Schuster).

Pianin, Eric. 1993. "Top Democrats Try to Stop House Spending-Cut Revolt." *Washington Post.* 23 November 1993, p.A23.

Pianin, Eric. 1994. "David Obey Appropriates a New Fiefdom." *The Washington Post National Weekly Edition.* 9-15 May 1994. p.11.

Pianin, Eric. 1998. "Bringing Home the Pork Can Pay Off at the Polls." *The Washington Post National Weekly Edition.* 15 June 1998. pp.10-11.

Plott, Charles R. 1968. "Some Organizational Influences on Urban Renewal Decisions." *American Economic Review* 58:306-321.

Polsby, Nelson W. 1968."The Institutionalization of the U.S. House of Representatives." *American Political Science Review* 62,2:144-168.

Pound, Edward T. and Douglas Pasternak 1994. "The Pork Barrel Barons." *U.S. News and World Report.* 21 February 1994. pp.32-40.

Preimesberger, Jon and David Tarr (eds.) 1993. *Congressional Districts in the 1990s: A Portrait of America.* (Washington, D.C.: Congressional Quarterly Inc.).

Price, David E. 1992. *The Congressional Experience: A View From the Hill.* (Boulder, CO: Westview).

Rabushka, Alvin. 1983. "A Constitutional Cure for Deficits." in Lawrence H. Meyer (ed.) *The Economic Consequences of Government Deficits.* (Boston: Kluwer-Nijhoff) pp.201-210.

Ray, Bruce A. 1980a. "Federal Spending and the Selection of Committee Assignments in the U.S. House of Representatives." *American Journal of Political Science* 24,3:494-510.

Ray, Bruce A. 1980b. "Congressional Promotion of District Interests: Does Power on the Hill Really Make a Difference?" in Barry S. Rundquist (ed.) *Political Benefits.* (Lexington. MA: Lexington Books).

Ray, Bruce A. 1980c. "Congressional Losers in the U.S. Federal Spending Process." *Legislative Studies Quarterly* 5,3:359-372.

Ray, Bruce A. 1981. "Military Committee Membership in the House of Representatives and the Allocation of Defense Department Outlays." *Western Political Quarterly* 34:222-234.

Ray, Bruce A. 1982. "Causation in the Relationship Between Congressional Positions and Federal Spending." *Polity* 14:676-690.

Reid, J. Norman. 1980. "Politics, Program Administration, and the Distribution of Grants-in-Aid: A Theory and a Test." in Barry S. Rundquist (ed.) *Political Benefits.* (Lexington. MA: Lexington Books).

Reid, T.R. 1980. *Congressional Odyssey.* (San Francisco: W.H. Freeman and Company)

Reischauer, Robert D. (ed.) 1997. *Setting National Priorities: Budget Choices for the Next Century.* (Washington, D.C.: The Brookings Institution).

Reisner, Marc. 1993. *Cadillac Desert: The American West and Its Disappearing Water.* (New York: Penguin Books).

Rich, Michael J. 1989. "Distributive Politics and the Allocation of Federal Grants." *American Political Science Review* 83,1:193-209.

Rich, Michael J. 1991. "Targeting Federal Grants: The Community Development Experience, 1950-1986." *Publius: The Journal of Federalism* 21:29-49.

Riker, William H. 1962. *The Theory of Political Coalitions.* (New Haven: Yale University Press)

Ritt, Leonard G. 1976. "Committee Position, Seniority, and the Distribution of Government Expenditures." *Public Policy* 24,4:461-489.

Rivers, Douglas and Morris P. Fiorina. 1989. "Constituency Service, Reputation, and the Incumbency Advantage." in Morris P. Fiorina and David W. Rhode (eds.) *Home Style and Washington Work: Studies of Congressional Politics.* (Ann Arbor: The University of Michigan Press).

Roberts, Brian E. 1990. "A Dead Senator Tells No Lies: Seniority and the Distribution of Federal Benefits." *American Journal of Political Science* 34,1:31-58.

Rourke, Francis E. 1993. "Whose Bureaucracy is it Anyway?" *PS Political Science and Politics* 24,4:687-691.

Rundquist, Barry and John Ferejohn. 1975. "Observations on a Distributive Theory of Policy-Making: Two American Expenditures Compared." in Craig Liske (et al. eds.) *Comparative Public Policy* (New York: John Wiley.).

Rundquist, Barry S. and David E. Griffith 1976. "An Interrupted Time-Series Test of the Distributive Theory of Military Policy-Making." *Western Political Quarterly* 29:620-626.

Rundquist, Barry S., Jeong-Hwa Lee, and Jungho Rhee. 1996. "The Distributive Politics of Cold War Defense Spending: Some State Level Evidence." *Legislative Studies Quarterly* 21,2:265-281.

Rundquist, Barry, Jungho Rhee, Jeong-Hwa Lee and Sharon E. Fox. 1997. "Modeling State Representation on Defense Committees in Congress, 1959-1989." *American Politics Quarterly* 25,1:35-55.

Safire, William. 1993. *Safire's New Political Dictionary.* (New York: Random House).

Saltzstein, Alan L. 1977. "Federal Categorical Aid to Cities: Who Needs It Versus Who Wants It. *Western Political Quarterly* 30:377-383.

Sanders, Arthur. 1988. "Rationality, Self-Interest, and Public Attitudes on Public Spending." *Social Science Quarterly* 69:311-324.

Savage, James D. 1988. *Balanced Budgets and American Politics.* (Ithaca: Cornell University Press).

Savage, James D. 1991. "Saints and Cardinals in Appropriations Committees and the Fight Against Distributive Politics." *Legislative Studies Quarterly.* 16,3:329-347.

Savage, James D. 1992a. "Trends in the Distribution of Apparent Academic Earmarks in the Federal Government's FY 1980-1992 Appropriations Bills." Prepared for the House Committee on Science, Space, and Technology by the Congressional Research Service of the Library of Congress. September, 1992.

Savage, James D. 1992b. "The Distribution of Apparent Earmarks in the Federal Government's FY 1992 Appropriations Bills." Prepared for the House Committee on Science, Space, and Technology by the Congressional Research Service of the Library of Congress. September, 1992.

Savage, James D. 1994. "Symposium: President Clinton's Budget and Fiscal Policy: An Evaluation Two Budgets Later." *Public Budgeting & Finance* Fall 1994.

Sawhill, Isabel V. 1986. "Reaganomics in Retrospect." in John L. Palmer (ed.) *Perspectives On The Reagan Years.* (Washington, D.C.: The Urban Institute Press).

Schick, Allen. 1983. "The Distributive Congress." in Allen Schick (ed.) *Making Economic Policy in Congress.* (Washington, D.C.: The American Enterprise Institute).

Schick, Allen. 1990. *The Capacity to Budget.* (Washington, D.C.: The Urban Institute).

Schick, Allen. 1994. "The Study of Microbudgeting." in Cogan et al. (eds.) *The Budget Puzzle.* (Stanford CA: Stanford University Press).

Schick, Allen. 1995. *The Federal Budget: Politics, Policy, Process.* (Washington, D.C.: The Brookings Institution).

Schick, Allen 1996. "The Majority Rules: Don't Look Now, but the Congressional Budget Process is Working." *The Brookings Review* Winter, 1996.

Schier, Steven E. 1992. A *Decade of Deficits: Congressional Thought and Fiscal Action.* (Albany, NY: State University of New York).

Schneider, Anne and Helen Ingram. 1993. "The Social Construction of Target Populations: Implications for Politics and Policy." *American Political Science Review* 87,2:334-347.

Schneider, William. 1993. "Whatever Happened to Tax and Spend?" *National Journal.* 4 December 1993; 2920.

Schroedel, Jean Reith. 1994. *Congress, The President, and Policymaking.* (Armonk, NY: M.E. Sharpe).

Schultze, Charles L. 1984. "Comments." in Mills, Gregory B. and John L. Palmer (eds.) *Federal Budget Policy in the 1980s* (Washington, D.C.: The Urban Institute)

Schwartz, Thomas. 1994. "Representation as Agency and the Pork Barrel Paradox." *Public Choice.*

Sellers, Patrick J. 1997. "Fiscal Consistency and Federal District Spending in Congresional Elections." *American Journal of Political Science* 41,3: 1024-1041.

Shear, Jeff. 1996. "Power Loss." *National Journal* 20 April 1996 pp.874-878.

Shepsle, Kenneth A. 1978. *The Giant Jigsaw Puzzle* (Chicago: The University of Chicago Press).

Shepsle, Kenneth A. 1983a. "Overgrazing the Budgetary Commons: Incentive-Compatible Solutions to the Problem of Deficits." in Lawrence H. Meyer (ed.) *The Economic Consequences of Government Deficits.* (Boston: Kluwer-Nijhoff) pp.201-210.

Shepsle, Kenneth A. 1983b. "The failure of Congressional Budgeting." *Society* 20:4-10.

Shepsle, Kenneth A. 1984. "The Congressional Budget Process: Diagnosis, Prescription, Prognosis." in W. Thomas Wander, F. Ted Hebert, and Gary W. Copeland (eds.) *Congressional Budgeting: Politics, Process and Power.* (Baltimore: The Johns Hopkins University Press).

Shepsle, Kenneth A. 1986. "Institutional Equilibrium and Equilibrium Institutions." in Herbert Weisberg (ed.) *Political Science: The Science of Politics.* (New York: Agathon).

Shepsle, Kenneth A. and Barry R. Weingast. 1981. "Political Preferences for the Pork Barrel: A Generalization." *American Journal of Political Science* 25,1:96-111.

Shepsle, Kenneth A. and Barry R. Weingast. 1984. "Legislative Politics and Budget Outcomes." in Gregory B. Mills and John L. Palmer (eds.) *Federal Budget Policy in the 1980s.* (Washington, D.C.: The Urban Institute Press).

Shepsle, Kenneth A. and Barry R. Weingast. 1985. "Policy Consequences of Government by Congressional Subcommittees." *Control of Federal Spending; Proceedings of the Academy of Political Science* 35,5:114-131.

Shepsle, Kenneth A. and Barry R. Weingast. 1994. "Positive Theories of Congressional Institutions." *Legislative Studies Quarterly* 19,2:149-179.

Shepsle, Kenneth A. and Barry R. Weingast 1995. *Positive Theories of Congressional Institutions.* (Ann Arbor, MI: University of Michigan Press).

Shuman, Howard E. 1988. *Politics and the Budget: the Struggle Between President and Congress.* (Englewood Cliffs, N.J.: Prentice Hall).

Smith, Hedrick. 1988. *The Power Game: How Washington Works.* (New York: Random House).

Smith, Hedrick. 1996. "The People & The Power Game: The Elected—The Presidency and Congress" (video: PBS airdate September 10, 1996) (South Carolina ETV: Hedrick Smith Productions).

Smith, Neal. 1994. "Congressional Newsletter" 28 June 1994.

Smith, Steven S. and Christopher J. Deering. 1984. *Committees in Congress.* (Washington, D.C.: CQ Press).

Snyder, Jim. 1995. "An Example of Academic Pork that Brings Home Some Actual Bacon." *The Chronicle of Higher Education.* 8 September 1995. p.A43.

Soherr-Hadwider, David. 1993. "Balancing National Interest and Constituency Demands: Congressional Voting on Military Base Closures." Paper presented at the Western Political Science Association Annual Conference, March 1993.

Soherr-Hadwiger, David. 1998. "Military Construction Policy: A Test of Competing Explanations of Universalism in Congress." *Legislative Studies Quarterly* 23,1:57-78.

Solomon, Burt. 1987. "Staff at Work." *National Journal.* 16 May 1987. pp.1174-1176.

Stanfield, Rochelle L. 1978. "Playing Computer Politics with Local Aid Formulas." *National Journal.* 9 December 1978. pp.1977-1981.

Starobin, Paul. 1993. "Bringing It Home." *National Journal* 27 March 1993.

Stein, Robert M. 1981. "The Allocation of Federal Aid Monies: The Synthesis of Demand-Side Explanations." The *American Political Science Review* 75:334-343.

Stein, Robert M. and Kenneth N. Bickers. 1994a. "Congressional Elections and the Pork Barrel." *The Journal of Politics* 56,3:377-99.

Stein, Robert M. and Kenneth N. Bickers. 1994b. "Universalism and the Electoral Connection: A Test and Some Doubts." *Political Research Quarterly* 47,2:295-318.

Stein, Robert M. and Kenneth N. Bickers. 1995. *Perpetuating the Pork Barrel.* (Cambridge: Cambridge University Press).

Stewart, Charles H. III. 1989. *Budget Reform Politics: The Design of the Appropriations Process in the House of Representatives, 1865-1921.* (Cambridge: Cambridge University Press).

Stockman, David. 1975. "The Social Pork Barrel." *The Public Interest* 39:3-30.

Stockman, David. 1986. *Triumph of Politics.* (New York: Harper and Row).

Strahan, Randall. 1990. *New Ways and Means: Reform and Change in a Congressional Committee.* (Chapel Hill, NC: University of North Carolina Press).

Strom, Gerald S. 1975. "Congressional Policy Making: A Test of a Theory." *The Journal of Politics.* 37:711-735.

Svorny, Shirley V. 1996. "Congressional Allocation of Federal Funds: The Job Training Partnership Act of 1982." *Public Choice* 87: 229-242.

Taylor, Andrew 1993. "In My Backyard, Please." *Congressional Quarterly Special Report: Where the Money Goes.* 11 December 1993. p.139.

Taylor, Andrew. 1996a. "Congress Hands President A Budgetary Scalpel." *Congressional Quarterly Weekly Report.* 30 March 1996. 864-867.

Taylor, Andrew. 1996b. "GOP Pet Projects Give Boost to Shaky Incumbents." *Congressional Quarterly Weekly Report.* 3 August 1996. 2169-2173.

Towell, Pat. 1996. "Protecting Pet Projects—Cautiously." *Congressional Quarterly Weekly Report.* 3 August 1996. 2172.

United States Advisory Commission on Intergovernmental Relations (ACIR). 1994. "Characteristics of Federal Grant-in-Aid Programs to State and Local Governments: Grants Funded FY 1993."

United States Bureau of the Census. 1993. *Congressional District Atlas,* 103 Congress of the United States. (Washington, D.C.:U.S. GPO).

United States Bureau of the Census. 1993. *Population and Housing Characteristics for Congressional Districts of the 103rd Congress.* (Washington, D.C.:U.S. GPO).

United States Department of Agriculture, Cooperative State Research, Education, and Extension Service. 1994. "National Research Initiative Competitive Grants Program: Abstracts of Funded Research Fiscal Year 1994." November 1994.

United States Department of Agriculture, Cooperative State Research, Education, and Extension Service. 1993. "National Research Initiative Competitive Grants Program: Abstracts of Funded Research Fiscal Year 1993." November 1993.

United States Department of Housing and Urban Development. 1993. "Annual Report to Congress on the Community Development Block Grant Program." 26 July 1993.

United States Department of Housing and Urban Development. 1994. "Community Development Block Grant Program: Directory of Allocations for Fiscal Years 1988-1994."

United States General Accounting Office (GAO). 1980. "Assessment of Whether the Federal Grant Process is Being Politicized During Election Years." Letter B-201644; 31 December 1980.

United States General Accounting Office (GAO). 1987. "Grant Formulas: A Catalog of Federal Aid to States and Localities." GAO/HRD-87-28. March 1987.

United States General Services Administration. 1994. *Catalog of Federal Domestic Assistance* (Washington, D.C. :GPO).

Warren, Charles. 1932. *Congress as Santa Claus or National Donations and the General Welfare Clause of the Constitution.* (Charlottesville, VA: TheMichie Company, Publishers.)

Weiner, Tim. 1994. "Sending Money to Home District: Earmarking and Congressional Pork Barrel." *New York Times.* 13 July 1994. p.A1.

Weingast, Barry. 1979. "A Rational Choice Perspective on Congressional Norms." *American Journal of Political Science* 23:245-262.

Weingast, Barry 1994. "Reflections on Distributive Politics and Universalism." *Political Research Quarterly* 47,2:319-328.

Weingast, Barry R., Kenneth A. Shepsle, and Christopher Johnsen. 1981. "The Political Economy of Benefits and Costs: A Neoclassical Approach to Distributive Politics." *Journal of Political Economy* 89,41: 642-664.

Weingast, Barry, and William J. Marshall. 1988. "The Industrial Organization of Congress; or, Why Legislatures, Like Firms, Are not Organized as Markets." *Journal of Political Economy* 96,1:132-163.

Whicker, Marcia Lynn and Nicholas A Giannataiso. 1997. "The Politics of Military Base Closing: A New Theory of Influence." *Public Affairs Quarterly.* (Summer)

White, Joseph. 1993. "Decision Making in the Appropriations Subcommittees on Defense and Foreign Operations." in Randall B. Ripley and James M. Lindsay (eds.) *Congress Resurgent: Foreign and Defense Policy on Capitol Hill.* (Ann Arbor: University of Michigan Press).

White, Joseph and Aaron Wildavsky. 1989a. "How to Fix the Deficit—Really." *The Public Interest* 94:3-24.

White, Joseph and Aaron Wildavsky. 1989b. *The Deficit and the Public Interest.* (Berkeley: University of California Press).

Wildavsky, Aaron 1964. *The Politics of the Budgetary Process.* (Boston: Little, Brown and Company).

Wildavsky, Aaron. 1988. *The New Politics of the Budgetary Process.* (Glenview, IL: Scott Foresman).

Willen, Mark (ed.) 1994. "The Freshmen-Elect: Profiles of the New Members of the 104th Congress." *Congressional Quarterly Special Report* 52,44. 12 November 1994.

Wilmerding, Lucius Jr. 1943. *The Spending Power: A History of the Efforts of Congress to Control Expenditures.* (New Haven: Yale University Press).

Wilson, James Q. 1973. *Political Organizations* (New York: Basic Books).

Wilson, James Q. 1980. "The Politics of Regulation." in James Q. Wilson (ed.) *The Politics of Regulation* (New York: Basic Books).

Wilson, James Q. 1989. *Bureaucracy: What Government Agencies Do and Why They Do It.* (New York: Basic Books).

Wilson, Rick K. 1986a. "What was it worth to be on a committee in the U.S. House, 1889-1913?" *Legislative Studies Quarterly* 11,1:47-63.

Wilson, Rick K. 1986b. "An Empirical Test of Preferences for the Pork Barrel: District-Level Appropriations for Rivers and Harbors Legislation, 1889-1913." *American Journal of Political Science* 4:729-754.

Woodward, Bob. 1994. *The Agenda: Inside the Clinton White House.* (New York: Simon & Schuster).

Yiannakis, Diana Evans. 1981. "The Grateful Electorate: Casework and Congressional Elections." *American Journal of Political Science* 25,3:568-580.

Yiannakis, Diana Evans. 1982. "House Members' Communication Styles: Newsletters and Press Releases." *Journal of Politics* 44:1049-1071.

Zaroya, Gregg. 1996. "Top Ten Pork-Barrelers." *George* September 1996. pp.96-101.

Index